T0305082

A Research Agenda for Experimental Economics

Elgar Research Agendas outline the future of research in a given area. Leading scholars are given the space to explore their subject in provocative ways, and map out the potential directions of travel. They are relevant but also visionary.

Forward-looking and innovative, Elgar Research Agendas are an essential resource for PhD students, scholars and anybody who wants to be at the forefront of research.

Titles in the series include:

A Research Agenda for Experimental Economics

Edited by

ANANISH CHAUDHURI

Professor of Experimental Economics, University of Auckland, Auckland, New Zealand

Elgar Research Agendas

 Edward Elgar
PUBLISHING

Cheltenham, UK • Northampton, MA, USA

Published by
Edward Elgar Publishing Limited
The Lypiatts
15 Lansdown Road
Cheltenham
Glos GL50 2JA
UK

Edward Elgar Publishing, Inc.
William Pratt House
9 Dewey Court
Northampton
Massachusetts 01060
USA

A catalogue record for this book
is available from the British Library

Library of Congress Control Number: 2021938671

This book is available electronically in the **Elgar**online
Economics subject collection
http://dx.doi.org/10.4337/9781789909852

ISBN 978 1 78990 984 5 (cased)
ISBN 978 1 78990 985 2 (eBook)

Printed and bound by CPI Group (UK) Ltd, Croydon, CR0 4YY

For my mother, Ila Chaudhuri

Contents

About the editor

Ananish Chaudhuri is Professor of Experimental Economics at the University of Auckland. He is the author of numerous articles in leading scholarly journals, and the books *Experiments in Economics: Playing Fair with Money* and *Behavioural Economics and Experiments*, both published by Routledge. Between 2013 and 2019, he served as the Chair of the Department of Economics at Auckland. He has also taught at Harvard Kennedy School, Wellesley College, Rutgers University and Washington State University. In 2018, he received the Distinguished Contribution Award from the Faculty of Business and Economics at Auckland. He has been a member of the Economics, Human and Behavioural Sciences panel of the Royal Society of New Zealand Marsden Fund. He has served in an editorial capacity at *Journal of Economic Behavior and Organization*, *Journal of Economic Psychology*, *Journal of Behavioral and Experimental Economics*, *New Zealand Economic Papers*, *Games* and *Scientific Reports*.

Contributors

Quentin D. Atkinson is Professor of Psychology at the University of Auckland, Auckland, New Zealand, and a Royal Society of New Zealand Rutherford Discovery Fellow.

Timothy N. Cason is Professor of Economics at Purdue University, West Lafayette, Indiana, USA, former co-Editor of *Experimental Economics* and former President of the Economic Science Association.

Ananish Chaudhuri is Professor of Experimental Economics at the University of Auckland, Auckland, New Zealand, and a research affiliate of CESifo, Munich.

Sarah Cowie is Lecturer (Assistant Professor) in the School of Psychology at the University of Auckland, Auckland, New Zealand.

David L. Dickinson is Professor of Economics at Appalachian State University, Research Fellow of IZA (Institute of Labor Economics), Bonn, and a Research Affiliate of the Economic Science Institute at Chapman University.

Catherine Eckel is Sara and John Lindsey Professor in the Liberal Arts, University Distinguished Professor in the Department of Economics at Texas A&M University and former President of the Economic Science Association.

Kyle Fischer is a PhD student in Psychology at the University of Auckland, Auckland, New Zealand.

Lana Friesen is Associate Professor of Economics at the University of Queensland, St. Lucia, Queensland, Australia.

Lata Gangadharan is Professor of Economics and Joe Isaac Chair of Business and Economics at Monash University, Clayton, Victoria, Australia, and current co-Editor of *Experimental Economics*.

John Gibson is Professor of Economics at Waikato University, Hamilton, New Zealand, a Fellow of the Royal Society of New Zealand and a Distinguished Fellow of the New Zealand Association of Economists.

Philip J. Grossman is Professor of Economics at Monash University, Clayton, Victoria, Australia.

Alice Guerra is Assistant Professor of Economics at the University of Bologna, Rimini, Italy.

Ian Kirk is Professor of Psychology, co-Director of the Cognitive Neuroimaging, Neuroplasticity and Neurodevelopment Laboratory and Associate Director of the Centre for Brain Research at the University of Auckland, Auckland, New Zealand.

Olav Krigolson is Associate Professor, School of Exercise Science, Physical and Health Education, University of Victoria, Victoria, British Columbia, Canada.

Pushkar Maitra is Professor of Economics at Monash University, Clayton, Victoria, Australia.

Ananta Neelim is Lecturer (Assistant Professor), School of Economics, Finance and Marketing, Royal Melbourne Institute of Technology University, Melbourne, Australia.

James Tremewan is Senior Lecturer in Economics at the University of Auckland, Auckland, New Zealand.

Alexander Vostroknutov is Associate Professor of Economics at Maastricht University, Maastricht, Netherlands.

Nina Xue is a PhD student in the Department of Economics at Monash University, Clayton, Victoria, Australia.

1 Introduction to *A Research Agenda for Experimental Economics*

Ananish Chaudhuri

1. Introduction

Experimental economics is an empirical approach to understanding behaviour in economic transactions. Researchers analyse decisions made by participants in a variety of economic "games" (or "experiments") that have been specifically designed to simulate a particular economic transaction that the researcher wishes to study. Participants in such experiments are remunerated, and the amount they receive depends on the decisions they make during the experiment.[1] By this definition, experimental studies that are not properly incentivised—because they either do not pay participants or they pay people a flat amount that is independent of their decisions—are not properly called experiments. The same argument applies for other methods, such as discrete choice experiments, that are applied in several areas including health policy (de Bekker-Grob, Ryan, & Gerard, 2012).

As we complete the second decade of the 21st century, experimental economics is firmly entrenched in the mainstream of economics, so much so that, almost a decade ago, Oswald (2010) commented:

> experimental papers are becoming common in the highest impact-factor journals... Some economists think that experimental-method papers may even take over as the dominant style of work. I am not sure; it is easy to get carried away with the latest fashions...But true-experiment papers will surely make up a much bigger slice of the future of economics than has been common up to this point. (p. 5)

Noussair (2011) explored trends in publishing in experimental economics for the first decade of the 21st century (2001–2010) by focusing on papers

1

published in six general-interest journals and three specialised ones. Noussair reports that the number of experimental papers published in these nine journals increased from 260 between 2001 and 2005 to 456 between 2006 and 2010, a 75% increase.[2] While there may be no real risk of economics becoming an experimental science in the near future, experiments are making rapid inroads into different areas of the discipline. Equally importantly, however, incentivised decision-making experiments are now finding increasing acceptance and application in other social sciences.

There is a long tradition of using experiments (though not always ones where participants were remunerated on the basis of their decisions) in psychology. In recent years, there has been a much greater concordance between the two disciplines, with psychologists paying more attention to monetary payments and reward salience and economists engaging in less structured (and less theory-driven) experiments in order to understand the basic drivers of human behaviour. Other sciences—both social and natural—have started adopting experimental games to study questions of interest, such as evolutionary approaches to understanding politics and political ideology and the evolution of cooperation and its consequent impact on cultural group selection and neuro-economics (which brings together scholars from economics, psychology, neuroscience and evolutionary biology). Before I provide an overview of the volume's coverage, given our interest in reaching a wide cross-section of researchers, it might be useful to address a few questions (and concerns) that come up regularly in discussions of experimental methods.

2.   Experiments in Economics and Psychology: Similarities and Differences

Experimental economists are generally interested in how human beings make decisions in a variety of economic interactions, especially those requiring strategic thinking. Given this interest in decision-making, the research agendas of experimental economists have broad overlaps with those of both cognitive and social psychologists. A partial list of ways in which experiments in economics and psychology differ appears below.

First, many, if not most, economics experiments were traditionally designed as tests of economic theories. Psychology, on the other hand, places less emphasis on writing down formal models of human behaviour, and data collection often takes precedence. The development of "theory" in psychology typically follows the demonstration of empirical regularities in the data. It is only after voluminous data have been collected that a new theory or concept is coined in an attempt to explain those empirical findings. Second, economists are typically interested in understanding the impact of specific institutions (such as markets) or changes in those institutional structures on behaviour, while in psychology there is less emphasis on institutional structure and constraints.

Third, experimental economists emphasise a clear incentive structure in the laboratory where the payments to participants are directly related to the decisions that they make. According to economists, the salience of the reward structure is what gets participants to focus on the task at hand and make good decisions. Psychologists often do not make performance-dependent payments, choosing at times to reward participants with course credits, extra credit, a fixed fee or random payments to a subset of participants. Psychologists also often emphasise the role of intrinsic motivation. In fact, some psychologists, as well as other social scientists, argue against providing salient monetary rewards that are task dependent. They argue that such extrinsically provided motivation in the form of monetary rewards to participants might, in fact, crowd out intrinsic motivations, which are often the primary focus.

Finally, psychologists often use deception in their experiments, while economists are typically opposed to this. Economists believe that, if subjects are deceived in one experiment and are later informed about such deception, then they might be less inclined to take the instructions at face value in the next experiment. Subjects might automatically suspect deception and assume that the experimenter wants to study something other than what the instructions suggest. Psychologists, on the other hand, believe that deceptions do not make a difference in behaviour, and extensive debriefings at the end of the session will take care of mistaken impressions and assumptions on the part of the participants. Psychologists also aver that, in some experiments, it is virtually impossible to address the research question adequately in the absence of such deception—see, for instance, the classic studies by Asch (1951, 1956) on conformity and by Milgram (1974) on obedience to authority. It is also the case that in recent years there has been considerable debate about what exactly constitutes deception (Bonetti, 1998; Cooper, 2014).

However, it is safe to say that, at present, incentivised experiments where participants are paid on the basis of decisions made and are not deceived in any way (except under the most extenuating circumstances, followed by extensive debriefing) constitute the gold standard in research in experimental social science.

3.   Payment Protocols in Experiments

I have addressed above why experimental economists insist on performance-dependent and salient rewards to motivate good decisions, but one topic that has generated controversy in recent times is: How do you pay subjects, especially when they have interacted for more than one game or for more than one round, as is often the case?

The traditional approach is to pay for all games/rounds. However, some argue that this may create a "wealth effect", implying that, as the experiment progresses, the subject is earning more and more money, which may alter decisions. Given that the payments are small, this is not a big issue, in my opinion. One way of avoiding this is to avoid telling subjects how much they are making over time. This is, obviously, easier if they are taking part in a series of distinct tasks as opposed to repeating the same task many times. At times, information about earnings is crucial if one is interested in learning. One alternative proposed by those who are suspicious of the "pay for all rounds" approach, especially where subjects are repeatedly undertaking the same task numerous times, is to select one round at random at the end of the session and pay for that round, but that does not necessarily solve the problem.

Suppose in an experiment a subject makes 50 (100) decisions but is paid for only one of those. The subject then knows that each decision has only a 1/50th (1/100th) chance of being relevant. This leads to a loss of reward salience because each decision now has a small probability of paying off; this is not all that different from survey responses. Finally, it has been argued by some that, if the task is complex and there is significant learning involved, then it may make sense to pay for the very last round, which best reflects the subject's facility at the task. Merlo and Schotter (1999) explore this payment question in a series of experiments where subjects are asked to make a prediction in a complex mathematical task. Getting the answer correct is difficult and somewhat beside the point. The idea is to see how close subjects come to the correct answer (much like throwing darts and trying to hit the bullseye) and whether they get better at it (come closer to the correct answer) over time. Subjects in these experiments take part in two treatments: learn-while-you-earn and learn-before-you-earn. As would be obvious from the names of the treatments, in the first, the subjects earn a small amount of money in each round, as is the traditional practice. In the second treatment, however, subjects play a number of rounds without pay and then earn a much larger amount (a large multiple of the per-round earning in the learn-while-you-earn treatment) in the last round. Merlo and Schotter (1999) find that subjects who take part in the learn-before-you-earn treatment do much better at coming closer to the correct answer. This is, at least partly, because the subjects who get paid every round adopt a more myopic approach where they focus on whether they "won" or "lost" in each round. The subjects in the other treatment, who do not have to worry about getting paid each round, engage in much greater experimentation and, in doing so, end up learning about the underlying problem much better over time.

Once again, there is no clear-cut answer. Paying for a single random round may make sense if there are not too many rounds, especially if there are significant constraints on research budgets, as there often are. Another way of avoiding potential wealth effects is to not reveal earnings information during the session, if this is practicable.

4.   Oft-Expressed Concerns With Experiments

In spite of the impressive growth that experimental economics has enjoyed in recent decades, there are still lingering questions about the external validity of experiments, as articulated by Levitt and List (2007a, 2007b). For instance, Levitt and List (2007a) write: "Yet unless considerable changes are made in the manner in which we conduct lab experiments, our model highlights that the relevant factors will rarely converge across the lab and many field settings" (p. 364). The implication here is that it is the results in field settings that matter and, unless laboratory experiments can tell us something about behaviour in the field, then these experiments are meaningless. In many ways, this criticism echoes the traditional idea (Lipsey, 1979) that the only meaningful way to learn anything important about economic phenomena is to study economies in the wild, or at least to create "field" experiments that are close approximations of the natural economy (e.g. Harrison & List, 2004; Carpenter et al., 2005). This view represents a misunderstanding of the function of experiments.

Experiments can play multiple roles. One of these is to test the empirical validity of economic theories, of course bearing in mind the caveat that such attempts may run into the Duhem–Quine problem (Harding, 1975).[3] But as Smith (1982) argues, to the extent that laboratory experiments create a small-scale microeconomic society, then the theoretical predictions that are supposed to hold true for complex, real-life phenomena should still be valid within the controlled conditions of the laboratory. It seems to defy reason that theoretical predictions that are wildly off the mark within the laboratory would still perform well in conditions with more confounding and uncontrolled variables.

Another major role of experiments is to demonstrate empirical regularities, and in doing so economic experiments essentially play the role of economic models that can lead to further theory building. Moreover, to the extent that many experiments are often comparing the impact on behaviour from changing various institutional parameters, it is not a big concern whether the experiments are carried out with the traditional participant pool of students or other non-traditional participants. In many cases, the different pools will produce changes in behaviour in the same direction, though perhaps of differing magnitudes in response to different treatments. This may be of little concern if it is the direction of change (comparative statics) rather than its magnitude that is of primary interest. It is also the case that differences in the behaviour of students and professionals are less pronounced than is usually presumed (Frechette, 2015).

The area where the issue of external validity does loom large is when experiments are utilised to design policy. Here there are two responses. If the data generated using student participants are considered unreliable, then an obvious response would be to run the experiments with more sophisticated participants. The student experiments can be thought of as pilot studies guiding the design of further experiments with non-student subjects. But in many cases—as with the design of spectrum auctions—the questions are difficult enough that there are not too many other options besides relying on lab experiments prior to implementation in the field. Chapter 4 of this volume, by Timothy N. Cason, Lana Friesen and Lata Gangadharan, highlights this point by showing how lab experiments in environmental management can serve as "wind tunnel tests" prior to field implementation.

As Camerer (2015) points out, while it is true that experimental results may not always translate directly to a particular context, it is also true that there might be problems with transferring from one field study to another. Given that a lot of parameters are specific to a particular field context, it is not clear that the results of these field studies are more generalisable to other contexts than are the results of lab experiments. Camerer writes:

> The guiding idea here is..."parallelism"...(the assumption) that the same general laws apply in all settings...For example, parallelism does not require that students in a lab setting designed to resemble foreign exchange traders behave in the same way as professional foreign exchange traders behave on trading floors...The maintained assumption of parallelism simply asserts that if those differences could be held constant (or controlled for econometrically), behaviour in the lab and the trading floor would be the same. Put differently, if many experimental and field data sets were combined, with sufficient variation among variables like stakes, experience, and

subject characteristics, a "Lab" dummy variable would not be significant (assuming it did not plausibly correlate with omitted variables). (p. 252)

Plott (1991) echoes the point that the emphasis on realism is misguided. Experiments are often designed to expose things that are hidden by nature. Therefore, designing experiments to replicate natural settings is not necessarily illuminating. Often the very simplicity of experiments is what makes them useful. According to Plott, economics is a study of principles that govern the behaviour of humankind in the ordinary business of life. Simple experiments are often sufficient to uncover those principles at least in part because those principles are better understood, not by studying them in equilibrium, but by understanding the structure and institutions that govern that equilibrium.

Having said this, I also note that currently economists are carrying out extremely elaborate field experiments (at times referred to as randomised controlled trials, or RCTs), and the 2019 Nobel Prize in Economics went to three practitioners in this area. An excellent resource for an overview of this line of work is Banerjee and Duflo (2011), two of the winners of the 2019 Nobel Prize, with the third being Michael Kremer. A similar example from other social sciences is provided by Henrich et al. (2004).

5.   The Scope of This Volume

The opportunity to put together this volume was both exciting and challenging, primarily because it was not immediately clear as to what topics the volume should cover. Incentivised experimental games are now used routinely in a wide range of fields. Given the increasing use of economic experiments in mainstream economics, this volume does not try to provide a comprehensive overview of this work. One intended group of readers includes people working in areas that may not automatically turn towards using experiments in studying their own research questions. Here, the aim is two-fold: (1) to reach out to these potential readers and inform them of ways in which experiments are being used by pioneers in those fields, and (2) to point out useful avenues of further research. To that end, the chapters in the volume are not intended to summarise work in those fields, but rather to provide a selection of how experiments are being utilised to address interesting research questions and what potential future extensions are.

Equally, however, we also wish to reach out to experienced experimentalists and point out how they can use the items in their toolkit to address other interesting research questions that are amenable to experimental study. Thus, our hope is to reach social scientists who want to learn about using experiments in their work as well as experimentalists who may be looking for new and exciting research ideas that rely on the experimental methodology. We will consider this volume to be successful if it manages to start fruitful conversations, and hopefully collaborations, between the two groups of researchers identified above.

The volume, then, is deeply influenced by this desire to take an interdisciplinary view and to talk to people who may not routinely think of running experiments in pursuing their research agenda. A different editor may have chosen an entirely different set of topics and contributors. These choices reflect both my own preferences and my assessment of what some of the more promising areas for further study are.

The current volume is divided into two parts. Part 1 consists of five chapters that are more "economic" in focus, while Part 2 contains four chapters that cover topics that venture further afield. Chapter 2, by James Tremewan and Alexander Vostroknutov, provides an elegant and tractable way of pinning down what social scientists mean when they talk about social norms (Bicchieri, 2006, 2016; Chaudhuri, 2009; Elster, 2009; Skyrms, 2004). As the authors point out, there seems to be no general acceptance of what social norms are and whether these are rules that members of a society "are" abiding by or "ought" to. Given the importance and ubiquity of appeals to social norms, both to explain behaviour and to make policy recommendations, the authors provide a way in which we should approach the topic; important distinctions that we should bear in mind; and a discussion of how we can design experiments that address and analyse related yet distinct components of the concept of norms. This chapter may be a little technical for some readers, but the effort will be worthwhile. In any event, researchers will still gain many insights from the chapter, even if they completely skip the mathematical bits.

In Chapter 3, Alice Guerra moves from norms to explicit rules and laws. She considers applications of experimental methods to legal issues, focusing primarily on three areas: bargaining and the Coase Theorem; pre-trial settlement and the litigation process; and torts and liability rules. As Guerra points out, understanding how people's behaviours interact with the law is crucial for any policymaker who seeks to use the law to encourage socially desirable behaviours and discourage socially undesirable ones. The questions of how legal institutions shape individuals' incentives and how people respond to changes in their legal environment remain relatively unexplored areas. However, they are eminently suitable for study using experimental methods, and recent decades have seen the emergence of substantial research in experimental law and economics. Taking off from the previous chapter by Tremewan and Vostroknutov, Guerra suggests that the roles of social norms and preferences in legal bargaining have received less attention than other economic parameters, such as transactions costs. Exploring the roles of such norms in the context of Coasian bargaining, pre-trial settlements and tort litigations may well be a fruitful area of further research. Those who wish to embark on that research agenda will be well served by the insights provided in the Tremewan and Vostroknutov chapter.

Chapter 4, by Timothy N. Cason, Lana Friesen and Lata Gangadharan, continues the regulatory theme set by Guerra and summarises experimental studies that focus on environmental regulations and compliance. I am sure I do not need to emphasise the importance of this line of research given our current focus on climate change issues. Among other things, Chapter 4 highlights the scope of experiments that, according to Roth (1995), "whisper in the ears of princes". These are experiments with enormous policy implications. As Cason et al. point out, one significant advantage to these experiments is that they can serve as "wind-tunnel tests" prior to the implementation of a particular policy, which is typically resource intensive and the costs of getting the implementation wrong can be high. Cason et al. state,

> for novel policy approaches, the data required for empirical testing are simply unavailable, either in a timely fashion, or at all. Laboratory experiments provide perhaps the only opportunity to explore empirically different policy options and counterfactuals. Field experiments are also useful to explore new regulatory policies—but they can be more difficult to conduct.

This has been true for other areas, such as the auctioning of broad-spectrum radio-waves (McAfee & McMillan, 1996; Binmore & Klemperer, 2002), but it is only recently that we have applied an experimental lens to environmental regulations, and the authors of this chapter are among the pioneers in this area.

In Chapter 5, Pushkar Maitra and Ananta Neelim take on yet another huge topic: behavioural development economics. However, in recognition of the fact that this broad area contains numerous potential subject matters, Maitra and Neelim focus on one such sphere, entrepreneurship. This choice is motivated by the fact that the formal sector in developing countries often fails to generate enough employment, leading people to depend on other sources of income generally characterised by low levels of formality and low productivity. Further, returns to education and experience in the formal labour markets are low in developing countries relative to high-income countries. All of this makes entrepreneurship a critical vehicle of economic growth in developing countries. Maitra and Neelim provide an overview of behavioural preferences and non-cognitive traits that affect entrepreneurial choice and success.

John Gibson rounds out Part I with a chapter on behavioural nudges on health. This is a relatively short chapter, which reflects, in part, the paucity of work in this area and the significant scope for further research. As Gibson notes, while much work in this area adopts the sobriquet of "experiments", these are not typically incentivised and are more along the lines of survey responses. Gibson also points out that this area presents many potential applications for RCTs that have recently become highly popular in other areas of economics, such as economic development. Nevertheless, the area of behavioural health appears to have remained somewhat immune to the RCT revolution. In his chapter, Gibson provides an overview of existing incentivised experiments in health and suggests that this area remains particularly fertile for the application of experimental techniques.

Part II begins with a chapter on gender and leadership written by scholars who have had significant impact in this area. Differences in the economic decisions and labour market outcomes of women and men are widely documented and sit squarely within the purview of economics. The reason I have chosen to place this chapter in the second part is that, in spite of the immediate relevance of the topic to economics, it still inspires considerable controversy, even now at the end of the second decade of the 21st century. The other reason for the chapter's placement here is the interdisciplinary nature of the topic, which elicits interest from researchers in diverse fields, ranging from sociology and feminist studies to psychology, management and leadership.

Eckel et al. focus primarily on the gender gap in leadership roles and start by summarising gender differences in preferences that are related to women's willingness to lead. Then they consider the selection of women as leaders and gender differences in perceptions, beliefs and behaviour that contribute to the leadership gap. They address the literature on stereotypes and discrimination, which play important roles in the evaluation and selection of women leaders, and they conclude with a discussion of possible interventions, their effectiveness and policy directions.

With Chapter 8, we begin to venture further away from economics. In this chapter, Kyle Fischer, Quentin D. Atkinson and Ananish Chaudhuri provide an overview of experiments that aim to understand political beliefs and preferences. Traditionally, political scientists have tended to take a unidimensional view of political ideology, placing people along a liberal–conservative (left–

right) spectrum. Liberals are generally egalitarian, more open to novelty, and supportive of redistributive policies, while conservatives are more concerned with preserving and enforcing traditional values, group conformity and justifying existing hierarchies (Jost et al., 2003). However, scholars across diverse disciplines have repeatedly and independently found two primary dimensions of political ideology, often referred to as economic conservatism (vs economic progressivism), and social conservatism (vs social progressivism).

Recently, Claessens et al. (2020) showed that there is a striking concordance between these dual dimensions of ideology and independent evidence for two key shifts in the evolution of human group living. First, humans began to cooperate more widely. Second, humans became more group-minded, conforming to and enforcing social norms in culturally marked groups. They propose that fitness trade-offs and environmental pressures have maintained variation in these tendencies to cooperate and conform, naturally giving rise to the two dimensions of political ideology. In Chapter 8, Fischer et al. start with an overview of studies that adopt a unidimensional view of politics before discussing the nascent, yet growing, work on the dual foundations of political ideology.

Chapter 9 tackles neuroeconomics. In this chapter, Sarah Cowie, Ian Kirk and Olav Krigolson explore examples of how a combination of neuroscientific, psychological, and economic approaches has shed light on why we behave in particular ways, over and above what any one of these individual approaches can reveal. This chapter focuses on specific examples of research that have contributed to the understanding of how decision-making depends on expected value, emotion and personality, and how learning and decision-making are influenced by prediction error, delay, ownership and cognitive load. These examples demonstrate how experiments have answered key questions or posed novel questions that set the direction for future research.

Chapter 10, by David L. Dickinson, looks at the impact of sleep or lack thereof on decision-making. Dickinson, who has undertaken path-breaking work in this area, points out that a large number of adults across countries suffer from insufficient sleep. Poor sleep, in general, impacts not only physical but also behavioural health via the type of thought processes used during decision-making. Research into how adverse sleep states impact decision-making stems from a larger research agenda on bounded rationality and the role of cognitive loads on decision-making. This chapter surveys the research on sleep and decision-making with a focus on decision paradigms that use rigorous and incentivised methods common to the field of experimental economics. Dickinson provides an overview of methodological issues for those who may wish to undertake this line of work, and then goes on to review the research on adverse sleep states and high-level decision-making, which covers both individual and social/interactive decisions.

6. Acknowledgements

I am deeply grateful to all the contributors for taking the time to write the chapters. I believe that together they constitute a major and exciting resource for researchers and provide pointers for fruitful future avenues of research. I ended up learning an enormous amount from each of the chapters. The contributors to this volume have devoted an enormous amount of time and effort in crafting very high-quality chapters at my request and I am deeply indebted to all of them for agreeing to do so.

More importantly, a large group of people has freely given time to reading and providing feedback on the chapters. I thank all of them sincerely. This group includes Marco Castillo, Scott Claessens, Sean Drummond, Tim Friehe, Ryan Greenaway-McGrevy, Robert Hoffman, Erik Kimbrough, Martin Kocher, Henrik Lando, Guy Lavendar-Forsyth, Sherry Li, Minhaj Mahmud, Matthew Miller, Sergio Rubens Mittländer, Gerd Mühlheusser, Jim Murphy, Susan Olivia, Francesco Parisi, Chris Sibley, John Stranlund, Christian Thöni and, last but certainly not least, Marie-Claire Villeval, who, in spite of her tremendous workload, read and commented on two chapters in this volume. Furthermore, these two groups—the authors and the reviewers—have done this work in the midst of the COVID-19 pandemic, which created tremendous disruptions to personal and academic lives. In spite of those vicissitudes, we have managed to put this volume together within the anticipated deadline.

I am grateful to Lana Friesen and David L. Dickinson for feedback on this chapter. Finally, I owe a debt of gratitude to Alex O'Connell at Edward Elgar who approached me with the idea of assembling this volume. I would not have thought of doing this had Alex not approached me. I am delighted that we have managed to make progress through the COVID-19 pandemic and will be able to see the results of our efforts in printed form in the near future. I hope that you enjoy reading this volume and that it leads to fruitful cross-disciplinary conversations in the future.

Nga mihi nui.

Notes

1. The terms "experimental economics" and "behavioural economics" are often used interchangeably in common parlance, but traditionally there has been a dichotomy between these two research areas. Experimental economists were those who hailed primarily from a background in economics and used incentivised economic experiments to test theoretical propositions. Behavioural economics, on the other hand, referred to the branch of study that attempted to infuse neo-classical economic models with psychological insights, such as bounded rationality as well as heuristics and biases. But in recent times, there has been greater blending of the two, caused by the natural overlap in the research agendas of these two streams. This has occurred so frequently that it is probably not controversial to say that, at present, the branch of economics that infuses neo-classical economics with insights from psychology is given the nomenclature of "behavioural economics", with incentivised decision-making experiments (or experimental economics) being a powerful toolkit in the behavioural economist's arsenal.
2. The six general-interest journals include *American Economic Review*, *Econometrica*, *Review of Economic Studies*, *Quarterly Journal of Economics*, *Journal of Political Economy* and *Economic Journal*. The three specialised journals are *Games and Economic Behavior*, *Journal of Economic Behavior* and *Organization and Experimental Economics*.
3. The Duhem–Quine thesis, or the Duhem–Quine problem, named after Pierre Duhem and Willard Van Orman Quine, suggests that it is impossible to test a scientific hypothesis in isolation. This is because any empirical test of the hypothesis requires one or more auxiliary assumptions or auxiliary hypotheses. So, even if a theory is falsified, it is not clear whether this is because the theory is wrong or because one or more of the auxiliary assumptions are wrong.

References

Asch, S. E. (1951). Effects of group pressure upon the modification and distortion of judgment. In H. Guetzkow (Ed.), *Groups, leadership and men*. Pittsburgh: Carnegie Press.

Asch, S. E. (1956). Studies of independence and conformity: A minority of one against a unanimous majority. *Psychological Monographs: General and Applied, 70*(9), 1–70.

Banerjee, A., & Duflo, E. (2011). *Poor economics*. New York: Public Affairs.

Bicchieri, C. (2006). *The grammar of society: The nature and dynamics of social norms*. Cambridge, UK: Cambridge University Press.

Bicchieri, C. (2016). *Norms in the wild: How to diagnose, measure and change social norms*. Oxford: Oxford University Press.

Binmore, K., & Klemperer, P. (2002). The biggest auction ever: The sale of the British 3G telecom licences. *Economic Journal, 112*(478), C74–C96.

Bonetti, S. (1998). Experimental economics and deception. *Journal of Economic Psychology, 19*(3), 377–395.

Camerer, C. (2015). The promise and success of lab-field generalizability in experimental economics: A critical reply to Levitt and List. In A. Schotter & G. Frechette (Eds.),

Handbook of experimental economic methodology (pp. 249–295). Oxford: Oxford University Press.

Carpenter, J., Harrison, G., & List, J. (2005). *Field experiments in economics.* London: JAI Press.

Chaudhuri, A. (2009). *Experiments in economics: Playing fair with money.* London: Routledge.

Claessens, S., Fischer, K., Chaudhuri, A., Sibley, C. G., & Atkinson, Q. D. (2020). The dual evolutionary foundations of political ideology. *Nature Human Behaviour, 4,* 336–335.

Cooper, D. J. (2014). A note on deception in economic experiments. *Journal of Wine Economics, 9*(2), 111–114.

de Bekker-Grob, E., Ryan, M., & Gerard, K. (2012). Discrete choice experiments in health economics: A review of the literature. *Health Economics, 21*(2), 145–172.

Elster, J. (2009). Norms. In P. Bearman & P. Hedström (Eds.), *The Oxford handbook of analytical sociology* (pp. 195–217). Oxford: Oxford University Press.

Frechette, G. (2015). Laboratory experiments: Professionals versus students. In G. Frechette & A. Schotter (Eds.), *Handbook of experimental economic methodology* (pp. 360–390). Oxford: Oxford University Press.

Harding, S. (Ed.). (1975). *Can theories be refuted? Essays on the Duhem–Quine thesis* (Vol. 81). Dordrecht, Netherlands: Springer Science & Business Media.

Harrison, G. W., & List, J. (2004). Field experiments. *Journal of Economic Literature, 42,* 1009–1055.

Henrich, J. P., Boyd, R., Bowles, S., Camerer, C., Fehr, E., & Gintis, H. (Eds.). (2004). *Foundations of human sociality: Economic experiments and ethnographic evidence from fifteen small-scale societies.* Oxford: Oxford University Press.

Jost, J. T., Glaser, J., Kruglanski, A. W., & Sulloway, F. J. (2003). Political conservatism as motivated social cognition. *Psychological Bulletin, 129*(3), 339–375.

Levitt, S., & List, J. (2007a). Viewpoint: On the generalizability of lab behavior to the field. *Canadian Journal of Economics, 40*(2), 347–370.

Levitt, S., & List, J. (2007b). What do laboratory experiments measuring social preferences reveal about the real world? *Journal of Economic Perspectives, 21*(2), 153–174.

Lipsey, R. (1979). *An introduction to positive economics* (5th ed.). London: Weidenfeld and Nicolson.

McAfee, R., & McMillan, J. (1996). Analyzing the airwaves auction. *Journal of Economic Perspectives, 10*(1), 159–175.

Merlo, A., & Schotter, A. (1999). A surprise-quiz view of learning in economic experiments. *Games and Economic Behavior, 28,* 25–54.

Milgram, S. (1974). *Obedience to authority: An experimental view.* New York: Harper & Row.

Noussair, C. (2011, November). Trends in academic publishing in experimental economics. *Communications with economists: Current and future trends.* Keynote address conducted at the meeting of the Wiley Economics Online Conference.

Oswald, A. (2010). *Notes on economics and the future of quantitative social science* (Unpublished manuscript). Department of Economics, University of Warwick. http://www2.warwick.ac.uk/fac/soc/economics/staff/academic/oswald/maysciencedata2010.pdf

Plott, C. R. (1991). Will economics become an experimental science? *Southern Economic Journal, 57*(4), 901–919.

Roth, A. (1995). Introduction to experimental economics. In J. Kagel & A. Roth (Eds.), *Handbook of experimental economics* (pp. 3–109), Princeton, NJ: Princeton University Press.

Skyrms, B. (2004). *The stag hunt and the evolution of social structure.* Cambridge, UK: Cambridge University Press.

Smith, V. L. (1982). Microeconomic systems as an experimental science. *American Economic Review, 72*(5), 923–955.

PART I

2 An informational framework for studying social norms

James Tremewan and Alexander Vostroknutov

1.   Introduction

The greatest achievements of humankind have resulted from our extraordinary ability to act together, and to formulate and achieve common goals that benefit the community as a whole—in other words, to cooperate. Comparisons between humans and other closely related species, such as apes and primates, unambiguously demonstrate that one crucial thing that distinguishes us from them is the presence of sophisticated culture—a collection of packages of social norms enhanced with high-fidelity information-transmission mechanisms (e.g. language)—that allows us to sustain vital community-oriented behaviours across many generations (Henrich, 2017; Laland, 2018). Given the highly cooperative nature of the societies we live in, it is thus not surprising that social norms permeate all aspects of our daily lives. Consequently, concepts related to social norms have featured in most social sciences and philosophy at least since the time of Aristotle.

Mainstream economics has traditionally put very little weight on the role of social norms in economic behaviour. Nevertheless, its mathematical concepts, including preferences, utility, rationality and game theory, combined with experimental methods have produced a set of valuable tools that have been used successfully to study incentivized social behaviour (Vostroknutov, 2020). Experimental economics was a latecomer to the topic of social norms. However, it can be a crucial addition to the methodological arsenal for studying them exactly because of its mathematically precise approach to formulating testable hypotheses.

Despite achieving various important insights, experimental economics' treatment of social norms remains sporadic, unstructured and terminologically vague. We believe that, to make progress in the field, a general framework should be put forward that would allow researchers to speak the same language and to expand the applicability of experimental economics methods to broader sets of problems related to norm-related behaviour. In this chapter, we propose such a framework based on the recent developments in experimental methodology and behavioural economic theory. The framework puts specific emphasis on the transmission of information relevant for normative reasoning, which is an integral part of understanding social learning, norm stability and norm uncertainty, among other topics, and their reflections in social behaviour. In essence, we construct an environment in which multimodal information (private information, learned opinions, observed actions) is processed by norm-following agents to act in a world inhabited by other norm-following agents. We show how this framework can prove useful in interpreting the results of existing experiments, and in designing future experiments to carefully avoid confounds.

In the spirit of this book, after developing a comprehensive framework for the study of social norms, we use it to structure both a compendium of experimental methods that have been developed for studying this topic, and our views on the most important avenues for future research. The chapter continues as follows: Section 2 gives a brief overview of terminology related to social norms and definitions proposed by researchers from various social sciences to assist readers who are new to the topic in parsing the existing literature; in Section 3 we outline and discuss our proposed framework; in Section 4 we describe the tools that can be used for the experimental study of social norms, cite papers that illustrate these tools and suggest how they might be used to further our knowledge of this fundamental aspect of human nature. Finally, given the space constraints of this chapter, we have omitted a number of interesting and important topics related to social norms (notably punishment). We would like to refer the readers to the extended version of this chapter available online (Tremewan & Vostroknutov, 2020), which is broader in scope and contains a deeper and more theoretical treatment of the material presented here.

2.   Definitions of Norms

An initial confusion to be cleared up in definitions of norms is the dual use of the words norm and normative. For many economists, the first association with these words will be in relation to the distinction between positive and normative economics, the former being the study of "what is" and the latter the study of "what ought to be". That is, the word normative has a moral flavour. On the other hand, normative often refers in common usage to "what is typical", which is an "is" rather than an "ought" concept. Both uses of the words are ingrained in the literature on norms, and the words will be used in both ways in this chapter. Often in the literature, people differentiate between "is" and "ought" using the terms descriptive and injunctive, simply defining descriptive norms as "what most people do" and injunctive norms as "what most people think is right". Many papers refer to one or the other of these concepts as a social norm.

The only general agreement regarding the definition of the term social norm seems to be that there is no general agreement. In preparation for this chapter, we ran a short survey among subscribers to an experimental economics discussion group to gauge the personal views of researchers in the field on some key definitional issues, and we indeed found considerable diversity.[1] For example, 46% of the 201 respondents regarded social norms and social preferences as completely distinct phenomena, while the other half viewed one as a subset of the other, or identified a partial overlap. While there were points of disagreement, there was also strong consensus on some issues, as will be seen later in this section.

Economic theorists have often viewed social norms as devices to enable coordination in the presence of multiple equilibria (e.g. Gintis, 2010). However, 84% of respondents in our survey disagreed with the statement that coordination on one of multiple equilibria is a sufficient definition of the term social norm. A more widely accepted view of social norms is that they relate explicitly to beliefs about what others believe ought to be done. We follow the terminology of Bicchieri (2016) and call individual's beliefs about what ought to be done "personal norms" and beliefs about others' personal norms "normative expectations".[2] In our survey, 85% of respondents agreed that normative expectations should be part of a definition of social norms, much more than any other statement we suggested in this question. The idea that social norms are commonly held perceptions of what society believes is acceptable (i.e. shared normative expectations) is present in two of the most prominent definitions, those of Bicchieri (2016) and Elster (1989). Beyond this there is less agreement, and we now highlight some of the additional conditions that some authors impose.

In some definitions, it must be the case not only that there are shared normative expectations, but also that these expectations are correct. For example, the definition by Fehr and Schurtenberger (2018) states that social norms are "commonly known standards of behaviour that are based on *widely shared views* of how individual group members ought to behave" (p. 458, emphasis added). In other words, personal norms and normative expectations generally coincide. Such a definition excludes an important class of phenomena that are regarded by others as social norms; specifically, this refers to behaviour underpinned by pluralistic ignorance (Bicchieri, 2016). This is a situation where personal norms are different from shared normative expectations. For example, in the folktale "The Emperor's New Clothes", the observers understand that the Emperor is naked, however, they keep pretending that he is not due to shared normative expectations (everyone believes that everyone believes that the Emperor is clothed). The opinions in our survey on whether personal norms should be included as a part of the definition of social norms are split: 40% of the respondents thought that "what one believes one ought to do" should be part of a definition of a social norm.

Elster (2009) includes in his definition that social norms are only adhered to due to fear of punishment ("the operation of social norms depends crucially on the agent *being observed by others*", p. 196, emphasis in original). An integral part of the definition of Bicchieri (2016) is that shared normative expectations only constitute a social norm when behaviour is conditional on those expectations as well as on empirical expectations, or beliefs about what others actually do. Bicchieri also requires conditionality in her definition of a descriptive norm, which is only defined as such if people are conforming to a behaviour because they believe others will do the same.

Overall, we see a large diversity of opinions on what norms are. The general framework we outline in the next section is rich enough to test the assumptions implicit in many of these definitions, while being relatively parsimonious in that the set of assumptions from which the framework itself is derived is small. Furthermore, there are hints that personal norms and empirical expectations may play an important role. Indeed, one of the important insights of our framework is that the effect of social norms, as represented by normative expectations, cannot be effectively studied without simultaneously accounting for these other types of "norm-related beliefs", which therefore play a major role in the remainder of the chapter.

3.   A Framework for Norms

In this section we develop a framework for investigating the relationship between norms and behaviour. In Section 3.1, we provide the basics of a general theory of "injunctive norms", showing how the normative acceptability or otherwise of an outcome can be derived from a game form. In Section 3.2, we follow the categorization of Bicchieri (2016) and give precise mathematical meaning to the four types of norm-related beliefs that she defines: factual beliefs, personal norms, normative expectations and empirical expectations. With this at hand, we show how different kinds of informative signals, social or otherwise, lead to the updating of these norm-related beliefs. In Section 3.3 we incorporate all four types of beliefs into the utility function, through which they may influence behaviour.

Given the constraints of this chapter, we give only simple examples to illustrate the mechanisms of the framework. We emphasize here that, although many of the specific details of our framework as we outline it here may be debated, the main insights are likely to hold in any model with two general assumptions: 1) agents are influenced to some degree in their choices by normative concerns; and 2) agents have some understanding of how others' normative views relate to factual beliefs, allowing information to be inferred from those normative views, and actions to be based upon them.

The main value of our framework is that it clearly separates the channels through which information, whether it be factual or related to social injunctive or descriptive norms, can affect behaviour: by shaping factual beliefs, personal norms, or normative or empirical expectations (Section 3.2); or through a direct impact on utility caused by a desire to act in accordance with norms (Section 3.3). We think that bearing this framework in mind when designing and interpreting experiments will help researchers place their work in a broader context and avoid possible confounds.

3.1   A Theory of Injunctive Norms

In this section we present a general theory of injunctive norms following Kimbrough and Vostroknutov (2020), henceforth KV. While a general theory is not essential for the remainder of our framework (and can be easily replaced by another theory), it will give us a firm basis on which to build the definitions and examples we develop in the following sections. Furthermore, we believe that some theory of injunctive norms—that defines which injunctive norm should arise in each situation—is necessary to study social decision-making because assuming that norms can vary freely with no structure allows everything to be explained in an ad hoc manner and is therefore unfalsifiable (Vostroknutov, 2020). Thus, KV's theory can be used as a starting point for future research on general theories of injunctive norms, which we will make use of in Section 4.1.

The theory builds on three premises: 1) that an individual feels (prospective) dissatisfaction about a certain outcome that can happen because of other materially better outcomes that could have happened instead; 2) that people are able to empathize with others (they understand others' dissatisfactions); and 3) the process of gene-culture co-evolution favours social norms that minimize aggregate dissatisfaction because individuals tend to bargain, argue, negotiate, and so on with one another, so the norm produces a balance between the interests of all parties involved.

To put this in mathematical terms, consider a finite set of players N and a set C of consequences that represent all possible outcomes of some interaction of the players.[3] Let us assume that there are consumption utility functions $u_i : C \rightarrow R$ defined for each player i that associate with each consequence $c \in C$ a consumption utility that i receives in it. In this section we assume that all u_i's are common knowledge. Then,

$$d_i(c_1, c) = \max \{u_i(c) - u_i(c_1), 0\}$$

denotes the dissatisfaction that player i feels about c_1 because of the possibility of c. Thus, player i is dissatisfied to the degree $u_i(c) - u_i(c_1)$ if c gives her higher consumption utility, and is not dissatisfied at all if c gives her lower consumption utility.[4] The total dissatisfaction that player i feels with respect to c_1 can then be defined as:

$$D_i(c_1) = \int_{c \in C} d_i(c_1, c) dc \qquad (2.1)$$

This is just a summation of all dissatisfactions that are felt in c_1 because of all other consequences in C (if there are finitely many consequences in C, then the integral is replaced by a sum). The overall dissatisfaction in c_1, which takes into account the dissatisfactions of all players, can be computed as:

$$D(c_1) = \sum_{i \in N} D_i(c_1).$$

Here we use the assumption that, because players can empathize with each other, they can compute the total dissatisfactions of other players. The knowledge of $D(c)$ for all consequences $c \in C$ gives each player an idea about how much dissatisfaction should be expected if c is achieved.

Next, KV postulate that the feeling of social appropriateness, associated with a consequence in C, which is also called normative valence, is inversely proportional to the overall dissatisfaction in this consequence. To capture this idea, we define the norm function, η as $\eta(c) = [-D(c)]$, where [.] stands for the linear normalization of the function $-D$ to the interval $[-1, 1]$ (this normalization is necessary to have a common "normative space" for all games). So, for all consequences c that minimize the overall dissatisfaction D we have $\eta(c) = 1$, while for all consequences that maximize the overall dissatisfaction we have $\eta(c) = -1$.

To illustrate this concept, consider the Dictator game. Suppose that there is a pie of size 1 and that a dictator chooses to give $c \leq 1$ to a receiver and is left with $1-c$. The set of consequences is given by all possible values of c and can be defined as $C = [0, 1]$. The consumption utilities are given by $u_d(c) = 1-c$ for the dictator and $u_r(c) = c$ for the receiver. For any consequence $c \in C$, the total dissatisfaction of the dictator is $D_d(c) = c^2/2$, and the total dissatisfaction of the receiver is given by $D_r(c) = (1 - c^2/2)$, both computed using equation (1). Thus, the overall dissatisfaction is given by:

$$D(c) = D_d(c) + D_r(c) = c^2/2 + (1 - c^2/2)$$

This is a parabola with a minimum at $c^* = 1/2$. Thus, the norm function $\eta(c)$ is a downward-sloping parabola with the equal split c^* being the most socially appropriate consequence, which we also call the injunctive norm, defined as any consequence c in which $\eta(c)$ reaches its maximum. The consequences $c = 0$ and $c = 1$ are the least appropriate ones, with $\eta(0) = \eta(1) = -1$.

To use this theory to predict behaviour, KV assume that players maximize norm-dependent utility of the form

$$w_i(c) = u_i(c) + \phi_i \eta(c) \tag{2.2}$$

where $\phi_i \geq 0$ is an individual propensity to follow norms. This utility function represents the trade-off between increasing own consumption utility u_i and acting in accordance with the injunctive norm function η. In the Dictator game, the optimal choice that maximizes $w_i(c)$ is

$$\frac{8\phi_i - 1}{16\phi_i} \text{ for } \phi_i \geq 1/8 \text{ and } 0 \text{ for } \phi_i < 1/8.$$

This example demonstrates how the theory predicts behaviour in *allocation games*—that is, games with a single move by one player who chooses among a set of possible allocations. For general games, special care should be taken when introducing the norm-dependent utility. For example, in games with sequential moves, normative punishment should be explicitly modelled to account for norm violations as the game unfolds. We suggest that readers who are interested in normative behaviour in generic games follow KV, who show how to deal with norm-dependent utility in games with observable actions.

3.2   Norm-Related Beliefs

In this section we describe how various norm-related beliefs are formed in the presence of uncertainty, and how they can be affected by different types of new information. We take as our starting point the classification of Bicchieri (2016), which distinguishes four types of beliefs that we present here, together with the corresponding mathematical objects from the model in the previous section:

- Factual beliefs: beliefs about the world (beliefs about u_k for all $k \in N$);
- Personal norm: what an individual believes is morally correct behaviour given factual information (represented by player i's own η_i);[5]
- Normative expectations: perceptions of the personal norms of others given factual information (i's beliefs about η_j for all $j \neq i$)—*normative information* can come from, for example, credible statements by individuals about their moral views, or the outcome of a referendum on a moral issue;
- Empirical expectations: perceptions of how other players will behave given current information (model's predictions about the choices of players $j \neq i$ given normative expectations and beliefs about ϕ_k for all $k \in N$)— *empirical information* may come from personal observation of others' behaviour, government statistics and so on.

The main idea we wish to get across in this section is the interdependence of these four types of beliefs and the information that underlies them. Some of these relationships are obvious, but others are less so. We discuss a series of examples to illustrate some key insights that arise from thinking about norms in this framework. All of these insights can be derived from a simple model with Bayesian agents that is laid out in Tremewan and Vostroknutov (2020).

To give a concrete example of how uncertainty and asymmetric information influence norm-related beliefs, consider the social acceptability of flying to a holiday destination, related to the modern phenomenon of "flight-shaming" (Gossling et al., 2020). Holiday-makers must decide how much convenience to sacrifice in order to benefit future generations by decreasing the potential costs resulting from anthropogenic climate change, but there is uncertainty over the degree to which emissions from the aviation industry will accelerate global warming.

How does factual information affect norm-related beliefs? First, imagine a situation where the latest and most reliable climate model is common knowledge. Because each individual's factual information is identical, personal norms and normative expectations coincide. Now suppose that you read an article that suggests that climate change will proceed at a faster pace than previously thought (new factual information). You update your personal norm accordingly (flying becomes less personally acceptable); however, you know that only some fraction of the population will have read the article, so you update your normative expectations to a lesser degree. Thus, personal norms in a population can differ due to asymmetric information, but are likely to be correlated. How much you update empirical expectations depends on your beliefs about how influenced other people are by normative concerns (ϕ_k).

Now consider new normative information, for example, a speech by Greta Thunberg emphasizing our moral duty to fly less. Clearly this will cause us to update our normative expectations, both because of direct information about Greta's personal norm and because this is likely to be a view shared by a broader swathe of the population. Empirical expectations will be updated to the degree to which we believe people are influenced in their choices by their normative beliefs. Furthermore, Greta's speech may influence our factual beliefs, and thereby our personal norms: knowing that Greta's personal norms are based on factual information, we can infer something about information she has that we may not be aware of. If she finds flying less acceptable than us, we can infer that her information suggests that flying is more harmful to future generations than we believed, and as far as we believe that her information sources are broader or more accurate than our own, we will update both our factual beliefs and personal norms.

New empirical information, for example, a newspaper article showing that people are choosing to fly less and holiday more in their own country, will directly cause us to update our empirical expectations. But again, this may suggest that others have information we do not about the harms of flying, causing us to also update our factual beliefs, personal norms derived from those beliefs and normative expectations.

Four important intuitions are illustrated by these examples. First, it is always the case that, with symmetric information about utilities and payoffs, personal norms coincide with normative expectations. Second, personal norms and normative expectations can differ when one is aware that others have different information, but will be correlated if information about the true state of the world received by different players is correlated. This suggests that in situations when there is a reason to believe that people have correlated information, both personal norms and normative expectations should be measured. Third, empirical information about the choices of others can change behaviour, even if one does not directly care about conforming with others' behaviour, because it reveals information about the state of the world and causes people to update their personal norms and normative expectations. In this case, it is possible that an individual's actions will be closer to a commonly observed action, but for purely informational reasons that have nothing to do with conformism per se. Fourth, normative and empirical information (e.g. opinions and actions) can have asymmetric effects on beliefs and behaviour because the latter is modulated by beliefs about the degree to which others follow norms (as defined by ϕ_k), whereas the former is not.

3.3   Generalised Norm-Dependent Utility

In the previous sections we discussed how norm-related beliefs can be formed and reshaped by new information. In this section we look at how these beliefs might affect decision-making through a generalized norm-dependent utility function that includes all four types of norm-related beliefs. In what follows, we do not explicitly refer to their relationships, but consider them only after all updating has taken place. For practical purposes, this is not a problem as long as one can measure beliefs between the arrival of the last piece of relevant information and when choices are made.

It is commonly believed that people have an intrinsic desire to follow norms. In our survey, 92% of respondents stated that people's choices are influenced by personal norms, as we assumed in the model in the previous section, and 96% agreed that people follow "social norms" even when anonymous.[6, 7] Norm-dependent utility functions have already been proposed. For example, Krupka and Weber (2013) consider a utility function with only material payoffs and normative expectations. Bašić and Verrina (2020) extend this utility function to include personal norms. We simply propose the further inclusion of empirical expectations, giving us the following generalized norm-dependent utility function:

$$W_i(c) = u_i(c) + \phi_i \eta_i(c) + \phi_i^N \eta_i^N(c) + \phi_i^E \delta_i(c) \tag{2.3}$$

where ϕ_i, ϕ_i^N and ϕ_i^E are intrinsic propensities to follow personal norms, normative expectations and empirical expectations, respectively. We view these parameters as individual constants that are context-independent. The function $\eta_i^N : C \to [-1,1]$ represents normative expectations as an "aggregated" norm function that depends on i's personal norm and her beliefs about others' personal norms $(\eta_k)_{k \in N}$, for example, averaging across all individuals. Similarly, $\delta_i : C \rightarrow [-1,1]$ is a function that depends on beliefs about the distribution of others' actions, for example, the distribution of actions normalized to [−1, 1]. These two functions capture the idea that utility is increasing in the degree to which a person conforms to what they believe others think is right, and what they believe others will do. However, it is not obvious what these functions should look like when the decision-maker believes there is heterogeneity in personal norms and actions, particularly if there are multiple modes. We return to this point in Section 4.2.

We are not claiming here that the parameters ϕ_i, ϕ_i^N and ϕ_i^E are necessarily all non-zero, which is an empirical question that has yet to be fully addressed. Rather, given the likely correlation in factual beliefs, normative and empirical expectations highlighted by the model in the previous section, failure to begin with such a general utility function runs the risk of biasing estimates of the remaining parameters. Finally, some current theories can be seen as imposing constraints on this general empirical model. For example, Elster's definition of norms implies that $\phi_i^N = 0$ under anonymity. The "conditionality" in Bicchieri's definition of a social norm implies that both ϕ_i^N and ϕ_i^E must be strictly positive.

3.4   Summary and Discussion

The framework we have outlined flows naturally from essentially only a few basic assumptions: people's behaviour is influenced by norms; there is uncertainty about the world; people can learn from others' behaviour and normative statements. It highlights two channels through which shocks to norm-related beliefs can influence behaviour: via the effect on other norm-related beliefs (Section 3.2), and through a direct effect on utility (Section 3.3). Separately identifying the existence or importance of each channel will require careful measurement and clever experimental designs, and may be challenging in many settings (especially field experiments). These challenges will be addressed in the following section. However, even when one cannot separately identify each factor, bearing in mind our framework will help to interpret patterns in norm-related behaviours.

4.   Experimental Methods and Research Directions

The purpose of this section is twofold. In addition to proposing various directions of research, informed by the framework described in Section 3, we also
aim to provide a reference for readers who are new to the field by explaining
various experimental methods that have been developed for the study of
norms. This chapter is not intended as a review of the literature, and the papers
we cite are chosen to illustrate methods and approaches rather than to provide
an overview of the current state of knowledge.

The structure mimics that of Section 3. In Section 4.1 we discuss building and
testing theories of (personal) injunctive norms. In Section 4.2 we focus on
norm-related beliefs, first describing methods for measuring such beliefs, then
discussing how one might explore their formation and transmission. Section
4.3 relates to the connection between beliefs and actions: how norm-related
information can change behaviour, and how to measure individuals' tendencies to follow norms. In this section we also discuss the challenges of eliciting
beliefs and actions from the same individual (order effects).

4.1   Injunctive Norms

There are many potential lines of research that are necessary to further our
understanding of injunctive norms. KV show that the model described in
Section 3.1 can account for behaviour in a wide variety of experimental games,
however, the evidence is based on previous experiments that were not specifically designed to test it. Therefore, there is a need for direct experimental evidence to support the theory or to determine strategic contexts in which it does
not work. Some tests along these lines can be found in Panizza et al. (2021) and
Merguei et al. (2020). In addition, many assumptions of the theory need to be
directly verified. For example, KV assume that injunctive norms are constructed solely from the dissatisfactions due to unachieved outcomes with
higher utility. However, it is not obvious that joy from not achieving outcomes
that bring lower utility does not play a role. In principle, dissatisfaction, joy or
some other reactions to counterfactual payoffs can enter the calculation of the
norm function η. Evolutionary models in the style of Gavrilets and Richerson
(2017) can be used to determine what kinds of norm functions have better
survival chances and thus have a higher probability of being internalized in the
process of evolution. In addition, the theory of KV contains a variety of "cultural" parameters that should be empirically estimated before the model can be
applied to a specific situation. These include the parameter that defines the
importance of punishment (σ in KV) and individual norm-aggregation weights

that determine social relationships that can influence injunctive norms, such as social status, ingroup/outgroup, kin, and ownership claims (see KV). Some of these parameters can be measured by means of third-party Dictator games (e.g. Chen & Li, 2009), however, currently there is no settled experimental methodology to estimate them.

4.2   Norm-Related Beliefs

In this section we first address the question of how to measure the four types of beliefs that provide the foundation of our framework, then we consider how to investigate belief formation and transmission.

4.2.1   Measuring Beliefs

There are numerous well-established methods for the incentivized elicitation of beliefs about actual outcomes or choices of others under the condition that these events can be later observed and compared to subjects' responses (for a survey, see Schlag et al., 2015). These methods allow us to directly measure a variety of factual beliefs, as well as empirical expectations. For some factual beliefs, such as the future impact of climate change, the objective truth is unknowable, so it cannot be used to incentivize elicitation. Prelec (2004) provides an incentivized mechanism for such cases when one's own beliefs are correlated with those of others.

Measuring personal norms is more problematic, as it is difficult to see how they can be elicited in an incentivized fashion. If it is true that normative and empirical expectations do not influence anonymous behaviour (as suggested by Elster, 2009), then anonymous third-party allocation and punishment games unconflated with self-interest (e.g. Fehr & Fischbacher, 2004) would be incentive-compatible for elicitation of personal norms. However, the role of normative and empirical expectations under anonymity is something that remains to be established.

The most straightforward way to measure personal norms is simply to ask subjects how appropriate each choice is from their perspective (to measure norm functions η_i), or which choice is the most appropriate (to measure norms c_i^*). Traditionally, economists have been suspicious of any beliefs elicited from people who have no explicit incentive to tell the truth. This attitude appears to be softening a little in some quarters, with increasing evidence that unincentivized responses can provide useful information.[8] However, there is good reason to believe that responses to questions about personal norms may in some circumstances be systematically biased: "social desirability bias" can lead subjects to misreport in the direction of their normative expectations, especially for sensitive topics (Krumpal, 2013). Possible partial remedies to ameliorate this concern are credibly ensuring anonymity (Hoffman et al., 1994) and having subjects sign oaths to tell the truth (Jacquemet et al., 2013).

One might think that it is necessary to incentivize elicitation of personal norms to achieve a fully incentivized elicitation of the higher-order normative expectations. However, the method introduced in Krupka and Weber (2013), henceforth KW, cleverly sidesteps this problem. Subjects are asked to state how socially appropriate each possible action is, and are paid if they guess the modal response of other subjects. This incentivizes subjects to state not the degree of appropriateness that they themselves believe is correct, but to match others' responses. This mechanism allows us to directly measure η_i^N.[9] This method has proved popular and has been used in many studies (e.g. Gächter et al., 2017; Barr et al., 2017; Hoeft et al., 2018; Chang et al., 2019).

A possible limitation of the KW task is that this method only elicits a central tendency of the belief distribution, while other features may also be important (see Section 3.3).[10] d'Adda et al. (2020) introduce a method for eliciting beliefs about the full distribution of personal norms of others (normative expectations); however, it relies on the preliminary unincentivized elicitation of personal norms.

We believe that there is room for improvement of the elicitation methods for norm-related beliefs. As discussed in Section 3.3, it is far from clear what aspects of normative expectations are important for behaviour, especially in the cases when there is a perception that personal norm functions are widely dispersed or have multiple modes. Optimal behaviour may depend on the values of η_i and η_i^N in all consequences C as well as on the uncertainty related to these objects. Or perhaps it is simply a central tendency that largely determines behaviour. To investigate this question, we need more precise estimates of norm functions. Following this direction, Merguei et al. (2020) propose a modified KW task where appropriateness levels are elicited on a continuous instead of a four-item Likert scale, as in KW. This allows for more accurate estimates that can be used for within-subjects analyses. However, this method still relies on eliciting only the mode of the belief distribution. There is a need for new methods that can estimate not only the whole norm functions, but also the uncertainty related to them.

4.2.2   Belief Formation

Few studies testing the impact of norm-related information measure its effect on beliefs, and instead look directly at behaviour (see Section 3.3). However, an experiment in d'Adda et al. (2020) shows that normative information influences all types of norm-related beliefs. Similarly, Bicchieri and Xiao (2009) find that presenting descriptive and/or normative information changes both empirical and normative expectations. Panizza et al. (2020) report an effect of descriptive information on normative expectations.

These studies provide some evidence on belief formation, however, much more systematic work needs to be done to better understand how norm-related information changes beliefs. In addition, there are few studies on the degree to which people use Bayesian updating when incorporating new normative information, or suffer from, for example, self-serving bias or confirmation bias. We know little about how uncertainty in the four types of norm-related beliefs affects the processing of new information. Finally, an interesting topic that has received a lot of attention in the fields of psychology and human evolutionary biology is how information from different sources is given different weight in the updating of beliefs, for example, selective attention to ingroups or those with higher status/prestige (e.g. Rendell et al., 2011; Henrich, 2017). An experimental economics methodology using incentivized games and a formal framework, such as the one proposed in this chapter, may have a lot to contribute in answering these questions.

4.3   Norm-Related Behaviour

In this section we discuss the connection between norm-related beliefs and behaviour, essentially the nature of the ϕs in the utility function (Equation 2.2). We begin with experiments that shock beliefs and look for a behavioural response, implicitly testing the hypothesis that at least one of ϕ_i, ϕ_i^N and ϕ_i^E is not equal to zero. As shown in Section 3.2, all kinds of information can affect all kinds of beliefs, so behavioural change resulting from a shock to empirical expectations, for example, does not imply that $\phi_i^E \neq 0$, as the change might result from an intermediate effect on personal norms or normative expectations. We then move on to experiments that estimate the average value of ϕ_i^N across a population, and finally we describe a method for measuring ϕ_i^N at the individual level.

4.3.1   Testing the Impact of Information on Behaviour

When looking at the relationship between norms and behaviour, it is, of course, not necessary to measure propensities to follow norms, or to identify intermediate effects through beliefs. While it may be useful to understand the precise channels through which behavioural change can occur—and is definitely of scientific interest—for many practical purposes it is only the ultimate effects on actions that are of concern. This is particularly the case for field experiments, where the objective is simply to find a solution to a specific problem.

Numerous lab experiments present subjects with normative or empirical information from subjects in earlier sessions and examine the effect on behaviour, in much the same way as the studies cited in Section 4.2. An alternative approach is to inform subjects of another subject's choice within the same session (Gächter et al., 2013). Such information may be seen as more relevant or credible than experimenter-supplied information from another session. Such distrust would not be unreasonable, given that typically experimenters choose to give information from extreme sessions in order to maximize possible treatment effects.

There is a substantial literature on field experiments investigating the potential of empirical or normative information to enact behavioural change in many domains with varying success. Empirical information about peer behaviour has been disseminated in a variety of ways, for example: posters and flyers on university campuses aimed at reducing alcohol consumption (Wechsler et al., 2003); reports on energy usage from an energy company to reduce consumption (Allcott, 2011); and letters from an employer to increase savings (Beshears et al., 2015). Normative information can be transmitted in a number of ways: emoticons signalling social approval or disapproval have been used in household energy consumption reports (Allcott, 2011) and on electronic displays near hand-sanitizer dispensers in hospitals (Gaube et al., 2018); Bursztyn et al. (2018) informed Saudi husbands of the results of a survey of their peers on the acceptability of female labour force participation.

Another valuable tool that researchers of social norms should be aware of is the "vignette study" (see Chapter 2 in Bicchieri, 2016). A vignette presents subjects with a description of a scenario, which can be used as the basis for eliciting norm-related beliefs. These are particularly useful when the behaviour under study is not easily replicated in the lab (e.g., child marriage), and when information from the experimenter is unlikely to be effective in shocking beliefs in the field (e.g., because members of the subject pool have firm beliefs based on long experience regarding the acceptability or prevalence of a behaviour in their community). In Brouwer et al. (2019), vignettes are used to refine understanding of treatment effects in a field experiment, illustrating how the advantages of a field experiment (external validity) can be combined with the advantages of a lab experiment (control and precision of measurement).

4.3.2   Measuring Norm-Following Propensities

The first attempt to measure the propensity to follow norms was undertaken by KW. They used dictator game choices combined with the normative expectations of a separate set of subjects in conditional logit regressions to estimate the population average of ϕ_i^N. They found that it is positive and significant, as expected, with subjects willing to sacrifice around \$5–\$6 to comply with the social norm.

Whether or not it is sufficient to use average normative expectations from subjects who are not making the decisions to estimate the propensity to follow norms is debatable. If there is an unambiguous social norm, in the sense that normative expectations in the population are reasonably well-aligned, then it is immaterial from whom the normative expectations are elicited. However, theoretically (as shown in Section 3.2) and empirically (Merguei et al., 2020), normative expectations can vary widely, and the measurement error resulting from using an average will bias estimates of ϕ_i^N.

One reason to elicit actions and normative expectations from separate subjects is to avoid possible order effects. The concern is that subjects may select an action to be consistent with their previously stated norms, or state norms to justify an earlier taken action, inflating the correlation between norms and behaviour. One study (d'Adda et al., 2016) did not find any order effects for the KW task, and at least two papers have analyzed the effect of the within-subjects norm elicitation on behaviour (Thomsson & Vostroknutov, 2017; Panizza et al., 2021). However, it remains to be seen how robust the absence of order effects is across games and subject pools, so it seems prudent to take precautions when eliciting both actions and normative expectations from the same subjects.[11] Bašić and Verrina (2020) guard against order effects by eliciting normative beliefs online, four weeks before a lab experiment where actions are elicited. If such a time delay is impractical, beliefs can be elicited "behind the veil of ignorance", for example, before subjects know whether they will take the role of dictator or receiver in an allocation game (d'Adda et al., 2020).

KW, and the subsequent studies using their method, estimate a utility function that only contains utility from money and concern for normative expectations (i.e. they assume $\phi_i = \phi_i^N = 0$). If, as argued in Section 3.2, personal norms and normative expectations are likely to be positively correlated, there will be an omitted variable bias inflating estimates of ϕ_i^N. Bašić and Verrina (2020) follow a similar methodology to KW, but elicit both normative expectations and personal norms from the same subjects, who make decisions in an assortment of games. They find that, while normative expectations and personal norms are highly correlated, there is sufficient variation to estimate the separate impact of each on decision-making.

While many questions can be addressed with estimates of population averages, it is also important to investigate heterogeneity in individual propensity to follow norms. This is necessary, for example, to better understand the role of individual behaviour in repeated interactions. Measuring individual propensity to follow norms was the goal of Kimbrough and Vostroknutov (2016), who proposed an individual rule-following task to measure ϕ_i directly. In this task and its later modification (Kimbrough & Vostroknutov, 2018), subjects were offered a trade-off between having more money and following an artificial costly rule devised by the experimenters. "Rule-following" subjects chose to forego significant amounts of money in order to stick to this rule, whereas "rule-breaking" subjects kept most of the money and broke the rule. The important part of the experiment was to see how these individual measures of rule following correlate with behaviour in various social dilemmas. Kimbrough and Vostroknutov (2016) found that rule-followers give more money in the Dictator game, have a higher rejection threshold in the Ultimatum game, give a higher percentage back in the Trust game, and when grouped with other rule-followers, sustain cooperation in the repeated Public Goods game. These findings validated both the measure of ϕ_i obtained from the rule-following task and the norm-dependent utility specification (Equation 2.2).[12]

The advantage of the rule-following tasks in measuring ϕ_i is that they are "assumption-free" in the sense that we do not need to assume anything specific about the norm-dependent utility to obtain these measures. A more assumption-dependent approach is to use "heavy" within-subjects designs. For example, in Panizza et al. (2021), each subject makes choices in over 100 mini-allocation games with two outcomes and two players. These binary choices are then plugged into an individual logit regression that assumes random utility of the form (as in Equation 2.2). Individual ϕ_i then comes out as a coefficient on the normative term in the utility. Panizza et al. (2021) also use the rule-following task within the same subjects and show that the estimates of ϕ_i obtained from the logit regression correlate with the estimates from the rule-following task, thus indicating that the logit estimates are reliable.

One of the most interesting and urgent directions of research suggested by our framework is to carefully establish which of personal norms, normative expectations and empirical expectations influence behaviour the most. As far as we are aware, there are as yet no studies that carefully account for all of these beliefs simultaneously and, therefore, given their likely correlations, no convincing evidence for any of them. Clearly, this will be easier in the laboratory, where anonymity can easily remove confounds due to possible changes in expected punishment. However, the relative importance of different types of beliefs is likely to be highly context dependent, so field experiments are crucial, and could perhaps be supported by auxiliary information from vignette studies. One such field experiment is reported in Rössler et al. (2019).

Another fascinating question is the degree to which a tendency towards rule-following is genetically or culturally determined. Rejection in the ultimatum game was found to be heritable (Wallace et al., 2007), but further evidence is required from tasks focussed specifically on norm following, such as that in Kimbrough and Vostroknutov (2018). To answer this and other related questions, such as whether ϕ_i changes with age, we will need evidence from neuroeconomics and cross-cultural, developmental and twin studies. Some initial evidence is provided in House et al. (2020), who find that children across societies start following norms and responding to novel norms at a similar age, suggesting a universal psychology for norm following.

5.   Conclusion

In this chapter we have outlined a framework that describes how norm-following agents make decisions and process various types of information to update their norm-related beliefs. On the theoretical side, we demonstrate with simple examples that norm-related beliefs—personal norms, normative and empirical expectations—are interconnected, and that a change in any one of them can result in updating the rest. This suggests that care should be taken when estimating the effects of various beliefs on behaviour. Specifically, given that all types of norm-related beliefs are correlated, inferences regarding their effects may be incorrect when only some are considered. Fortunately, as described in

Section 4, experimental methodology for the meticulous study of norms and norm-related behaviour is already reasonably well-developed. We hope that this chapter is of use in aiding the design of future experiments, and in informing researchers of the tools at their disposal.

Acknowledgements

We would like to thank Erik Kimbrough and Marie Claire Villeval for invaluable comments. All mistakes are our own.

Notes

1. The full survey and results can be found in Tremewan and Vostroknutov (2020).
2. Some authors use the terms moral norms (Charness and Schram, 2013) or private values (d'Adda et al., 2020) instead of personal norms.
3. Typically, C represents the terminal nodes of the game. However, the game form (that defines the players' strategies) does not need to be precisely specified, in which case C can be seen as a set of all possible outcomes of some unstructured bargaining process.
4. This is the formulation proposed by KV. However, it has never been directly compared (yet) to other possible models in this framework. In Section 4.1 we discuss these alternatives in more detail.
5. It may seem more natural to economists to think of personal norms as preferences rather than beliefs. Here we are using the word "belief" in a more colloquial sense for convenience.
6. In the question about social norms, we did not specify whether we were referring to injunctive or descriptive norms, so it is unclear whether they believed that either normative or empirical expectations, or both, were important.
7. For an explanation of why such preferences may have evolved, see Henrich (2017).
8. For risk, time and social preference elicitation, see Falk et al. (2016); for a review of experimental comparisons of non-incentivized and incentivized belief elicitation, see Charness et al. (forthcoming).
9. In a situation where information is common knowledge (and the subject pool is homogeneous), the method of KW also elicits personal norms, which in this context should be identical to normative expectations (see Section 3.2).
10. In KW, subjects were incentivized to guess the modal appropriateness level. However, other payment schemes can be used to elicit beliefs about the mean or median. See Schlag et al. (2015) for a review of possible methods.
11. Similar issues have been studied with respect to elicitation of empirical expectations, and evidence for the existence, and even direction, of order effects has been mixed. See Schlag et al. (2015) for a survey.

12. Kimbrough and Vostroknutov (2018) also tested the robustness of the Dictator game result in five countries and found even stronger correlations between dictator choices and the proxies for ϕ_i measured in the rule-following task.

References

Allcott, H. (2011). Social norms and energy conservation. *Journal of Public Economics*, *95*(9–10), 1082–1095.

Barr, A., Lane, T., & Nosenzo, D. (2017). On the social appropriateness of discrimination. *CeDEx Discussion Paper Series*.

Bašić, Z., & Verrina, E. (2020). *Personal norms—and not only social norms—shape economic behavior* (Working paper). Max Planck Institute for Research on Collective Goods, GATE-LAB, University of Lyon. https://www.coll.mpg.de/184912/2020_25online.pdf

Beshears, J., Choi, J. J., Laibson, D., Madrian, B. C., & Milkman, K. L. (2015). The effect of providing peer information on retirement savings decisions. *Journal of Finance*, *70*(3), 1161–1201.

Bicchieri, C. (2016). *Norms in the wild: How to diagnose, measure, and change social norms*. Oxford: Oxford University Press.

Bicchieri, C., & Xiao, E. (2009). Do the right thing: But only if others do so. *Journal of Behavioral Decision-Making*, *22*(2), 191–208.

Brouwer, T., Galeotti, F., & Villeval, M. C. (2019). *Teaching norms in the streets: An experimental study* (Unpublished manuscript). Tilburg University, Tilburg, Netherlands. https://econpapers.repec.org/paper/haljournl/halshs-02466113.htm

Bursztyn, L., Gonzalez, A. L., & Yanagizawa-Drott, D. (2018). *Misperceived social norms: Female labor force participation in Saudi Arabia* (Working Paper No. 2018-042). Human Capital and Economic Opportunity Global Working Group, University of Chicago. https://ideas.repec.org/p/hka/wpaper/2018-042.html

Chang, D., Chen, R., & Krupka, E. (2019). Rhetoric matters: A social norms explanation for the anomaly of framing. *Games and Economic Behavior*, *116*, 158–178.

Charness, G., Gneezy, U., & Rasocha, V. (Forthcoming). Experimental methods: Eliciting beliefs. *Journal of Economic Behavior & Organization*.

Charness, G., & Schram, A. (2013). *Social and moral norms in allocation choices in the laboratory* (Unpublished manuscript). University of California at Santa Barbara and University of Amsterdam.

Chen, Y., & Li, S. X. (2009). Group identity and social preferences. *American Economic Review*, *99*(1), 431–457.

d'Adda, G., Drouvelis, M., & Nosenzo, D. (2016). Norm elicitation in within-subjects designs: Testing for order effects. *Journal of Behavioral and Experimental Economics*, *62*, 1–7.

d'Adda, G., Dufwenberg, M., Passarelli, F., & Tabellini, G. (2020). Social norms with private values: Theory and experiments. *Games and Economic Behavior*, *124*(120), 288–304.

Elster, J. (1989). Social norms and economic theory. *Journal of Economic Perspectives*, *3*(4), 99–117.

Elster, J. (2009). Norms. In P. S. Bearman & P. Hedström (Eds.), *The Oxford handbook of analytical sociology* (pp. 195–217). Oxford: Oxford University Press.

Falk, A., Becker, A., Dohmen, T. J., Huffman, D., & Sunde, U. (2016). *The preference survey module: A validated instrument for measuring risk, time, and social preferences.* Retrieved from the Institute of Labor Economics website: https://www.iza .org/publications/dp/9674/the-preference-survey-module-a-validated-instrument -for-measuring-risk-time-and-social-preferences

Fehr, E., & Fischbacher, U. (2004). Third-party punishment and social norms. *Evolution and Human Behavior, 25*(2), 63–87.

Fehr, E., & Schurtenberger, I. (2018). Normative foundations of human cooperation. *Nature Human Behaviour, 2*(7), 458–468.

Gächter, S., Gerhards, L., & Nosenzo, D. (2017). The importance of peers for compliance with norms of fair sharing. *European Economic Review, 97,* 72–86.

Gächter, S., Nosenzo, D., & Sefton, M. (2013). Peer effects in pro-social behavior: Social norms or social preferences? *Journal of the European Economic Association, 11*(3), 548–573.

Gaube, S., Tsivrikos, D., Dollinger, D., & Lermer, E. (2018). How a smiley protects health: A pilot intervention to improve hand hygiene in hospitals by activating injunctive norms through emoticons. *PLOS ONE, 13*(5), e0197465.

Gavrilets, S., & Richerson, P. J. (2017). Collective action and the evolution of social norm internalization. *Proceedings of the National Academy of Sciences, 114*(23), 6068–6073.

Gintis, H. (2010). Social norms as choreography. *Politics, Philosophy & Economics, 9*(3), 251–264.

Gossling, S., Humpe, A., & Bausch, T. (2020). Does "flight shame" affect social norms? Changing perspectives on the desirability of air travel in Germany. *Journal of Cleaner Production, 266,* 122015.

Henrich, J. (2017). *The secret of our success: How culture is driving human evolution, domesticating our species, and making us smarter.* Princeton, NJ: Princeton University Press.

Hoeft, L., Mill, W., & Vostroknutov, A. (2018). *Normative acceptance of power abuse* (Unpublished manuscript). University of Mannheim, MPI Bonn, Maastricht University. http://www.vostroknutov.com/pdfs/abuse_HMV_02.pdf

Hoffman, E., McCabe, K., Shachat, K., & Smith, V. (1994). Preferences, property rights, and anonymity in bargaining games. *Games and Economic Behavior, 7,* 346–380.

House, B. R., Kanngiesser, P., Barrett, H. C., Broesch, T., Cebioglu, S., Crittenden, A. N., … Silk, J. B. (2020). Universal norm psychology leads to societal diversity in prosocial behaviour and development. *Nature Human Behaviour, 4*(1), 36–44.

Jacquemet, N., Joule, R.-V., Luchini, S., & Shogren, J. F. (2013). Preference elicitation under oath. *Journal of Environmental Economics and Management, 65*(1), 110–132.

Kimbrough, E., & Vostroknutov, A. (2016). Norms make preferences social. *Journal of the European Economic Association, 14*(3), 608–638.

Kimbrough, E., & Vostroknutov, A. (2018). A portable method of eliciting respect for social norms. *Economics Letters, 168,* 147–150.

Kimbrough, E., & Vostroknutov, A. (2020). *A theory of injunctive norms* (Unpublished manuscript). Chapman University and Maastricht University. http://www .vostroknutov.com/pdfs/axinorms12_02.pdf

Krumpal, I. (2013). Determinants of social desirability bias in sensitive surveys: A literature review. *Quality & Quantity, 47*(4), 2025–2047.

Krupka, E. L., & Weber, R. A. (2013). Identifying social norms using coordination games: Why does dictator game sharing vary? *Journal of the European Economic Association, 11*(3), 495–524.

Laland, K. N. (2018). *Darwin's unfinished symphony: How culture made the human mind.* Princeton, NJ: Princeton University Press.

Merguei, N., Strobel, M., & Vostroknutov, A. (2020). *Moral opportunism and excess in punishment decisions* (Unpublished manuscript). Maastricht University. http://www.vostroknutov.com/pdfs/MSV-00.pdf

Panizza, F., Vostroknutov, A., & Coricelli, G. (2020). *How conformity can lead to extreme social behaviour* (Unpublished manuscript). University of Trento, Maastricht University, University of Southern California. https://psyarxiv.com/q4n35

Panizza, F., Vostroknutov, A., & Coricelli, G. (2021). *The role of meta-context in moral decisions* (Unpublished manuscript). University of Trento and University of Southern California. http://www.vostroknutov.com/pdfs/metacontextPVCnext00.pdf

Prelec, D. (2004). A Bayesian truth serum for subjective data. *Science, 306*(5695), 462–466.

Rendell, L., Fogarty, L., Hoppitt, W. J., Morgan, T. J., Webster, M. M., & Laland, K. N. (2011). Cognitive culture: Theoretical and empirical insights into social learning strategies. *Trends in Cognitive Sciences, 15*(2), 68–76.

Rössler, C., Rusch, H., & Friehe, T. (2019). Do norms make preferences social? Supporting evidence from the field. *Economics Letters, 183*, 108569.

Schlag, K. H., Tremewan, J., & Van der Weele, J. J. (2015). A penny for your thoughts: A survey of methods for eliciting beliefs. *Experimental Economics, 18*(3), 457–490.

Thomsson, K., & Vostroknutov, A. (2017). Small-world conservatives and rigid liberals: Attitudes towards sharing in self-proclaimed left and right. *Journal of Economic Behavior and Organization, 135*, 181–192.

Tremewan, J., & Vostroknutov, A. (2020). *An informational framework for studying social norms: An extended version* (Unpublished manuscript). Maastricht University. http://www.vostroknutov.com/pdfs/tv-normsframework.pdf

Vostroknutov, A. (2020). Social norms in experimental economics: Towards a unified theory of normative decision-making. *Analyse & Kritik, 42*(1), 3–39.

Wallace, B., Cesarini, D., Lichtenstein, P., & Johannesson, M. (2007). Heritability of ultimatum game responder behavior. *Proceedings of the National Academy of Sciences, 104*(40), 15631–15634.

Wechsler, H., Nelson, T. E., Lee, J. E., Seibring, M., Lewis, C., & Keeling, R. P. (2003). Perception and reality: A national evaluation of social norms marketing interventions to reduce college students' heavy alcohol use. *Journal of Studies on Alcohol, 64*(4), 484–494.

3 Experiments in law and economics

Alice Guerra

1. Introduction

Laws inevitably affect individuals' behaviour. Property rules, liability systems, criminal penalties, legal fees and breach remedies in contract law are just some examples of legal instruments that influence individuals' decisions and affect their range of possible actions. Understanding how people's behaviour interacts with the law is critical for any lawmaker or enforcement authority whose task is to design legal rules to discourage socially undesirable behaviour. The questions of how legal rules shape individuals' incentives and how people respond to changes in their legal environment are still mostly unsettled. For nearly half a century, scholars in the field of law and economics have addressed this question assuming rational responses to changes in the legal environment and using theoretical perspectives. In recent decades, empirical and experimental testing of theoretical predictions has been gaining increasing importance in the literature. This has given rise to a set of experimental studies – both in the lab and in the field – that focus specifically on how individuals behave under different legal rules and institutions. This strand of the literature is referred to as "Experimental Law and Economics" (McAdams, 2000; Croson, 2009).

In this chapter, I provide examples of the application of experimental methods to leading topics in law and economics. The aim is to show people who are working in these fields, but not generally using experiments, how they can apply the experimental method to their work. Equally, however, this chapter seeks to reach people who already use economics experiments – particularly those focused on bargaining and risk preferences – but who do not generally work on law and economics, to show them how their toolkit can be applied to questions in these traditional domains.

This chapter is a selective survey of the literature: I highlight some specific topics in law and economics, and use them as examples of how economics experiments can be applied to traditional legal domains.[1] I select studies that document causal relationships, mostly laboratory economics experiments that are relevant to the law.[2]

In regards to the topics, I focus on three specific research areas: bargaining and the Coase theorem (Section 2); pre-trial settlement and the litigation process (Section 3); and torts and liability rules (Section 4). These are traditional, leading topics in the law and economics literature that have been extensively analysed from different theoretical perspectives, but have seen extremely divergent research progress in terms of their experimental applications – from the most developed bargaining experiments to the least used experiments in tort law and economics.

Specifically, experiments testing the predictive power of the Coase theorem (Coase, 1960) – which stem from the pioneering work by Hoffman and Spitzer (1982) – have achieved a critical mass and an exponential development, almost reaching a saturation point (Medema, 2017). Pre-trial settlement experiments – originating with Coursey and Stanley (1988) – have also reached a fairly advanced development. Experiments on the litigation process, including fee-shifting rules and split-award regimes, are relatively more recent (Spier, 1994) and are attracting a growing number of scholars. Finally, experiments on torts and liability rules deserve particular mention. While the theoretical, economic analysis of tort law is one of the most developed areas in law and economics, there are only a few experimental applications. Stemming from the pioneering work by Kornhauser and Schotter (1990), only five studies have so far experimentally tested the theoretical predictions of tort models. This calls for further experimental evidence to improve our understanding of how individuals' precautionary behaviours respond to different liability rules.

For each topic, I review the pioneering contributions and the most recent published papers. The aim is to offer examples on how economics experiments can be applied to traditional law and economics topics, as well as to provide fresh insights for future research.

2.   Bargaining and the Coase Theorem

Bargaining experiments analyse when and how frequently parties bargain on legal entitlements, and how often they reach an efficient agreement. This topic is widely acknowledged to be important for legal analyses, with relevance for a proper choice between liability and property rules, as well as an efficient selection of default rules in contracts (McAdams, 2000). Bargaining experiments are also useful to predict individuals' incentives to negotiate around pre-trial settlement instead of entering costly litigation (see Section 3).

The Coase theorem is one of the fundamental building blocks of bargaining theory. It generally states that if transaction costs are sufficiently low, individuals bargain and reach an efficient outcome (i.e. the outcome that maximises joint payoffs), regardless of the initial allocation of property rights (Coase, 1960). This theoretical prediction relies upon several assumptions: transaction costs are absent or minimal; property rights are clearly defined and perfectly enforced (i.e. the court system is costless); parties are rational utility maximisers; individuals' preferences and the value each party attaches to the various outcomes are common knowledge.

The first experiments in law and economics aimed at testing the predictive power of the Coase theorem. Here, the advantage of the experimental method over observational data is evident: in the lab, scholars can perfectly reproduce the theorem's assumptions. The pioneering study is by Hoffman and Spitzer (1982). They designed a two-party bargaining experiment to analyse whether parties reach the efficient outcome through bargaining, regardless of the initial allocation of legal entitlements, under the Coase theorem's assumptions. In their bargaining game, participants (students) were randomly matched in pairs and designated as A or B. In each pair, one subject was randomly (by coin flip) assigned to the role of controller and had the unilateral power to select an outcome from a payoff schedule. The outcome was a number indicating the dollars that the parties would receive as payment. See Figure 3.1 for sample instructions, as shown to participants in one treatment condition. In that condition, the efficient outcome was clearly number 1, with a joint payoff of $14.00.

The instructions to participants clarified that the non-controller "may attempt to influence the controller to reach a mutually acceptable joint decision" and "may offer to pay part of all of his or her earnings to the controller" (Hoffman and Spitzer, 1982, p. 83). The controller could talk face-to-face with the matched partner, and the final decision had to be mutually accepted. The two parties were asked to complete a binding agreement on the selected outcome and, hence, on their final payments, as shown in Figure 3.2.

In the treatment condition shown in Figure 3.1, without the possibility of bargaining, A would choose number 6 and B would choose number 0. Instead,

Controller's choice	Payoff schedules ($)	
Number	Payoff to A ($)	Payoff to B ($)
0	0.00	12.00
1	4.00	10.00
2	6.00	6.00
3	8.00	4.00
4	9.00	2.00
5	10.00	1.00
6	11.00	0.00

Source: Hoffman and Spitzer (1982; p. 86, Part A, Table 1).

Figure 3.1   Sample payoffs schedule in Hoffman and Spitzer (1982)

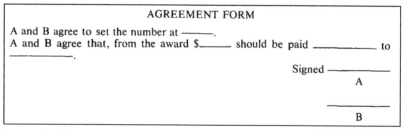

Source: Hoffman and Spitzer (1982; p. 84).

Figure 3.2   Sample agreement form in Hoffman and Spitzer (1982)

with the possibility of bargaining, the Coase theorem predicts that, regardless of the initial allocation of property rights (i.e. irrespective of which party was initially assigned the role of the controller), the matched pairs would bargain and reach an agreement to split the highest joint payoff – that is, number 1. Would subjects actually bargain to reach that efficient outcome? Hoffman and Spitzer (1982) provided an overall affirmative answer. Nearly all the pairs (91.6%) in the condition shown in Figure 3.1 did bargain and chose the highest joint payoff. Similarly, in the other experimental conditions – which included three-person bargaining and imperfect information on individual payoffs – almost 80% of the pairs still agreed on the efficient outcome.

The main limitation in Hoffman and Spitzer (1982) is that they were not able to detect the causal effect of bargaining on reaching the efficient outcomes because their experimental design did not include a control group wherein bargaining was not allowed. Harrison and McKee (1985) addressed this issue by conducting an experiment similar to Hoffman and Spitzer (1982) but including the control group with no bargaining possibility. They found that the efficient outcome was not generally reached when parties could not negotiate around side payments, thus showing a causal link between Coasean bargaining and the efficient outcome.

Several subsequent experiments – mainly conducted in the 1980s – confirmed the predictive power of the Coase theorem under different circumstances. For instance, Coase's predictions were proven to be robust to large group size (e.g. groups of 20 subjects; Hoffman and Spitzer, 1986); to different mechanisms assigning the role of the controller (e.g. random assignment vs earned the right to be the controller by competition; Hoffman and Spitzer, 1985a); to asymmetric and unpleasant (physical discomfort) payoffs associated with the negotiation process (Coursey et al., 1987); to trading in markets with externalities (Harrison et al., 1987) instead of bargaining over monetary outcomes, as in Hoffman and Spitzer (1982); to more complicated bargaining tasks (e.g. negotiating a labour contract with multiple possible outcomes under incomplete information; Schwab, 1988); and to bargaining around known but risky lottery tickets (Shogren, 1992) instead of certain outcomes, as in Hoffman and Spitzer (1982).[3] More recently, scholars have continued to stress-test the Coase theorem under different negotiation contexts (e.g. Anderlini and Felli, 2006; Robson and Skaperdas, 2008; Bar-Gill and Engel, 2016; Hong and Lim, 2016). For instance, Anderlini and Felli (2006) analysed a bargaining game where transaction costs were present (i.e. parties incurred some costs to negotiate). They found that ex-ante contractual costs led to inefficiencies (i.e. contractual agreements were either never reached or reached inefficient outcomes). Robson and Skaperdas (2008) analysed a context in which property rights were initially ambiguously defined and found that the Coase theorem still holds.

Prante et al. (2007) used a meta-analysis to collectively examine the experimental results of Coasean bargaining games. Their meta study provides clear evidence that greater transaction costs reduce the likelihood of efficient bargains, and that, in some cases, variables related to social dimensions (e.g. reciprocity, trust, communication channels, allocation mechanisms of property rights) significantly affect bargaining outcomes (see also Pecorino and Van Boening, 2010). This offers some insights for future research. The impacts of social dimensions in bargaining processes have received relatively less attention compared to those of economic parameters, such as transaction costs. Future studies could investigate how social contexts affect individuals' bargaining behaviour, including whether social connections, trust, and reputation formation among bargainers, and could help achieve efficient outcomes even in the presence of great transaction costs.

To summarise, a large literature – only partially reviewed here – experimentally tested the Coase theorem and provided support for its predictions (e.g. Prudencio, 1982; Harrison and McKee, 1985; Hoffman and Spitzer, 1982, 1985a, 1985b, 1986; Coursey et al., 1987; Harrison et al., 1987; Schwab, 1988). Some of those experiments showed an additional, unpredicted regularity: subjects were willing to divide the payoffs equally, even if this was not efficient. This result later gained growing attention among experimental economists, who extensively investigated fairness preferences and inequity aversion, also in bargaining processes (e.g. Bolton, 1991; Fehr and Schmidt, 1999; Bolton and Ockenfels, 2000).

However, some other experiments conducted from the 1990s onwards revealed that, in other contexts, the allocation of property rights do affect individuals' behaviour. In their influential experiment, Kahneman et al. (1990) tested the Coase theorem in a context where paired buyers and sellers bargained face-to-face over common consumer goods (e.g. chocolate bars) without any time limit. Their experiment departed from the typical Coasean bargaining game in that it considered consumption goods, and it did not introduce externalities. Specifically, half the subjects were randomly assigned the role of sellers and given the possibility to sell a good they own, whereas the other half were randomly assigned the role of buyers and given the possibility to purchase the good. Conventional economic theory predicts that half of the goods should be traded in voluntary exchanges (Kahneman et al., 1990, p. 1328). That is, half of the sellers should be willing to sell their good, whereas half of the buyers should be willing to purchase the good. By contrast, Kahneman et al. (1990) found under-trading and a willingness-to-accept greater than the willingness-to-pay. Roughly speaking, subjects were less willing to sell than to buy because they had the property rights over the good. This psychological bias – well known as the "endowment effect", as first reported by Thaler (1980) – undermines the Coase theorem: initial entitlement does matter, and the exchange rate between goods may vary if they are either sold or bought. Later, several experiments stress-tested the endowment effect in different contexts, including auctions, contests and simulated markets (e.g. Ortona and Scacciati, 1992; Franciosi et al., 1996; Plott and Zeiler, 2005; Bordalo et al., 2012), with implications for law and economics, and welfare economics (Hanemann, 1991; Hovenkamp, 1991). Along similar lines, Bigoni et al. (2017) tested Coasean predictions when parties faced the opportunity for an efficient breach of contract. Promisees were given a right to enforce the contract with specific performance. The experiment showed that the promisees required higher compensation and often refused to resolve the contract if the purpose of the breach was the pursuit of a gain by the promisor. The Coasean outcome was more easily achieved when the purpose of the breach was the avoidance of a loss.

To conclude, Coasean bargaining games represent the first set of economics experiments applied to law and economics, and demonstrate that this methodology can be fruitfully used to answer research questions in traditional legal domains. Apart from stress-testing theories, controlled lab experiments can reveal some novel aspects – such as inequity aversion and prosocial preferences – that refine theory and foster our understanding of individuals' responses to legal instruments.

3.   Pre-Trial Settlement and the Litigation Process

Law and economics scholars have increasingly used experimental methods to analyse litigants' incentives for pre-trial settlement. Those experiments are similar to the Coasean bargaining games reviewed in Section 2. The main difference is that settlement experiments specifically focus on bargaining under conditions of risk (i.e. different likelihoods for alternative litigation outcomes), whereas the Coasean bargaining games do not generally involve any risk or uncertainty about the final outcome. Another difference is that, if people fail to settle a dispute, they enter into costly litigation processes. In the litigation stage, parties are faced with legal fee structures – generally, either the American Rule (each party bears its own legal expenses independent of the trial outcome) or the English Rule (the loser pays the prevailing party's attorney fees in addition to their own expenses). Those alternative fee structures affect individuals' litigation expenditures and their ex-ante settlement incentives differently. Scholars in this field have increasingly used the experimental methodology to address two main questions: (1) Why do people fail to settle?; (2) Do alternative legal instruments (e.g. fee-shifting rules; split award regimes) affect individuals' settlement incentives and litigation expenditures, and if so, how? In this section, I provide some examples of contributions that have addressed those questions, and I discuss possible avenues for future research.

3.1   Why Do People Fail to Settle?

Why do people fail to settle their disputes and enter costly trial litigations? The basic economic models of settlement bargaining predict that, since any trial is costly, litigants should prefer bargaining to reach a private settlement, rather than entering trial litigation (Daughety and Reinganum, 2005). However, in the real world, people often fail to settle their disputes, and do enter costly litigation. Which factors explain this behaviour?

One popular explanation for settlement failure is that litigants form biased expectations about their own likelihood of winning the case. Roughly speaking, each litigant interprets the facts of the dispute in their own favour, and thus believes that the final court decision will favour their case. This kind of judgment error –referred to in the literature as self-serving bias (e.g. Landeo et al., 2013) – narrows the settlement range and increases the likelihood of trial litigation. The self-serving bias hypothesis – which was first developed by Priest and Klein (1984) as the selection hypothesis – has found support in several experimental studies (e.g. Stanley and Coursey, 1990; Loewenstein et al., 1993; Babcock and Loewenstein, 1997).

In their pioneering work, Loewenstein et al. (1993) designed a settlement experiment – framed as a highly realistic mock tort dispute (see Figure 3.3 for sample instructions) – that can be described as follows. Subjects (all students) were randomly paired and assigned roles as either plaintiff or defendant in a tort dispute. Each subject was provided with 27 pages of case materials – including, for example, testimony and reports – from a real accident case. Both parties were given the same information and the same time to read the material before entering a bargaining stage.

Participants knew that a real judge had rendered a verdict regarding the damage awarded to the plaintiff, but they were not informed about the amount awarded. Rather, they were asked to guess it before engaging in any bargaining. Those guesses remained confidential and were monetarily rewarded if sufficiently close to the judge's actual award. In the bargaining stage, each pair was given a half-hour to negotiate face-to-face over a private settlement. If litigants failed to reach a settlement agreement, the plaintiff was awarded the amount specified by the judge, and the parties had to pay litigation costs, which were announced in advance and varied across subjects.[4] The results revealed strong evidence of self-serving bias: each plaintiff's guess of the judge's award was systematically higher than each defendant's estimate. Moreover, such bias correlated with subsequent settlement failure during negotiation.

A similar study by the same authors confirmed the effect of the self-serving bias hypothesis on settlement failure. Babcock et al. (1995) had subjects (all students) negotiating face-to-face, as in Loewenstein et al. (1993), but manipulated the order in which participants received their assigned role and the case material. When subjects received their assigned roles (either plaintiff or defendant) after the case materials, they settled 94% of the time. In contrast, when subjects received their assigned roles before the case materials, the settlement rate significantly decreased to 72%. The parties differed in guessing the judge's award only when they were assigned their roles before reading the case

---

INSTRUCTIONS FOR CONDITION A

Sudden Impact: Elmo Johnson, Defendant

In this experiment you will play the role of Elmo Johnson. Your goal is to settle a civil suit brought against you by Rick Jones. The case is a distilled version of an actual lawsuit that took place in Texas. Jones accuses you of hitting his motorcycle with your car and causing him injuries. He is asking for $100,000 in damages, but if the case goes to trial the actual award could be anything between $0 and $100,000.

You will have thirty minutes to read the case and thirty minutes to settle the case by negotiating with Jones. We have secured a judgment from a retired Texas judge who was not involved in the original case. If you are unable to settle the case with Jones, you will "go to trial," and the judge's decision will determine the magnitude of the settlement. The judgment is contained in an envelope in our possession.

If you are unable to settle, you will need to add $10,000 to whatever the judge determines that you owe Jones. The $10,000 is for legal expenses incurred in going to trial. Jones will also bear $10,000 in legal expenses so that, if you go to trial, he will need to deduct $10,000 in costs from whatever you end up paying him.

We have given you $12 to start off with. Please do not discuss this amount with the other subject. But you are responsible for any payments to the other subject as well as legal costs. Every $10,000 loss to Johnson is a $1 loss for you. So, for example, if you settled at $50,000, you would pay the other subject $5.00. If you failed to settle, and the judge awarded Jones $50,000, then you would pay the other subject $5.00, and you would pay the experimenter $1.00 in legal expenses. The other subject would get the $5.00 you pay but would also pay the experimenter $1.00 in legal expenses.

Source: Loewenstein et al. (1993; p. 159).

Figure 3.3   Sample instructions for Condition A in Loewenstein et al. (1993)

material – and such bias significantly increased settlement failures. This result reveals that, contrary to the findings of classical economic analysis of settlement, parties are less likely to settle when they are provided with additional information. This happens because the additional information is likely subject to self-serving interpretations (i.e. it increases the divergence in litigants' beliefs about the objective merit of the case).

Beyond the self-serving bias hypothesis, another popular explanation for settlement failure is that litigants have asymmetric, verdict-relevant information (the asymmetric-information hypothesis). Economic theory predicts settlement failure and settlement delay under asymmetric information (e.g. Spier, 1992, 1994). The rationale behind those inefficiencies (failure and delay) is that litigants proceed to trial in the attempt to signal and/or extract information (e.g. Bebchuk, 1984; Reinganum and Wilde, 1986; Kennan and

Wilson, 1993). Roth (1995) provided a survey of bargaining experiments under asymmetric information. Here, I focus on one specific bargaining experiment – Sullivan (2016) – that cleanly provided empirical support for the asymmetric-information hypothesis. In Sullivan's experiment, negotiation was designed in abstract terms (i.e. not contextualised, as was done in most of the self-serving bias experiments described above). Participants were asked to bargain over a tort dispute. Instead of reports with factual evidence, they were given numerical details about the case, including the plaintiff's probability of winning at trial, the probability distribution of damage awards, and the legal fees. Instead of face-to-face interactions, subjects were provided the possibility of bargaining a settlement agreement anonymously using computer software and with a virtual (i.e. computerised) judge resolving the disputes that failed to settle. Instead of 30 minutes, subjects had two minutes per round to negotiate a settlement in real time. To detect the causal effect of asymmetric information on settlement outcomes, Sullivan introduced one treatment with symmetric information about the case, and another treatment with asymmetric information, wherein one litigant in each pair was provided with additional information (i.e. the damage amount the judge would award in court litigation). The results provided strong support for the asymmetric-information hypothesis. Specifically, subjects negotiating under symmetric information were 50% more likely to settle a dispute than those negotiating under asymmetric information. In addition, among subjects who reached a settlement agreement, those negotiating under asymmetric information took approximately twice the time spent by subjects negotiating under symmetric information.

3.2   Do Legal Rules Affect Individuals' Litigation Behaviour?

Another growing strand of the experimental literature is focused on the effect of legal instruments (e.g. fee-shifting rules, settlement escrows, split awards) on the relevant outcomes of a lawsuit, including the likelihood of pretrial settlement and litigation expenditures at trial. Two influential papers experimentally compared alternative fee-shifting rules (Coursey and Stanley, 1988; Coughlan and Plott, 1998): the American Rule vs the English Rule.[5] The results confirmed the theoretical predictions: if compared to the American Rule, the English Rule increases settlement rates (Coursey and Stanley, 1988; Coughlan and Plott, 1998) but also legal expenditures at trial (Coughlan and Plott, 1998).

In the pioneering work by Coursey and Stanley (1988), the experimental design can be most easily described as follows. Participants (all students) were randomly matched in pairs and asked to anonymously bargain to divide 100 tokens. Participants who reached an agreement on the division within five minutes earned their tokens (according to the agreement), and the game ended.

Absent an agreement, a division of the 100 tokens was imposed by a random draw. The random draw was designed to map the trial outcome according to a probability distribution known to participants. Specifically, the authors considered two alternative probability distributions: in one case, the parties were equally likely to win; in the other case, one (randomly selected) party was more likely to win. Total trial costs (legal fees) amounted to 40 tokens, which were borne by one or both litigants according to the cost rule in place. Specifically, under the American Rule treatment, each side was charged 20 tokens; under the English Rule treatment, the losing side was charged 40 tokens, whereas the winning side was not charged at all.[6] In line with the theory, the authors found that settlement rates were significantly higher under the English Rule than the American Rule (80% vs 61.1%). The authors interpreted this finding through the lens of risk preferences: under the English Rule, the risk of paying the opponent's fees, in addition to one's own expenses, led risk-averse litigants to settle more often than under the American Rule.

In later research, Coughlan and Plott (1998) added some complexities to Coursey and Stanley's (1988) experimental design by providing participants the possibility to choose how much to spend at trial. In Coughlan and Plott (1998), the probability of winning the lawsuit was no longer exogeneous, as in Coursey and Stanley (1988), but rather a function of legal expenditures, the objective merit of the case,[7] and the effectiveness (or abilities) of parties' lawyers. The research aim was to analyse the effects of the American Rule vs the English Rule on settlement rates and litigation expenditures. Coughlan and Plott's (1998) litigation game proceeds as follows. The plaintiff observed the merit of the case and was asked to decide whether to incur a fixed cost to file for the suit. If the plaintiff filed, the defendant was provided the possibility to settle the case by paying the entire amount requested by the plaintiff. Note that, differently from prior contributions, here there is no pre-trial bargaining over the amount of settlement. If the case was not settled, participants went to trial where they were asked to choose how much to spend in legal expenditures. The plaintiff's probability of winning the lawsuit depended upon parties' relative legal expenditures – in addition to the merit of the case and the relative effectiveness of parties' lawyers. The case was then solved by a random draw consistent with that probability. The results showed that settlement rates were higher under the English Rule than under the American Rule (88% vs 20%) – which is consistent with Coursey and Stanley (1988) and in line with theory. However, when settlement failed and parties proceeded to trial, average expenditures per dispute were significantly higher under the English Rule than under the American Rule (75.5 vs 35.9). These results – which hold for any level of merit and lawyer ability – support the predictions of litigation models and open some questions for future research. For instance, further evidence is needed to understand the reasons why individuals spend more resources under the English Rule than the American Rule. Such investigation could include the role of fairness, inequity aversion, risk preferences in the litigation process, and alternative fee-shifting rules.

After Coursey and Stanley (1988) and Coughlan and Plott (1998), only a few other laboratory experiments have analysed the effects of fee-shifting rules on individuals' litigation behaviour (Main and Park, 2000, 2002; Inglis et al., 2005; Massenot et al., 2016). The findings are mixed. For instance, while Coursey and Stanley (1988) and Coughlan and Plott (1998) both found that settlement rates were significantly higher under the English Rule than under the American Rule, Massenot et al. (2016) observed no significant differences. Importantly, Massenot et al. (2016) revealed that each rule had its own costs and benefits (e.g. the American Rule was more efficient at the trial stage, whereas the English Rule performed better in incentivising ex-ante precautionary behaviours). Hence, one rule did not unequivocally dominate the other, which might explain why the two rules coexist in real-world litigation systems.

The mixed results might be driven by the different experimental designs implemented. Massenot et al. (2016) framed the experiment in a medical malpractice context (see Figure 3.4 for sample instructions), whereas Coursey and Stanley (1988) and Coughlan and Plott (1998) used a neutral, non-framed design. Differently from Coursey and Stanley (1988) and Coughlan and Plott (1998), Massenot et al. (2016) considered a three-stage game: the first stage involved a doctor's care decisions to avoid a medical error, hence, a monetary loss to a patient; the second stage involved settlement bargaining; the third stage was the (eventual) litigation game (in case of settlement failure). This experimental design allowed the authors to simultaneously study some of the most relevant litigation outcomes: ex-ante precautionary behaviour, pretrial settlement rates, and trial litigation expenditures. At the beginning of the experiment, participants were randomly matched in pairs and assigned to the role of either doctor or patient. The "doctors" were asked to decide how much to invest in care to avoid an accident (medical error). In the case of an accident, the "patients" (plaintiffs) suffered a loss of 100.[8]

Investing in care was costly but reduced the probability of the accident from 0.5 in case the defendant (the doctor) was negligent, to 0.1 in case they were careful. In the settlement stage, plaintiffs were informed about the care decision of their paired defendant. Then, both players were asked to report their reservation prices, which determined whether the case was settled or proceeded to the court stage. If the case was settled, the game was over, and subjects were informed about their final payoff. If the case was not settled, subjects proceeded to the third stage of the game to solve their dispute in court. During the trial, both subjects were simultaneously asked to choose their legal expenditures.[9]

First stage of the game - Medical consultation

The first stage is only played by the doctor.

The doctor treats the patient and decides to be either negligent or careful. If the doctor is careful, it reduces the risk of medical error but it costs him some ECU.

In case of medical error, the patient loses 100 ECU.

If the doctor is careful:

- The doctor loses a variable number of ECU. This number will be communicated to the doctor at the beginning of each game. This number will not be communicated to the patient.

- The patient has 1 chance in 10 (10 percent) of being victim of a medical error and thus of losing 100 ECU.

If the doctor is negligent:

- The doctor does not lose any ECU.

- The patient has 1 chance in 2 (50 percent) of being victim of a medical error and thus of losing 100 ECU.

Source: Massenot et al. (2016).

Figure 3.4   Sample instructions in Massenot et al. (2016)

The authors manipulated two dimensions: the fee-shifting rule (American Rule vs English Rule), and the settlement stage (present vs absent). Specifically, they considered two fee-shifting rules: (1) the "American Rule" treatment, where there is no fee shifting, and (2) the "English Rule" treatment, where the losing party has to reimburse the winning side's expenses in court, up to 75 tokens. In addition, the authors manipulated the possibility for the parties to avoid the court stage through settlement bargaining. In the "three-stage" game, parties were provided the possibility to enter their reservation price to avoid court litigation, whereas in the "two-stage" game, the settlement stage was dropped from the design and all cases directly proceeded to the court stage.

The results showed that the English Rule did not reduce litigation rates through more settlements, for any merit of the case. This is clearly in contrast with theory and prior experimental evidence. The findings also revealed that the English Rule was associated with substantially greater litigation spending, but also with greater ex-ante legal compliance with precautionary standards. Hence, Massenot et al. (2016) showed that there are pros and cons associated with each legal rule, and that one rule cannot be unequivocally preferred to the other. Massenot et al.'s (2016) experiment provides insights for future research. For instance, it would be interesting to test whether their results – which hold within a framed medical malpractice case – hold in other tort contexts (e.g. car accident) or non-framed games (as in Coursey and Stanley, 1988; Coughlan and Plott, 1998).

Moving beyond fee-shifting rules, recent contributions examined the effects on litigation outcomes of other legal instruments – including settlement escrows (Babcock and Landeo, 2004) and split awards (Landeo et al. 2007). Even if litigation experiments have already attracted growing attention among law and economics scholars, the mixed results achieved so far call for additional evidence. As pointed out by Spier (2007), the predictions of litigation models greatly depend on the specific characteristics of the legal procedures and on the context analysed. To what extent does context matter? Future contributions could explore how individuals respond to the interaction between legal instruments and contexts. Further evidence is also needed on other important yet underexplored characteristics of legal procedures, including sequential litigation (Bernhardt and Lee, 2015), court errors and parties' probatory difficulties (Kaplow, 2017), and different standards of proof (Guerra et al., 2019).

4.   Torts and Liability Rules

Theoretical models of tort law have been extensively used to analyse the effects of alternative liability rules on individual precautionary incentives from different angles and perspectives (see Faure, 2009, for an extensive review). Even though tort law and economics represent one of the first and most well-developed applications of economic methodology in the analysis of the law, the process of testing its basic assumptions and predictions is still incomplete. Very little is known about individuals' precautionary behaviour under different liability rules. This is partly explained by the fact that precautions are difficult to observe and practically impossible to measure empirically (van Velthoven, 2009). The experimental methodology can overcome this empirical shortcoming since it allows us to observe precautionary investments at the individual level while keeping other factors constant.

In spite of the advantages of the experimental method in overcoming observation difficulties, only a few experiments have been so far conducted (e.g.

Kornhauser and Schotter, 1990, 1992; Wittman et al., 1997; Angelova et al., 2014; Deffains et al., 2019; Guerra and Parisi, 2019). Most of these contributions compared precautionary behaviour under different liability rules.[10] For instance, Kornhauser and Schotter (1990) compared strict liability vs negligence in a single-actor accident context (only the injurer can take care); Kornhauser and Schotter (1992) compared simple negligence vs negligence with contributory negligence in a two-actor accident context (both the injurer and victim can take care); Wittman et al. (1997) studied contributory negligence vs comparative negligence vs no-fault rules in a dynamic context; Angelova et al. (2014) examined no liability vs strict liability vs negligence; and Deffains et al. (2019) analysed social norms under no law vs strict liability vs negligence, with either mild or severe rule enforcement. Those experiments – except Kornhauser and Schotter (1990) and Deffains et al. (2019) – generally supported the theoretical predictions. Specifically, in line with theory, rules of simple negligence and negligence with contributory negligence generate equivalent care levels (Kornhauser and Schotter, 1992); the no-fault equilibrium yields suboptimal amounts of care effort, if compared to negligence with contributory negligence and comparative negligence (Wittman et al., 1997); and strict liability and negligence are equally effective, and both perform better than no liability (Angelova et al., 2014). However, some results are contradictory. For instance, in contrast with theory and Angelova et al.'s (2014) experimental results, Kornhauser and Schotter (1990) found that negligence is more effective than strict liability in generating optimal care incentives, whereas Deffains et al. (2019) showed that negligence is less effective than strict liability in cases where causing harm is socially inefficient (i.e. when the losses imposed on others exceed the private gains accrued from the risky activity). Those divergent results suggest that one liability rule does not strictly dominate another: it depends on the accident circumstances – including, for example, the trade-off between individual gains vs harms to others – and on differential learning patterns through time and experience.

In a different yet related experiment, Guerra and Parisi (2019) tested one of the core assumptions of tort models – that is, the symmetric behaviour of potential tortfeasors and victims when faced by a threat of liability or a risk of harm without compensation, respectively. As opposed to prior contributions, Guerra and Parisi (2019) did not focus on the deterrent effects of specific legal rules, but instead analysed whether inflicting damages on others is perceived as equivalent to being damaged under symmetric liability rules (i.e. strict liability and no liability). In what follows, I first review the pioneering works by Kornhauser and Schotter (1990, 1992); then, I describe the more recent experiment conducted by Guerra and Parisi (2019); finally, I provide insights for future research.

The pioneering paper in this area – Kornhauser and Schotter (1990) – compared strict liability and negligence in a single-actor (or unilateral-care) accident context. In their experiment, all participants were potential tortfeasors and were asked to decide how much to spend in precautions to reduce the accident probability. This is an individual decision-making experiment: subjects took decisions individually (i.e. no interaction with others); their final payoff depended exclusively on their own chosen level of precautions; their choices did not affect others' payoffs. Subjects made their decisions knowing that, in case of accident, they would have to compensate damages to a hypothetical victim according to either a negligence standard or strict-liability rule. Their experimental results departed from the predicted efficiency equivalence between strict liability and negligence: under strict liability, subjects initially undertook more precautions and then fewer precautions than the optimal level; whereas they always undertook the optimal level of precautions under negligence.

In a later experiment, Kornhauser and Schotter (1992) compared simple negligence and negligence with contributory negligence in a two-actor (or bilateral-care) accident context, wherein investments in precautions by both subjects jointly affected the accident probability. As in real-life accident scenarios, at no point during the experiment was there any interaction between subjects. The results were largely consistent with predictions of tort theory. Specifically, those two rules created equivalent incentives when the standard of due care was set at the socially optimal level. The rule of negligence with contributory negligence, however, proved to be superior to simple negligence when the actors could choose the activity level of the risk-creating action. Further, neither rules performed well in terms of efficiency when individuals were asked to choose the level of care and the level of activity jointly. Finally, their experimental findings confirmed the theoretical prediction – that the agent who bears the loss in equilibrium has incentives to reduce the level of activity, and that the amount of information the subjects have on others' care choices does not increase the efficiency of any rule.

In the most recent research, Guerra and Parisi (2019) tested a core theoretical assumption widely used in law and economics models of accident law: tortfeasors and victims are expected to have symmetric reactions to symmetric accident risks. The authors used a within-subjects design with two treatments: tortfeasors under strict liability and victims under no liability. The experiment included two stages, with one treatment in each stage. Each stage consisted of ten independent and identical periods. At the beginning of the experiment, subjects were randomly assigned to the role of either "Player A" or "Player B"; the roles remained fixed throughout the experiment and were randomly paired with another participant in the opposite role. In each period, each subject received an endowment of 140 tokens, and each Player A was asked to decide how much to invest in precautions to avoid an accident with their matched Player B. Each additional investment in precaution reduced the accident probability by 10%, but also entailed an increasing marginal cost for Player A. The accident probability was defined as a function of Player A's precautionary investments and ranged between 25% (if Player A chose the maximum amount of precautions) and 85% (if Player A chose not to invest in precautions). The cost of precautions ranged from 0 (if Player A chose not to invest in precautions) to 60 (if Player A chose the maximum amount of precautions). If an accident occurred, the monetary loss was 80 tokens.[11]

This experiment mimics a unilateral-care setting wherein only Player A could take actions to avoid the accident. Player B was present in the lab but remained passive throughout the experiment. This design choice is different from the previous experiments analysing unilateral-care accidents: the accident harm falls on a real participant and not on a hypothetical person, as in, for example, Kornhauser and Schotter (1990).

The authors manipulated two treatments: tortfeasors under strict liability (TSL) and victims under no liability (VNL). In the TSL treatment, if an accident would have occurred, Player B would have suffered the initial loss, but Player A would have fully compensated them for the damage suffered. In the VNL treatment, if an accident would have occurred, the loss would have fallen upon Player A, and they would have not received any compensation. In both treatments, Player A's expected earnings were computed as the initial endowment minus precaution costs, minus expected accident loss. Importantly, Player A's expected earnings were identical in the two treatments: if an accident would have occurred, Player A would have always faced the full accident loss, either as liability (TSL treatment) or as uncompensated loss (VNL treatment). In this scenario, tort theory predicts that Players A under strict liability and Players A under no liability should exhibit the same precautionary behaviour. See Figure 3.5 for sample instructions, as shown to Players A in the TSL treatment.

The results confirmed the core theoretical prediction of tort models with respect to average precautionary investments, but also revealed interesting behavioural effects that the role of the parties played in the dynamics of precautionary behaviour. When looking at behavioural dynamics, the findings showed that victims' and tortfeasors' precautionary investments changed differently through time. Tortfeasors revealed greater sensitivity to their prior experience as victims of an accident, compared to tortfeasors who did not have such prior victim experience. By contrast, victims did not show any reaction

How many tokens you would like to invest in precautions to avoid an accident with your matched Player B?

- o   0 tokens
- o   5 tokens
- o   12 tokens
- o   21 tokens
- o   32 tokens
- o   45 tokens
- o   60 tokens

Summary of the instructions					
In each period:	Initial Endowment	Precaution Cost	Probability of Accident	Earnings PLAYER A	Earnings PLAYER B
• Only Player A can invest in precautions to avoid an accident. • In each period, If an accident occurs, Player B will suffer the accident loss of 80 tokens. • In this case, Player A will always have to fully compensate Player B for the accident loss (80 tokens).	140	- 0	85% Accident 15% No Accident	60 tokens 140 tokens	140 tokens 140 tokens
	140	- 5	75% Accident 25% No Accident	55 tokens 135 tokens	140 tokens 140 tokens
	140	- 12	65% Accident 35% No Accident	48 tokens 128 tokens	140 tokens 140 tokens
	140	- 21	55% Accident 45% No Accident	39 tokens 119 tokens	140 tokens 140 tokens
	140	- 32	45% Accident 55% No Accident	28 tokens 108 tokens	140 tokens 140 tokens
	140	- 45	35% Accident 65% No Accident	15 tokens 95 tokens	140 tokens 140 tokens
	140	- 60	25% Accident 75% No Accident	0 tokens 80 tokens	140 tokens 140 tokens

When you are done, please press "Continue" and kindly wait.

Source: Guerra and Parisi (2019)

Figure 3.5   Sample decision screen and payoff schedule in the TLS treatment, in Guerra and Parisi (2019)

to their prior experience as tortfeasors. Moreover, tortfeasors adjusted their precaution levels through time, and their average precautionary investments smoothly converged to the efficient level, with decreasing variance. By contrast, victims' behaviours continued to exhibit a more erratic reaction to the risk of an uncompensated accident loss, with a greater variance in the observed precautionary investments.

By considering this recent paper alongside prior experiments on tort law and economics (e.g. Kornhauser and Schotter, 1992; Wittman et al., 1997; Angelova et al., 2014), we can start observing experimental validations supporting the predictive power of the existing economic theory of tort law (Zamir, 2020), but also some mixed results (e.g. Kornhauser and Schotter, 1992, vs Deffains et al., 2019), which calls for further evidence. For instance, the findings by Guerra and Parisi (2019) suggest the need to revisit some of the conventional predictions of tort theory to account for dynamic factors of precautionary investments. Individuals learn through time (e.g. from past accident experiences and interactions with others), and legal instruments can generate different dynamic paths of convergence towards efficient precautionary investments.

Also, further experimental evidence is needed to investigate how individuals' precautionary choices and damage perceptions change depending upon the accident context and the type of harm, for example, pain and suffering vs pure monetary losses; neutral vs framed tort contexts (e.g. medical malpractice cases, car accidents); and first-time vs repeated offenders (Guerra and Hlobil, 2018). Future experimental designs can combine the presence of liability rules with the possibility for individuals to purchase insurance coverage (see Kunreuther et al., 2013, on insurance and behavioural economics), or to retaliate against tortfeasors (see Mittlaender, 2020). Another avenue for future research is to investigate whether individuals' social dimensions variables (e.g. fairness, guilt aversion) affect their precautionary behaviour, and whether such influences vary under alternative liability rules.

5.   Conclusion

Experimental law and economics is a growing area of research, but it is still at a relative early stage of development. This chapter provides examples of relevant laboratory experiments as applied to three specific research topics: (1) bargaining and the Coase theorem; (2) settlement bargaining and the litigation process; and (3) torts and liability rules. These topics – which have been extensively analysed from different theoretical perspectives – have seen divergent developments of experimental applications: from the widely studied bargaining experiments, to the fairly advanced pretrial settlement and litigation experiments, to the embryonic stage of tort experiments. The hope here is to offer examples of each field and insights for future research – which is especially needed in some undeveloped areas, such as tort experiments. The topics reviewed here are not comprehensive; there are other research areas in law and economics where experiments can be fruitfully used, such as contract breach, illegal behaviours, and the enforcement of the law. For recent, extensive reviews on other law and economics topics, see Sullivan and Holt (2017) and Zamir and Teichman (2018).

This chapter focuses on laboratory experiments, but obviously there are other experimental methodologies (e.g. natural experiments, vignette studies) that have been applied to law and economics topics. There is no methodology that dominates the others tout court; each methodology offers advantages and disadvantages, and the choice of one over the other ultimately depends upon the research question and scope of application. Engel (2013) provided an extensive discussion on alternative experimental methods in law and economics, with their respective advantages and disadvantages. Differently from observational data, lab experiments can provide clean tests of law and economics theories by illuminating the counterfactual: How would individuals' behaviour change if, all else being equal, a different legal institution is in place? This methodology surely has its limitations (Hertwig and Ortmann, 2001; Croson, 2009; Engel, 2013) – the most discussed being its weak external validity. But it also has its strengths, which make it a crucial component in the toolbox of any scholar who seeks to foster our understanding of how individuals react to alternative legal instruments.

Acknowledgements

The author would like to thank Ananish Chaudhuri, Tim Friehe, Henrik Lando, Sergio Rubens Mittlaender, Gerd Muehlheusser, Francesco Parisi, and Christian Thoeni for useful comments.

Notes

1. For excellent and exhaustive reviews on experimental law and economics, see: Hoffman and Spitzer (1985b), Davis and Holt (1993), Kagel and Roth (1995), McAdams (2000), Sunstein (2000), Talley and Camerer (2007), Arlen and Talley (2008), Croson (2009), Sullivan and Holt (2017), Charness and DeAngelo (2018), and Zamir and Teichman (2018).
2. This chapter does not review either psychology experiments or uncontrolled (natural) experiments, including observational studies. See Engel (2013) for an extensive discussion on the key experimental methods generally applied to law and economics – including field experiments, survey data, and vignettes, in addition to lab experiments.
3. For extensive reviews of some of the contributions that stress-tested the Coase theorem, see, among others, McAdams (2000) and Croson (2009).
4. The authors introduced four experimental conditions, each of which detailed different trial costs on the parties in the event of non-settlement: Condition A, $10 000 each; Condition B, $20 000 to the defendant, none to the plaintiff; Condition C, $20 000 to the plaintiff, none to the defendant; Condition D, $5 000 each.
5. In addition to the English Rule and the American Rule, Coursey and Stanley (1988) also considered a modified version of Rule 68 of the Federal Rules of Civil Procedure, wherein either the plaintiff pays both litigants' costs if she does no better at trial than the defendant's final settlement offer, or each side pays their own costs.
6. The losing party is defined as the subject that was randomly allotted fewer than half the tokens.
7. The authors considered three alternative objective merits: frivolous cases, where the plaintiff's merit was 25%; closely contested cases, where the merit was 50%; and strong cases, where the merit was 75%.

8. In this experiment, the judge did not decide the damage award. The plaintiff, if winning the dispute, would have been awarded the same amount as the accident loss (100).
9. For the sake of clarity, it is worth mentioning that the settlement stage was invoked only in case of accident, but the authors let all subjects proceed to the settlement stage to avoid "losing" observations of those subjects who experienced no accident. Roughly speaking, the authors asked subjects to take their settlement decisions before knowing whether an accident happened or not. Only at the end of the experiment did they know about the occurrence of the accident. If there was no accident, all their decisions in the settlement and court stage were irrelevant for their payoff.
10. Other contributions – which lie outside the focus of this chapter – experimentally tested the deterrent effect of tort liability compared to other deterrence mechanisms, such as, fines vs damages and ex-ante regulation vs ex-post liability (e.g. Cardi et al., 2012; Eisenberg and Engel, 2014; Baumann et al., 2020).
11. At the end of each period, participants were informed about whether an accident happened, their own period earnings, and their matched participant's period earnings. Players A's precaution investments remained private information – though can be guessed. After the ten periods in the first stage, the second stage began with a set of new instructions to participants. They were informed that their role and task remained the same as in the first stage, but the liability scenario would have changed.

References

Anderlini, L., and Felli, L. (2006). Transaction costs and the robustness of the Coase theorem. *The Economic Journal*, 116(508), 223–245.

Angelova, V., Armantier, O., Attanasi, G., and Hiriart, Y. (2014). Relative performance of liability rules: Experimental evidence. *Theory and Decision*, 77(4), 531–556.

Arlen J., and Tally E. (2008). *Experimental Law and Economics*. Cheltenham, UK: Edward Elgar Publishing.

Babcock, L., and Landeo, C. M. (2004). Settlement escrows: An experimental study of a bilateral bargaining game. *Journal of Economic Behavior & Organization*, 53(3), 401–417.

Babcock, L., and Loewenstein, G. (1997). Explaining bargaining impasse: The role of self-serving biases. *Journal of Economic Perspectives*, 11(1), 109–126.

Babcock, L., Loewenstein, G., Issacharoff, S., and Camerer, C. (1995). Biased judgments of fairness in bargaining. *The American Economic Review*, 85(5), 1337–1343.

Bar-Gill, O., and Engel, C. (2016). Bargaining in the absence of property rights: An experiment. *The Journal of Law and Economics*, 59(2), 477–495.

Baumann, F., Friehe, T., and Langenbach, P. (2020). Fines versus damages: Experimental evidence on care investments. *MPI Collective Goods Discussion Paper* (2020/8).

Bebchuk, L. A. (1984). Litigation and settlement under imperfect information. *RAND Journal of Economics*, 15(3), 404–415.

Bernhardt, D., and Lee, F. Z. X. (2015). Trial incentives in sequential litigation. *American Law and Economics Review*, 17(1), 214–244.

Bigoni, M., Bortolotti, S., Parisi, F., and Porat, A. (2017). Unbundling efficient breach: An experiment. *Journal of Empirical Legal Studies*, 14(3), 527–547.

Bolton, G. (1991). A comparative model of bargaining: Theory and evidence. *American Economic Review*, 81, 1096–1136.

Bolton, G., and Ockenfels, A. (2000). ERC: A theory of equity, reciprocity, and competition. *American Economic Review*, 90, 166–193

Bordalo, P., Gennaioli, N., and Shleifer, A. (2012). Salience in experimental tests of the endowment effect. *American Economic Review*, 102(3), 47–52.

Cardi, W. J., Penfield, R. D., and Yoon, A. H. (2012). Does tort law deter individuals? A behavioural science study. *Journal of Empirical Legal Studies*, 9(3), 567–603.

Charness, G., and DeAngelo, G. (2018). Law and economics in the laboratory. In J. C. Teitelbaum and K. Zeiler (Eds.), *Research Handbook on Behavioural Law and Economics* (pp. 321–346). Cheltenham, UK: Edward Elgar Publishing. doi: 10.4337/9781849805681.00023

Coase, R. H. (1960). The problem of social cost. *The Journal of Law & Economics*, 56(4), 837–877.

Coughlan, P. J., and Plott, C. R. (1998). An experimental analysis of the structure of legal fees: American Rule vs. English Rule. *Social Science Working Paper no. 1025*. California Institute of Technology, Pasadena.

Coursey, D., Hoffman, E., and Spitzer, M. (1987). Fear and loathing in the Coase theorem: Experimental tests involving physical discomfort. *The Journal of Legal Studies*, 16, 217–248. doi: 10.1086/467829

Coursey, D. L., and Stanley, L. R. (1988). Pretrial bargaining behavior within the shadow of the law: Theory and experimental evidence. *International Review of Law and Economics*, 8(2), 161–179.

Croson, R. (2009). Experimental law and economics. *Annual Review of Law and Social Science*, 5, 25–44.

Daughety, A. F., and Reinganum, J. F. (2005). Economic theories of settlement bargaining. *Annual Review of Law and Social Science*, 1, 35–59.

Davis, D., and Holt, C. A. (1993). *Experimental Economics*. Princeton, NJ: Princeton University Press.

Deffains, B., Espinosa, R., and Fluet, C. (2019). Laws and norms: Experimental evidence with liability rules. *International Review of Law and Economics*, 60, 105858.

Eisenberg, T., and Engel, C. (2014). Assuring civil damages adequately deter: A public good experiment. *Journal of Empirical Legal Studies*, 11(2), 301–349.

Engel, C. (2013). Behavioural law and economics: Empirical methods. *MPI Collective Goods Preprint* (2013/1). Available at: https://ssrn.com/abstract=2207921 or doi: 10.2139/ssrn.2207921

Faure, M. (2009). *Tort Law and Economics* (Vol. 1). Cheltenham, UK: Edward Elgar Publishing.

Fehr, E., and Schmidt, K. (1999). A theory of fairness, competition, and cooperation. *Quarterly Journal of Economics*, 114, 817–868.

Franciosi, R., Kujal, P., Michelitsch, R., Smith, V., and Deng, G. (1996). Experimental tests of the endowment effect. *Journal of Economic Behaviour and Organization*, 30(2), 213–226.

Guerra, A., and Hlobil, T. M. (2018). Tailoring negligence standards to accident records. *The Journal of Legal Studies*, 47(2), 325–348.

Guerra, A., Luppi, B., and Parisi, F. (2019). Standards of proof and civil litigation: A game-theoretic analysis. *The BE Journal of Theoretical Economics*, 19(1), 1–19.

Guerra, A., and Parisi, F. (2019). Victims versus tortfeasors: A(symmetric) reactions to symmetric incentives. Available at: https://ssrn.com/abstract=3133168 or doi: 10.2139/ssrn.3133168

Hanemann, W. M. (1991). Willingness to pay and willingness to accept: How much can they differ? *American Economic Review*, 81(3), 635–647. doi: 10.1257/000282803321455449

Harrison, G., Hoffman, E., Rutstrom, E., and Spitzer, M. (1987). Coasean solutions to the externality problem in experimental markets. *The Economic Journal*, 97, 388–402. doi: 10.2307/2232885

Harrison, G., and McKee, M. (1985). Experimental evaluation of the Coase theorem. *The Journal of Law and Economics*, 28, 653–670. doi: 10.1086/467104

Hertwig, R., and Ortmann, A. (2001). Experimental practices in economics: A methodological challenge for psychologists? *Behavioral and Brain Sciences*, 24(3), 383–403.

Hoffman, E., and Spitzer, M. L. (1982). The Coase theorem: Some experimental tests. *Journal of Law and Economics*, 25(1), 73–98.

Hoffman, E., and Spitzer, M. L. (1985a). Entitlements, rights, and fairness: An experimental examination of subjects' concepts of distributive justice. *Journal of Legal Studies*, 14, 259–297.

Hoffman, E., and Spitzer, M. L. (1985b). Experimental law and economics: An introduction. *Columbia Law Review*, 85, 991–1024.

Hoffman, E., and Spitzer, M. L. (1986). Experimental tests of the Coase theorem with large bargaining groups. *Journal of Legal Studies*, 15(1), 149–171.

Hong, F., and Lim, W. (2016). Voluntary participation in public goods provision with Coasean bargaining. *Journal of Economic Behaviour and Organization*, 126, 102–119.

Hovenkamp, H. (1991). Legal policy and the endowment effect. *The Journal of Legal Studies*, 20(2), 225–247. doi:10.1086/467886

Inglis, L., McCabe, K., Rassenti, S., Simmons, D., and Tallroth, E. (2005). Experiments on the effects of cost-shifting, court costs, and discovery on the efficient settlement of tort claims. *Florida State University Law Review*, 33, 89–117.

Kagel, J. H., and Roth, A. E. (1995). *Handbook of Experimental Economics*. Princeton, NJ: Princeton University Press.

Kahneman, D., Knetsch, J., and Thaler, R. (1990). Experimental tests of the endowment effect and the Coase theorem. *Journal of Political Economy*, 98, 1325–1348. doi: 10.1086/261737

Kaplow, L. (2017). Optimal design of private litigation. *Journal of Public Economics*, 155, 64–73.

Kennan, J., and Wilson, R. (1993). Bargaining with private information. *Journal of Economic Literature*, 31(1), 45–104.

Kornhauser, L. A., and Schotter, A. (1990). An experimental study of single-actor accidents. *The Journal of Legal Studies*, 19, 203–233.

Kornhauser, L. A., and Schotter, A. (1992). An experimental study of two-actor accidents. *C.V. Starr Center for Applied Economics*, Research Report No. 92–57.

Kunreuther, H. C., Pauly, M. V., and McMorrow, S. (2013). *Insurance and Behavioural Economics: Improving Decisions in the Most Misunderstood Industry*. Cambridge, UK: Cambridge University Press.

Landeo, C. M., Nikitin, M., and Babcock, L. (2007). Split-awards and disputes: An experimental study of a strategic model of litigation. *Journal of Economic Behavior & Organization*, 63(3), 553–572.

Landeo, C. M., Nikitin, M., and Izmalkov, S. (2013). Incentives for care, litigation, and tort reform under self-serving bias. In T. J. Miceli and M. J. Baker (Eds.), *Research*

Handbook on Economic Models of Law (pp. 112–155). Cheltenham, UK: Edward Elgar Publishing.

Loewenstein, G., Issacharoff, S., Camerer, C., and Babcock, L. (1993). Self-serving assessments of fairness and pretrial bargaining. *Journal of Legal Studies*, 22(1), 135–159.

Main, B. G. M., and Park, A. (2000). The British and American rules: An experimental examination of pre-trial bargaining in the shadow of the law. *Scottish Journal of Political Economy*, 47(1), 37–60.

Main, B. G. M., and Park, A. (2002). The impact of defendant offers into court on negotiation in the shadow of the law: Experimental evidence. *International Review of Law and Economics*, 22(2), 177–192.

Massenot, B., Maraki, M., and Thöni, C. (2016). Legal compliance and litigation spending under the English and American rule: Experimental evidence. Université de Lausanne, Faculté des hautes études commerciales (HEC), Département d'économétrie et économie politique.

McAdams, R. (2000). Experimental law and economics. In B. Bouckaert and G. de Geest (Eds.), *Encyclopedia of Law and Economics* (Vol. 1, pp. 539–561). Cheltenham, UK: Edward Elgar Publishing.

Medema, S. G. (2017). The Coase theorem at sixty. *Journal of Economic Literature*, 58(4), 1045–1128.

Mittlaender, S. (2020). Retaliation, remedies, and torts. *MPI Social Law and Social Policy* (preprint).

Ortona, G., and Scacciati, F. (1992). New experiments on the endowment effect. *Journal of Economic Psychology*, 13(2), 277–296.

Pecorino, P., and Van Boening, M. (2010). Fairness in an embedded ultimatum game. *The Journal of Law and Economics*, 53(2), 263–287.

Plott, C. R., and Zeiler, K. (2005). The willingness to pay–willingness to accept gap, the "endowment effect," subject misconceptions, and experimental procedures for eliciting valuations. *American Economic Review*, 95(3), 530–545.

Prante, T., Thacher, J. A., and Berrens, R. P. (2007). Evaluating Coasean bargaining games with meta-analysis. *Economics Bulletin*, 3(68), 1–7.

Priest, G. L., and Klein, B. (1984). Selection of disputes for litigation. *Journal of Legal Studies*, 13(1), 1–55.

Prudencio, C. (1982). The voluntary approach to externality problems: An experimental test. *Journal of Environmental Economics and Management*, 9, 213–228. doi: 10.1016/0095-0696(82)90031-6

Reinganum, J. F., and Wilde, L. L. (1986). Settlement, litigation, and the allocation of litigation costs. *RAND Journal of Economics*, 17(4), 557–566.

Robson, A., and Skaperdas, S. (2008). Costly enforcement of property rights and the Coase theorem. *Economic Theory*, 36(1), 109–128.

Roth, A. E. (1995). Bargaining experiments. In J. H. Kagel and A. E. Roth (Eds.), *Handbook of Experimental Economics* (pp. 253–348). Princeton, NJ: Princeton University Press.

Schwab, S. (1988). A Coasean experiment on contract presumptions. *The Journal of Legal Studies*, 17, 237–268. doi: 10.1086/468129

Shogren, J. F. (1992). An experiment on Coasian bargaining over ex ante lotteries and ex post rewards. *Journal of Economic Behavior & Organization*, 17(1), 153–169.

Spier, K. E. (1992). The dynamics of pretrial negotiation. *Review of Economic Studies*, 59(1), 93–108.

Spier, K. E. (1994). Pretrial bargaining and the design of fee-shifting rules. *RAND Journal of Economics*, 25(2), 197–214.

Spier, K. E. (2007). Litigation. In A. M. Polinsky and S. Shavell (Eds.), *Handbook of Law and Economics* (Vol. 1, pp. 259–342). London: Elsevier.

Stanley, L. R., and Coursey, D. L. (1990). Empirical evidence on the selection hypothesis and the decision to litigate or settle. *Journal of Legal Studies*, 19(1), 145–172.

Sullivan, S. P. (2016). Why wait to settle? An experimental test of the asymmetric-information hypothesis. *The Journal of Law and Economics*, 59(3), 497–525.

Sullivan, S. P., and Holt, C. A. (2017). Experimental economics and the law. In F. Parisi (Ed.), *The Oxford Handbook of Law and Economics* (Vol. 1, pp. 78–103). Oxford: Oxford University Press.

Sunstein, C. (2000). *Behavioural Law and Economics*. Cambridge, UK: Cambridge University Press.

Talley, E., and Camerer, C. (2007). Experimental law and economics. In M. Polinsky and S. Shavell (Ed.), *Handbook of Law and Economics* (Vol. 2, pp. 1619–1650). Amsterdam: Elsevier.

Thaler, R. (1980). Toward a positive theory of consumer choice. *Journal of Economic Behaviour and Organization*, 1, 39–60. doi: 10.1016/0167-2681(80)90051-7

Van Velthoven, B. C. (2009). Empirics of tort. In G. de Geest (Ed.), *Encyclopedia of Law and Economics*. Cheltenham, UK: Edward Elgar Publishing.

Wittman, D., Friedman, D., Crevier, S., and Braskin, A. (1997). Learning liability rules. *The Journal of Legal Studies*, 26(1), 145–162.

Zamir, E. (2020). Refounding law and economics: Behavioural support for the predictions of standard economic analysis. *Review of Law and Economics*, 16(2). doi:10.1515/rle-2019-0023

Zamir, E., and Teichman, D. (2018). *Behavioural Law and Economics*. Oxford: Oxford University Press.

4 Complying with environmental regulations: experimental evidence

Timothy N. Cason, Lana Friesen and Lata Gangadharan

1. Introduction

The scope of laws and regulations is wide-reaching and encompasses environmental laws and regulations, tax compliance, occupational health and safety, tax exemptions for owner occupied housing, insurance fraud, claims for social security benefits, misbehaviour by banks and financial advisors, and much more. This chapter focuses on compliance with environmental laws and regulations, although many of the lessons can be applied more broadly.

Effective laws and regulations require adequate monitoring and enforcement. Even the best-designed environmental regulation can be ineffective if regulators fail to take steps to promote compliance. Yet this is costly and resources are limited. While systematic data on environmental enforcement is hard to find, Shimshack (2014) reports that between 1994 and 2011, the U.S. Environmental Protection Agency (EPA) conducted approximately 19 850 federal inspections per year. Combined with the additional enforcement expenditures at the state level, governments spend billions of dollars monitoring and enforcing environmental regulations each year. Policymakers therefore have incentives to find cost-effective ways to improve compliance among firms and individuals. Increasing compliance will help to achieve regulatory goals, such as cleaner air or fewer workplace accidents.

This chapter discusses the multiple ways that experimental economics can improve our understanding of the factors that affect compliance and lead to more effective use of limited enforcement resources. This includes testing theory, examining behavioural factors and the effectiveness of social observability, and test-bedding new methods in a low-cost and low-risk environment. We provide examples of all of these, and show that experiments are a useful complement to observational studies and are an essential methodology in the economics toolkit.

We demonstrate how experimental economics can improve our understanding of the factors affecting compliance in ways that are often impossible using naturally occurring data. Experiments, of course, also set the gold standard for causal inference. Although they typically study simplified and somewhat artificial settings, experiments can nevertheless provide highly relevant empirical evidence, particularly when guided by clear theoretical principles. For example, experiments can help test theoretical conclusions regarding the benefits of relative auditing rules versus random auditing of firms or individuals. Grounding an experimental design in theory can help generalise the lessons beyond the specific setting considered in the experiment.

Why should firms and individuals comply with regulations? Beginning with Becker (1968), a rich body of literature has explored the economics of compliance.[1] Key in the canonical model is the trade-off between the expected benefits and expected costs of compliance, where the benefits depend on both avoiding being detected as noncompliant and the potential penalty imposed if detected. While the empirical literature on compliance with environmental regulations demonstrates the importance of economic incentives (see, for example, surveys of the evidence by Shimshack, 2014, and Gray & Shimshack, 2011), these authors also recognise the potential role of other "socio-behavioural" factors (Alm & Shimshack, 2014), such as reputation and moral costs.

Empirical studies can document general relationships between enforcement and outcomes, such as pollution, but causality is harder to establish. One issue is that deterrence measures, such as inspections, are potentially endogenous; violators are more likely to be inspected, but for reasons that are unobservable to the analyst. In addition, assumptions need to be made and measures constructed regarding perceptions of key variables, such as inspection probabilities and penalties. Furthermore, obtaining data on compliance for uninspected firms is difficult, and it is often not available. Violators have a reason to stay silent. Firms' cost structures are also difficult for regulators to accurately observe. All of these issues, however, can be overcome with experiments.

A second major advantage of experiments in this context is the opportunity to investigate behavioural influences that are challenging to manipulate using naturally occurring data. Even if theory and empirical evidence exist, laboratory experiments can test the robustness of those results to behavioural factors, sometimes uncovering unanticipated behaviours that may undermine (or promote) the success of a policy. For example, experimental designs can observe or minimise reputation, social image, and other social motives and try to draw causal inferences. Experiments can also study the interactions between standard economic and behavioural factors.

Moving beyond understanding the basic determinants of compliance, a third significant advantage of experiments is their ability to trial (or "test-bed") different enforcement strategies in a low-cost and low-risk setting. For novel policy approaches, the data required for empirical testing are simply unavailable, either in a timely fashion, or at all. Laboratory experiments provide perhaps the only opportunity to explore empirically different policy options and counterfactuals. Field experiments are also useful for exploring new regulatory policies—but they can be more difficult to conduct. This chapter focuses on laboratory experiments.

Our aim is not to provide a comprehensive survey but to highlight some specific contributions and provide examples to illustrate how experiments can be used to investigate a range of applications on regulatory compliance, as well as suggesting areas for future study.[2] Section 2 illustrates how experiments can help in designing tools of monitoring and enforcement based on standard economic incentives (e.g. state-dependent enforcement, probability of detection versus fines, competitive audit mechanisms, contracts). Section 3 considers a specific environmental application in greater detail: compliance in "cap-and-trade" markets for pollution permits. Section 4 discusses how leveraging behavioural economic insights (framing, information, social pressure, reciprocity) can improve compliance. These nonbinding incentives show promise for behavioural change and in affecting social norms. We caution, however, against relying too heavily on such approaches intended to activate behavioural motivations in this compliance domain since the evidence is mixed. Section 5 concludes.

2.   Standard Economic Incentives

This section describes how economics experiments can provide valuable empirical evidence on the standard economic tools of deterrence. This includes the basic levers, such as the probability of detection and the penalties imposed. The main purpose of enforcement is to deter potential violators in the first place—so-called general deterrence. Experiments can be used to test theoretical predictions on the relationship between enforcement and compliance in a controlled way. Since enforcement is costly, understanding these relationships can inform budget-constrained regulators on how to deploy their limited resources in the most effective manner. Note that almost all of the experiments in this section are neutrally framed and therefore not specific to an environmental context. We briefly discuss this feature of the experimental designs in the concluding section.

2.1   General Deterrence

The seminal economics of crime model by Becker (1968) provides a framework for the compliance decisions of firms subject to environmental laws and regulations. In particular, when deciding on their level of compliance, environmental managers compare the expected costs of compliance (e.g. pollution-abatement costs) with the expected benefits of compliance. Typically, compliance benefits are determined by the avoidance of expected penalties. These expected penalties are comprised of two key components: the probability of punishment and the severity of punishment if detected.

The fundamental question is: Do polluters respond to these basic levers? That is, does general deterrence work, in that expected penalties deter violations from occurring in the first place? Friesen (2012) explores this question in the context of a regulatory compliance task where, in each decision period, participants in the experiment choose whether or not to comply with a generic regulation. Compliance incurs a certain cost, whereas violation entails a risk of being inspected and consequently incurring a penalty. The relevant parameters of compliance cost, likelihood of inspection, and penalty magnitude are varied systematically across 30 periods of choices. Friesen (2012) finds that the general deterrence hypothesis holds, as increases in either the probability of inspection or penalty (ceteris paribus) significantly increase compliance.[3] She also compares the effectiveness of the two levers of probability and severity of punishment, finding that an increase in the severity of punishment is a more effective deterrent than an equivalent increase in the probability of punishment. This is consistent with risk-averse expected utility maximisation.

Anderson and Stafford (2003) ask similar questions, but in the context of a public good experiment with an option to use a third-party punishment mechanism (neutrally framed as an earnings adjustment) to probabilistically punish free-riding. Consistent with Friesen (2012), they also find that compliance (here, public good contributions) increases with both levers, and that subjects respond more to increases in punishment severity than to punishment likelihood.

These findings can give regulators confidence in the basic underlying theoretical framework of the deterrence approach, and they provide information on the most effective lever to pull. The difference is that, in Friesen (2012), violations do not cause harm to others, whereas in the public good setting of Anderson and Stafford (2003), a violation reduces the public good, arguably capturing an important aspect of environmental compliance. This difference in design is evident in later studies as well. Consistent findings across settings increase confidence in the external validity of the findings.

2.2   Dynamic Enforcement

In contrast to random inspections, under conditional audit rules the regulator selects firms for inspection on the basis of certain characteristics. This kind of targeting is explicitly mentioned in the U.S. EPA's "Next Generation Compliance" initiative, which includes "Innovative Enforcement" approaches, including data analytics and targeting, as one of the five key and interconnected components to improve compliance.[4]

In this subsection, we emphasise the characteristic of past compliance status. While the experiments discussed in the previous subsection involve repeated decision-making, the enforcement parameters faced in a later period do not depend on earlier revealed compliance decisions. In contrast, many regulations invoke stricter penalties for repeat offenders, as well as increased scrutiny (likelihood of detection) for past violators. This can lead to stronger compliance incentives when individual penalty levels are limited by statute.

Theoretical models beginning with Harrington (1988) demonstrate the advantages of such dynamic enforcement. Specifically, Harrington (1988) models a simple approach where polluters are allocated into two groups based on their past compliance record, as determined by their inspection outcomes. Polluters in the non-targeted group face a relatively low detection probability and penalty. However, polluters that are revealed via an inspection to be in violation are moved to the target group for the next period. This structure enhances (leverages) compliance incentives because, in the targeted group, inspections are more frequent and penalties higher than in the non-targeted group. In addition, the opportunity to escape the target group (back to the less-scrutinised non-target group) if found to be in compliance gives polluters an additional incentive to comply. Harrington (1988) demonstrates theoretically how this approach can increase compliance without increasing the inspection budget, thereby leveraging enforcement resources. Friesen (2003) expands this case from what she labels as past compliance targeting to optimal targeting. Optimal targeting enhances compliance even further by fully concentrating inspection resources on polluters in the target group, while also employing a random mechanism to move polluters into the target group. Targeting is optimal as the best transition parameters are derived rather than assumed.

Clark et al. (2004) provide an experimental test of the Harrington (1988) model in comparison to both Friesen (2003) and the baseline case of purely random inspections. The theoretical prediction is that the same level of compliance can be achieved as under random audits, but with fewer inspections using past compliance targeting, and even fewer with optimal targeting. Clark et al.'s (2004) experimental results confirm this ranking of inspections, although only the difference between optimal targeting and random inspections was statistically significant. Unexpectedly, however, compliance rates were significantly lower with optimal targeting than in either random or past compliance targeting.

Cason and Gangadharan (2006a) also test the Harrington (1988) model but using natural rather than neutral language. The various treatments test different parameter values for the cost of compliance and the probability of being released from the target group. While they find that participants respond to the parameters in the expected direction, the responses are not as sharp as predicted by theory. Using a simple model of bounded rationality (noisy best response), Cason and Gangadharan (2006a) find that subjects are less likely to make errors that are more costly, and that accounting for this pattern of decision errors significantly improves the model fit. This suggests that how people act at the margin (where incentives to optimise are small) can influence the success of a policy.

In general, these experimental findings provide support for the greater effectiveness of dynamic enforcement through the mechanisms modelled by theory. However, they also suggest the need for caution when using more complex enforcement schemes to ensure these benefits are not undermined by bounded rationality and decision errors. More investigation of bounded rationality appears warranted in this context. Note that these experiments took considerable care to describe the multi-group inspection regimes. In practice, firms and individuals regulated under these schemes may not be as well informed. This further complicates interpretation of the benefits of such schemes.

2.3   Relative Conditional Audit Mechanisms

A more recent literature explores conditional audit mechanisms that use relative comparisons with other polluters, rather than just a firm's own past compliance information. These mechanisms create competition among pollut-ers to avoid being inspected, thus providing another means to leverage limited enforcement resources and increase compliance.[5] In particular, the probability of an audit depends on relative comparisons among peers, with inspections directed at polluters who are believed to be less compliant than other similar regulated entities.

Gilpatric et al. (2011) model a competitive audit regime where the regulator employs a rank-order tournament based on a noisy signal about compliance. Specifically, the regulator ranks facilities within a peer group based on a set of noisy signals and audits the facility expected to be the least compliant. Due to a strictly binding inspection budget, the regulator can only select a limited number of facilities to audit. The authors show theoretically that a rank-order tournament generates greater compliance than random audits using the same inspection budget. They then provide empirical support for this result in an experiment, and also find support for the model's comparative static predic-tions (e.g. the effect of increasing the penalty or audit cost).[6]

In Gilpatric et al. (2011), compliance means the truthfulness of reporting emis-sions, with emissions themselves treated as fixed. While accurate reporting is clearly a desirable outcome, later experiments also consider the impact that audit tournaments have on pollution itself. For example, Cason et al. (2016) report an experiment that considers both reporting and emissions choices. They find that audit tournaments lead to significantly lower misreporting than random audits, and that the benefit of audit tournaments does not erode with experience. Importantly, they also find that the benefits of audit tournaments extend beyond encouraging truthful reporting, with a reduction in emissions and the negative externality they generate. While these findings confirm that the basic mechanisms of the model work as expected theoretically, the impact on emissions is worthy of further exploration.

Gilpatric et al. (2015) combine both types of conditional audit mechanisms to create a dynamic tournament mechanism. The mechanism is based on the Harrington (1988) two-group approach but with tournaments to govern the transitions between the two groups. Specifically, audited firms in each group compete in a rank-order tournament, with the worst (largest violator) in the non-target group being moved to the target group, while the best escapes the target group for the next period. They compare this dynamic tournament mechanism to both static random audits and dynamic targeting based on a (non-competitive) standard. In the experiment, both dynamic mechanisms significantly increase compliance relative to random audits. However, while the results of the dynamic tournament mechanism are consistent with theory, the dynamic standards mechanism is not. Instead, compliance under the dynamic standards mechanism is insensitive to changes in either audit costs or the transition probabilities, which are both theoretically important parameters.

Gilpatric et al. (2015) suggest that the two dynamic tournaments perform differently because the incentives in the tournament mechanism are more obvious than in the dynamic standards mechanism, which requires individually solving a complicated dynamic problem. They argue that complexity might also explain the mixed findings in earlier experimental tests of targeting (Clark et al., 2004; Cason & Gangadharan, 2006a). In addition, Gilpatric et al. (2015) use a continuous choice setting compared to discrete choice in these two earlier studies, showing robustness to the choice of strategy space. Finally, note that while they also add heterogeneity in (pre-determined) pollution levels in their model, the experiment uses homogenous emissions, and the interaction between reporting and heterogeneous emission levels remains unexplored.[7]

2.4   Underexplored Topics

One aspect largely unexplored in the experimental literature is the impact of the organisational structure in which regulatory compliance decisions occur. Specifically, while a manager might make a decision to comply, the actions of others in the organisation (e.g. workers) significantly affect the outcome. In a recent paper, Cason et al. (2020) explore regulatory compliance in social dilemmas with and without a principal–agent relationship. In their experiment, agents choose costly effort levels that can reduce the probability of an accident (regulatory violation) occurring. This intra-firm decision is embedded in an inter-firm social dilemma whereby an accident at any firm within the group harms all firms. In this setting, Cason et al. (2020) investigate whether the principal can design a contract that incentivises the agent to take a desired (compliance) choice. Different treatments explore different contract forms: an unconditional wage plus a non-contractual bonus, a conditional (on outcome) wage, and a conditional wage plus a non-contractual bonus. These are compared to a baseline environment without an agent, so that the principal makes the compliance choice directly. Cason et al. (2020) find that principals use a combination of conditional wages and bonuses to help solve the agency problem. Hence, while the social dilemma still reduces overall welfare, the conditional contracts ensure that agency risk does not make this problem worse. In contrast, unconditional (gift exchange) contracts worsen the social dilemma (i.e. reciprocity is insufficient to incentivise the agent when there is outcome uncertainty). Future experiments can explore these issues further.

The experiments described above all involve inspection probabilities and penalties that are known and announced to participants. In reality, regulated firms must form beliefs of both the likelihood of being detected and the penalty if caught in violation. While legal scholars have long espoused the benefits of enforcement uncertainty (e.g. Harel & Segal, 1999), only two laboratory experiments specifically explore this topic, and neither is in an environmental compliance context. DeAngelo and Charness (2012) find that uncertainty about the enforcement regime (due to participants' failure to understand a more complex enforcement regime) significantly reduces violations in a laboratory experiment framed as speeding. On the other hand, in a study of tax compliance, Salmon and Shniderman (2019) find limited evidence of ambiguity aversion, which suggests that ambiguous enforcement might not improve compliance, and that instead it might be beneficial to reveal the parameters of the enforcement regime rather than conceal them. Given the prevalence of enforcement uncertainty in practice, this is clearly an important aspect for future study, and laboratory experiments are ideal to explore such topics in a controlled manner.

3.   Enforcement in Emissions Permit Markets

Considerable experimental research has investigated compliance in emissions permit markets. In this type of environmental regulation, sometimes referred to as "cap-and-trade," the regulator sets a limit on the total volume of pollution allowed, and allocates property rights over this allocation by distributing thousands of individual permits. A permit typically conveys the right to emit a specific amount of pollution over a specific time period (e.g. one tonne of CO_2 during calendar year 2021). The initial allocation for each time period can be auctioned, providing a source of government revenue, but sometimes a portion of the allocation is "grandfathered" to existing polluters at no cost. The government often reduces the number of permits allocated over time to achieve additional reductions in emissions.

A key distinguishing feature of this regulatory approach is that it provides flexibility for meeting pollution control goals, since individuals and firms can trade the emissions permits amongst each other. In many trading schemes, parties can bank unused permits for future use, or even borrow from future allocations. This flexibility means that firms face the same trade-off on the margin of incurring their marginal cost of an additional amount of pollution abatement or paying the market price for a permit to avoid the abatement. Firms with low marginal abatement costs can undertake abatement and sell permits, while those with high abatement costs can avoid abatement and buy permits. In a competitive market with zero transaction costs, this equates all firms' marginal abatement costs—at the common permit price—and this minimises the overall cost of meeting the original limit the regulator set for the total pollution allowed (Montgomery, 1972).

The first large-scale permit-trading scheme was implemented in Title IV of the 1990 Clean Air Act Amendments in the U.S., which effectively cut in half the amount of SO_2 released by large sources (e.g. coal-fired electricity genera-tors). Emissions trading is particularly suited for uniformly mixed pollutants (i.e. where the geographic location of the emissions source is not relevant to address the environmental problem), so the most important permit markets today are used to regulate greenhouse gas (GHG) emissions. The largest is the European Union Emissions Trading Scheme (EU ETS). Markets also exist in Australia, New Zealand, and many other countries, as well as regionally in the U.S. (such as the Regional Greenhouse Gas Initiative, RGGI, in the northeast, and a large GHG market in California).

Stranlund (2017) provides a comprehensive review of theoretical and empirical research on regulatory compliance in emissions permit markets. For the same reasons noted earlier regarding the difficulty of studying compliance with nat-urally occurring field data, many empirical studies of enforcement in permit markets have employed laboratory experiments. Laboratory experiments have also provided empirical evidence on other design features of emissions permit markets other than enforcement, as surveyed in Friesen and Gangadharan (2013a) and Cason (2010).

3.1   Measurement and Penalties

Measurement is the first challenge facing any regulatory scheme that is based on the quantity of pollution produced. Firms and the regulator must have some measurement or credible estimate of emissions. In some cases, Continuous Emissions Monitoring (CEM) is feasible.[8] This approach, however, is not feasible for other types of pollutants, or when individual sources are smaller or more numerous. For some important GHG emissions, accounting-based approaches are feasible. CO_2 emissions, for example, are approximately pro-portional to fossil fuel input, with the total emissions per unit of input depend-ing on the fuel type. Therefore, CO_2 emissions can be estimated based on the amount of fuel use and this can be the basis of self-reported emissions. These emissions reports are then subject to auditing, such as in the EU ETS and the California GHG market, analogous to the requirement that financial records require certified audits for tax and financial market regulation.[9]

A firm whose emissions in a particular period exceed current permit holdings can simply buy additional permits. Effective enforcement, therefore, requires that any (marginal) penalty must exceed the permit price for each "unit" of emissions that exceeds the permits held. Emissions trading markets often also require that excess emissions must be covered in subsequent years, either through a reduced future allocation or a requirement that the firm buy extra permits to account for prior year excess emissions. This makes part of the penalty market-based, as it is dependent on future permit prices. In some cases, permit violations require future period offsets or reduced allocations at a multiple of the violation size. For example, violations in California's GHG market are punished with a four-to-one offset (California Air Resources Board, 2011). These types of future-year permit reductions make the most environmental sense for a cumulative pollutant, such as GHG emissions, where the time dimension—at least the year-to-year variation—is not too relevant.

3.2   Unique Aspects of Permit Market Compliance

Given perfect enforcement, no market power, and zero transaction costs, firms minimise regulatory compliance costs by choosing emissions such that their marginal abatement costs equal the permit price. As noted above, these choices minimise aggregate abatement costs (Montgomery, 1972). If enforcement is imperfect, however, a firm that chooses to violate will hold enough permits so that the expected marginal penalty for noncompliance equals the permit price. Thus, the permit price endogenously determines the marginal compliance choice. Nevertheless, the marginal incentive is still the same for all firms when they face the same permit prices, so the aggregate abatement costs are still minimised even with imperfect enforcement (Malik, 1990). Stranlund et al. (2013) provide experimental support for this prediction, using laboratory markets with eight traders exchanging permits through a continuous double auction.[10] Although violations were lower than predicted in treatments when compliance incentives were weak, individual emissions control was distributed approximately as predicted.

Another implication of this common marginal incentive to comply, given by the prevailing permit price, is that a firm's compliance decision is independent of its individual characteristics. All firms are affected by the same margin (Stranlund & Dhanda, 1999). The policy implication of this theoretical result is clear: The regulator has no reason to target specific firms for more or less aggressive enforcement.[11] Murphy and Stranlund (2007) provide support for this implication using a laboratory experiment and by showing that cost effectiveness of enforcement would not improve if enforcement stringency was based on the firms' heterogeneity in abatement costs. Although these experimental markets appear to be competitive, this experiment also provides evidence of non-trivial transaction costs. In particular, those firms with higher marginal abatement costs, who should buy larger quantities of permits in equilibrium, buy fewer permits than predicted. They are therefore less compliant than firms with lower abatement costs who are net permit sellers.

Another unique aspect of compliance in emissions permit markets is that enforcement stringency affects the permit price. Murphy and Stranlund (2006) study the implications of this both theoretically and experimentally. They show that enforcement has a direct effect on prices: more enforcement, such as through a greater penalty for noncompliance, increases compliance rates, which increases permit demand; consequently, this raises the permit price. The higher permit price has a countervailing but smaller impact, reducing compliance. Because permits are more expensive, this raises the cost of compliance since this is achieved by buying more permits. Their experiment is able to decompose these direct and indirect impacts, providing valuable empirical evidence that the compliance benefits of increased enforcement are tempered in permit markets due to the resulting increase in compliance costs.

3.3   Intertemporal Complications

Another feature that makes emission permit markets unusual is banking, which links compliance across periods. When banking is allowed, firms can carry over unneeded permits from the current compliance period for use in later compliance periods. In some cases, such as in the EU ETS, firms can also borrow against future permit allocations if they hold insufficient permits (e.g. Chevallier, 2012). This ability to redeem permits for compliance in different time periods leads the potential for intertemporal arbitrage to limit price differences over time, as is the case for any durable asset.

Because banking smooths out permit prices across time, it can help promote the price stability needed to properly incentivise investments in new abatement technologies. Volatility can arise, for example, from the correlation of emissions with weather, since emissions increase directly with greater heating and cooling demands. Price variation can also arise from discrete changes in total permit allocations, and this can also motivate banking. For example, Phase I of the U.S. SO_2 trading scheme featured extensive banking in the late 1990s prior to the pre-announced reduction in total permits introduced in Phase II (in 2000).

Cason and Gangadharan (2006b) study compliance in a laboratory experiment with permit banking and emissions variability. Enforcement has a dynamic component based on a two-group version of Harrington's (1988) model of history-dependent performance. This experiment provides support for the theoretical prediction that banking smooths out permit price variability. Under-reporting emissions, however, increases the size of a firm's permit bank. Banking therefore increased noncompliance because it provides the incentive for even compliant firms to under-report emissions in order to bank permits that maintain considerable value in future periods.

Stranlund et al. (2011) use an experiment to study the role of self-reporting emissions in a dynamic market with permit banking, drawing a distinction between permit violations (i.e. not holding enough permits to cover emissions) and reporting violations (i.e. under-reporting emissions). Although a permit registry provides the regulator with perfect information about the number of permits held by the firm, the regulator does not learn the amount of emissions without auditing. A firm that holds sufficient permits to cover emissions in the current period may choose to under-report emissions to increase the size of its permit bank. Consistent with the theoretical results in Stranlund et al. (2005), higher permit violation penalties have little deterrence value in these markets with banking. Reporting violation penalties are more important to improve compliance and limit emissions.

3.4   Underexplored Topics

Several of the enforcement strategies discussed earlier in this chapter, such as dynamic enforcement and competitive audit mechanisms, have not been investigated for enforcement in emissions markets, either theoretically or experimentally (except to a limited extent in Cason and Gangadharan, 2006b). Another new enforcement approach that needs more investigation ties monitoring or fines to the level of permit prices. This approach has rarely been implemented in the field, but it featured prominently in some federally based emissions trading programs proposed in the U.S. in the 2000s.[12] Stranlund et al. (2019) report the only experiment conducted to study how this type of dynamic enforcement performs. While a treatment where the audit rate varied with permit prices effectively eliminated noncompliance as predicted, an alternative based on a fine level that varied with the price level was less successful. Permit markets, in practice, have often been implemented with administrative price floors and ceilings, and they are often expected to be binding (Borenstein et al., 2019). While the price and efficiency consequences of such price controls have been explored in experiments (Stranlund et al. 2014; Perkis et al., 2016; Friesen et al., 2020), and the enforcement implications of price controls have been studied in theory (Stranlund & Moffitt, 2014), compliance and enforcement implications of price controls have not been considered in experiments.

Permit markets are also likely to become increasingly linked, internationally and across states. This will change the compliance incentives in different jurisdictions as it will affect prices (see Stranlund, 2017, for a discussion). Different regions will also have variations in penalties and enforcement. Although some initial experiments have explored the implications of linking markets in different ways (Cason & Gangadharan, 2011), none has explored the effects of linking on compliance.

4.   Behavioural Levers

While many studies focus on the monetary incentives inherent in complying with regulatory programs, firms and individuals may also be motivated by additional factors, such as status, reputation, prevailing social norms, shame, and corporate social responsibility, which may influence their incentives to comply.[13] These extrinsic, intrinsic, and reputational motives have been studied extensively in the literature and studies have also shown that in some situations increasing monetary (extrinsic) incentives may crowd out intrinsic motives and dilute reputational effects (Benabou & Tirole, 2006). The combination of extrinsic, intrinsic, and reputational motives may be particularly important in the sphere of compliance with environmental programs in the field (Brent et al., 2016, provides a comprehensive review). In this section we highlight several papers that introduce non-monetary motives into the study of environmental compliance using laboratory experiments.

4.1   Social Observability

Information disclosure strategies have been considered a "third wave" of environmental regulation, in many cases replacing or supplementing traditional command-and-control and market-based instruments. The desire for social approval, leading to the positive impact of social observability on compliance rates could be effectively leveraged by regulators, especially if the costs associated with public disclosure are mostly negligible. The U.S. EPA's "Next Generation Compliance" initiative includes information disclosure ("Transparency") as another key component to tackle compliance.

Cason et al. (2016) compare the effectiveness of traditional audit mechanisms and social information policies in an environment where members of a group may impose direct negative externalities on others depending on their decisions. The externality introduces an important feature into the audit literature, which has traditionally focused on individual decision-making; it makes the setting more relevant for studying environmental issues and provides a platform to investigate non-monetary motives. Social observability policies, for example, rely on the premise that increasing the visibility of actions and audit outcomes can lead to improved compliance, which, due to the externality, benefits others.

The audit treatments examined in Cason et al. (2016), as discussed in Section 2, include a random audit treatment, in which firms are randomly inspected with a constant and exogenously determined probability, and the tournament audit treatment, in which firms are ranked based on their self-reporting. In the tournament, firms have an incentive to compete in terms of compliance since lower under-reporting compared to others in the regulatory group results in lower chances of an audit. The audit treatments include two levels of information disclosure. In the low-information condition, only the reporting choices of other participants are revealed, whereas in the high-information scenario, participants see digital photographs of everyone in the group and also learn the output and compliance of the inspected group members.

Revealing identities along with additional information about detected under-reporting may increase the stigma from noncompliance compared with the low information treatment. The additional information, however, could also provide a signal about the proportion of evaders in the population, which might cause individuals to update their beliefs about the social norm and the cost of deviating from that norm. Depending on the norm in the group, one could observe lower or higher compliance. The audit tournament treatment presents further challenges. While making reporting choices visible has no effect on others in the random treatment, greater under-reporting in the tournament treatment leads to positive externalities for other group members as it reduces their probability of being audited. This positive effect could reduce the social stigma from under-reporting.

As noted earlier and consistent with theoretical predictions, the treatment with audit tournaments leads to higher compliance levels as compared to the random audit treatment. Competition to avoid being audited reduces misreporting by 60 to 80 per cent on average. Reliance on the relative perceived performance amongst regulated individuals leads to improved efficiency by both reducing negative-externality-generating output and by increasing truthful reporting. Interestingly, however, social observability does not significantly affect output or reporting in either of the audit treatments. The offsetting incentives in the tournament mechanism apparently counteract any social stigma that might exist for misreporting. The findings suggest that social information could interact in unexpected ways with competitive schemes and needs to be examined closely before it can be considered an effective enforcement strategy in the field.

When individuals have different capacities to be compliant, this heterogeneity could influence the formation of norms relating to compliance. Those with higher endowments or higher abilities to comply may place different weights on the principles of group efficiency and equality as compared to those with lower capacity. Brent et al. (2019) evaluate the effectiveness of monetary and non-monetary approaches to improve environmental compliance in situations where agents are heterogenous. Their monetary mechanisms focus on tax and redistribution policies to improve compliance with extraction limits in a non-linear common-pool resource setting. Agents vary in their ability to extract a resource from a common pool. In one of their tax policies, each unit consumed is taxed, with the tax reflecting the scarcity of the resource. The other policy proposes higher rates for higher successive blocks of consumption, similar to the increasing block rate tariffs commonly used to price electricity and water use. Both policies also have an inequality-reduction dimension, achieved through an equal redistribution of the tax revenue towards all the group members.

Along the non-monetary dimension, observability is implemented such that each individual's extraction decision and payoff are publicly revealed to their group members. The authors find that both the tax and redistribution mechanisms significantly improve compliance by reducing extraction, while also increasing efficiency and reducing inequality, as compared to a baseline treatment with no policy. Social observability, interestingly, reduces compliance in the absence of a combined tax and redistribution mechanism. With a tax and redistribution mechanism, the negative effect of social information and observability disappears and there are no significant differences in compliance with or without observability. This means that social observability on its own encourages people to extract more. In particular, a majority of high-type subjects extract at their maximum capacity level knowing that their decision will be made public. The authors conjecture that the decisions of the high-types may be self-serving, to signal that they would not subsidise the low types and act to install a norm of high extraction to mitigate any potential guilt in case others in the group show intentions to comply.

4.2   Encouraging Honesty

As mentioned in Section 3, compliance in many environmental programs is measured with self-reports by individuals and firms. Self-reporting can improve compliance (as in some programs it offers lower penalties for those who voluntarily report environmental non-compliance) and reduce enforcement costs (EPA, 2000). Honesty, however, is an important part of this regulatory framework.[14] Self-reporting regimes can be designed in different ways that can consequently influence intrinsic motivations to be honest. Friesen and Gangadharan (2013b) examine the effectiveness of voluntary and compulsory self-reporting. Keeping economic incentives constant, theoretically one should not observe any difference between voluntary and compulsory reporting. Behavioural influences, however, may affect these regimes differently. This is because distinct differences may exist between failing to voluntarily submit a report (an act of omission) and telling an outright lie (an act of commission: knowingly submitting a false report). If agents are averse to blatant lies, this could result in greater reporting of violations in the compulsory self-reporting scenario than in the voluntary one. Conversely, being compelled to submit a report could lead to crowding out of the intrinsic motivation to voluntarily report violations and therefore may lead to less reporting in the compulsory case.

To examine the effectiveness of the two regimes, Friesen and Gangadharan (2013b) designed a production task with self-reporting of environmental accidents where some participants faced compulsory reporting while, for others, reporting was voluntary. They find that reporting of accidents was significantly more frequent with compulsory than with voluntary reporting. The aversion to overt lying therefore had a stronger effect than any potential crowding out of the intrinsic motivation to voluntarily report. Importantly, the compulsory regime led dishonest people (measured using an individual-level matrix task designed by Mazar et al., 2008) to be more truthful and report accidents more often. Many programs in the field use voluntary self-reporting systems, and this research suggests that the choice of self-reporting scheme can be critical in improving compliance in environmental programs. With increased use of online reporting, monitoring may become easier; on the other hand, this kind of reporting reduces social distance, which could increase dishonesty.

4.3   Underexplored Topics

Overall, the literature suggests that regulators need to exercise care when implementing policies that rely on behavioural motives to enhance compliance. The two policy levers from standard economic models of deterrence, frequency of inspections, and magnitude of fines appear to be less sensitive to context. In contrast, the experimental literature finds that environmental policies that rely on social information, norms, crowding out, and morality produce mixed results.[15] In some cases, they may also have perverse effects and can interact in unexpected ways with other features of the compliance policy.

The next generation of experiments in this area could focus on identifying the underlying reasons for these mixed results.[16]

5.   Summary and Conclusion

Compliance with laws and regulations is inherently difficult to study empirically since agents have the incentive to hide their illegal activity or over-report costly actions. While important lessons can be learned from studying detected violations, the presence of undetected violations means this leads to an incomplete picture of overall regulatory compliance. For over 50 years economists have developed models of enforcement and how agents should react to different compliance incentives. The combination of a solid, micro-founded theoretical framework and the inherent challenges of observing a complete picture of the key compliance choices using naturally occurring field data makes experimental studies in this area particularly useful.

The experiments we have summarised in this chapter investigate responses to differing inspection rates and penalties, testing some of the basic implications of the seminal model of Becker (1968). They also investigate alternatives that can improve on random inspections, including dynamic enforcement that applies greater scrutiny towards firms with past violations, and rank-order tournaments that inspect firms that are more likely to be non-compliant. We also provide an overview of a range of experiments that study compliance in markets for emission permits, and the use of social norms, triggered by transparency, to promote compliance.

Most of the experiments we describe were carried out in dedicated experimental economics laboratories on university campuses using college students as subjects. While this methodology is standard in this field, it raises the question of generalisability. Individuals and consumers sometimes make compliance decisions, but the most relevant population of decision-makers for regulatory compliance choices is firms and their managers. The theoretical models that motivate the research questions and the experimental designs discussed here do not make assumptions about the detailed characteristics of the relevant decision-makers; for example, they are silent about the amount of industry experience required before the models make relevant empirical predictions.

The use of a narrow class of subjects who are accustomed to making decisions in a controlled setting provides some benefits. Theory-oriented experimental studies, even those that have policy implications such as those considered here, can benefit from having a relatively homogeneous subject pool (Cason & Wu, 2019). Reducing the nuisance variation across treatments arising from subject heterogeneity increases experimental control—and the lower variance helps improve statistical power.

Another design feature of these laboratory studies that increases experimental control at the potential cost of generalisability is their use of neutral framing. Subjects in these experiments typically saw no references to the environment or pollution, although the experiments that study compliance often employ "inspections", "penalties", and other enforcement terms. The experiments avoid environmental terminology because individuals may have different attitudes towards environmental protection, which could influence behaviour in an uncontrolled way (Cason & Raymond, 2011). These attitudes are not part of the theoretical models that guide the experimental designs, with the exception of some experiments described in Section 4 that explore behavioural factors. Avoiding environmental terminology can help reduce variance that is beyond the models' scope. Additional research would be useful to determine how much framing affects behaviour in these types of experiments.

Compliance in environmental markets is studied mostly using a classical economic lens. Would social concerns about environmental issues influence the behavioural norms relating to compliance in these markets, or would competitive market forces dilute the impact of these norms (e.g. Bartling et al., 2015)? Would their impact differ depending on the direct harm caused by pollution? Would organisational structure affect compliance decisions? If managers can delegate compliance to another employee, does this give them some moral wiggle room, and what does this imply for compliance in these markets? It would be fruitful to explore these open questions in the future.

As resources for regulatory enforcement remain stretched, we anticipate research in environmental compliance will grow and an experimental approach would provide the scope for investigations that are systematic, rigorous, and rely on causal inferences.

Acknowledgments

We thank Jim Murphy and John Stranlund for their helpful suggestions.

Notes

1. Polinsky and Shavell (2000) survey the early theoretical literature.
2. Recent survey papers providing more details regarding laboratory experiments addressing specific environmental issues include Cason and Wu (2019), Friesen and Gangadharan (2013a), and Cason (2010). Surveys of relevant field experiments include Brent et al. (2016), List and Price (2016), and Price (2014).
3. Other laboratory experiments also confirm that the basic deterrence predictions hold, including DeAngelo and Charness (2012) in a task framed as speeding, and Salmon and Shniderman (2019) with respect to audit probabilities in a tax compliance experiment.
4. See https://www.epa.gov/compliance/next-generation-compliance, accessed 16 May, 2020.
5. Even compliant firms prefer to avoid inspections, as they are costly regardless of their compliance status.
6. Gilpatric et al. (2011) also study a more general relative evaluation mechanism that applies when the audit budget is not fixed. Under this mechanism, the probability of an audit depends on the entity's estimated compliance relative to its peer group. They demonstrate, both theoretically and experimentally, that this mechanism also increases compliance.
7. In theoretical work, Oestreich (2015) models the impact of competitive audit mechanisms (using a Tullock-style contest, which nests random audits and perfectly discriminating audits as limiting cases) on actual emissions, as well as the reporting of these emissions. Interestingly, he finds that excessive competition can backfire by increasing emissions, while still improving the truthfulness of reporting.
8. For example, the emissions permit scheme implemented in the 1990 U.S. Clean Air Act Amendments applied to large sources, and "smokestack-based" monitors were used to quantify each source's SO_2 and NO_x emissions. Emissions data were transferred to the regulator in real time, so this simplified measurement and reporting compliance was essentially for maintenance and accuracy of the CEM devices.
9. The certification of emissions reports is a potential source of noncompliance, and Shen et al. (2020) conducted an experiment in which the regulated firm may make side payments ("bribes") to a third party tasked with verifying report accuracy. They find that rotating both verifiers and inspection officials reduces corruption and improves truthful reporting.
10. In this trading institution, which is used for many laboratory studies of emissions permit markets, traders wishing to buy permits can submit bid prices to buy or accept sellers' offer prices in continuous time. Symmetrically, those wishing to sell permits can submit offer prices to sell or accept buyers' bid prices at any time. This centralised, multilateral negotiation process creates relatively competitive market conditions even with a relatively small number of traders.
11. This result does not hold in the presence of market power, however (van Egteren and Weber, 1996), nor does it hold in the presence of transaction costs. Transactions costs drive a wedge between what buyers pay for permits and the price that sellers receive (Stavins, 1995). Consequently, since buyers face a higher "effective" price, they are more likely to violate than are sellers.

12. Fines were also tied to permit prices in pilot programs implemented in China (Zhang, 2015). For example, in the Beijing pilot, the fine for excess emissions ranged between three and five times the prevailing average permit price in the previous six months. The rate depended on the extent of noncompliance, with the higher fine rate (5) applied to firms with emissions more than 20 per cent over their permit holdings.

13. Research using psychological measures and self-reports of emotions shows that emotional arousals are strongly associated with the likelihood of being compliant (e.g. Coricelli et al., 2010; Khadjavi, 2014). This may be one channel through which individuals take non-monetary factors (such as moral and social dimensions) into account when making compliance decisions. Additionally, limited evidence exists that affirmative motivations, such as belief that honest emissions reporting is appropriate or that levels of permit endowments are "fair", increase compliance (Raymond and Cason, 2011).

14. Using data from more than 90 experimental studies, Abeler et al. (2019) show that the main reasons for truth-telling in different contexts include a preference for being honest and a preference for being seen to be honest.

15. Slemrod (2019) also reports this mixed evidence of the effectiveness of intrinsic motives in the area of tax compliance.

16. Research using field data lend some support to these mixed effects. For example, while evidence from the field indicates that social information might change behaviour by triggering conformity to a social norm (e.g., Allcott and Mullainathan, 2010; Ferraro and Price, 2013), researchers also find that economic incentives provide much larger and more persistent effects as compared to intrinsic measures, such as moral suasion, which showed a diminishing effect when the interventions were repeated (Ito et al., 2018).

References

Abeler, J., Nosenzo, D., & Raymond, C. (2019). Preferences for truth-telling. *Econometrica*, *87*(4), 1115–1153.

Allcott, H., & Mullainathan, S. (2010). Behaviour and energy policy. *Science*, *327*(5970), 1204–1205.

Alm, J., & Shimshack, J. P. (2014). Environmental enforcement and compliance: Lessons from pollution, safety, and tax settings. *Foundations and Trends in Microeconomics*, *10*, 209–274.

Anderson, L., & Stafford, S. (2003). Punishment in a regulatory setting: Experimental evidence from the VCM. *Journal of Regulatory Economics*, *24*(1), 91–110.

Bartling, B., Weber, R. A., & Yao, L. (2015). Do markets erode social responsibility? *Quarterly Journal of Economics*, *130*, 219–266.

Becker, G. (1968). Crime and punishment: An economic approach. *Journal of Political Economy*, *76*, 169–217.

Benabou, R., & Tirole, J. (2006). Incentives and prosocial behavior. *American Economic Review*, *96*(5), 1652–1678.

Borenstein, S., Bushnell, J., Wolak, F. A., & Zaragoza-Watkins, M. (2019). Expecting the unexpected: Emissions uncertainty and environmental market design. *American Economic Review*, *109*, 3953–3977.

Brent, D., Friesen, L., Gangadharan, L., & Leibbrandt, A. (2016). Behavioral insights from field experiments in environmental economics. *International Review of Environmental and Resource Economics, 10*, 95–143.

Brent, D., Gangadharan, L., Mihut, A., & Villeval, M. C. (2019). Taxation, redistribution and observability in social dilemmas. *Journal of Public Economic Theory, 21*(5), 826–846.

California Air Resources Board. (2011). *Overview of ARB Emissions Trading Program.* Sacramento: California Environmental Protection Agency.

Cason, T. N. (2010). What can laboratory experiments teach us about emissions permit market design? *Agricultural and Resource Economics Review, 39*(2), 151–161.

Cason, T. N., Friesen, L., & Gangadharan, L. (2016). Regulatory performance of audit tournaments and compliance observability. *European Economic Review, 85*, 288–306.

Cason, T. N., Friesen, L., & Gangadharan, L. (2020). Inter-firm social dilemmas with agency risk. *European Economic Review, 129*, 103570. https://doi.org/10.1016/j.euroecorev.2020.103570

Cason, T. N., & Gangadharan, L. (2006a). An experimental study of compliance and leverage in auditing and regulatory enforcement. *Economic Inquiry, 44*, 352–366.

Cason, T. N., & Gangadharan, L. (2006b). Emissions variability in tradable permit markets with imperfect enforcement and banking. *Journal of Economic Behavior and Organization, 61*, 199–216.

Cason, T. N., & Gangadharan, L. (2011). Price discovery and intermediation in linked emissions trading markets: A laboratory study. *Ecological Economics, 70*, 1424–1433.

Cason, T. N., & Raymond, L. (2011). Framing effects in an emissions trading experiment with voluntary compliance. In R. M. Isaac & D. A. Norton (Eds.), *Research in experimental economics* (pp. 77–114). Bingley, UK: Emerald Group Publishing.

Cason, T. N., & Wu, S. (2019). Subject pools and deception in agricultural and resource economics experiments. *Environmental and Resource Economics, 73*, 743–758.

Chevallier, J. (2012). Banking and borrowing in the EU ETS: A review of economic modelling, current provisions and prospects for future design. *Journal of Economic Surveys, 26*, 157–176.

Clark, J., Friesen, L., & Muller, A. (2004). The good, the bad and the regulator: An experimental test of two conditional audit schemes. *Economic Inquiry, 42*, 69–87.

Coricelli, G., Joffily, M., Montmarquette, C., & Villeval, M. C. (2010). Cheating, emotions, and rationality: An experiment on tax evasion. *Experimental Economics, 13*, 226–247.

DeAngelo, G., & Charness, G. (2012). Deterrence, expected cost, uncertainty and voting: Experimental evidence. *Journal of Risk and Uncertainty, 44*, 73–100.

Environmental Protection Agency (EPA). (2000). Incentives for self-policing: Discovery, disclosure, correction and prevention of violations. *Federal Register 65*(70), 19617–19627.

Ferraro, P. J., & Price, M. K. (2013). Using non-pecuniary strategies to influence behavior: Evidence from a large-scale field experiment. *Review of Economics and Statistics, 95*(1), 64–73.

Friesen, L. (2003). Targeting enforcement to improve compliance with environmental regulations. *Journal of Environmental Economics and Management, 46*(1), 72–86.

Friesen, L. (2012). Certainty of punishment versus severity of punishment: An experimental investigation. *Southern Economic Journal, 79*(2), 399–421.

Friesen, L., & Gangadharan, L. (2013a). Environmental markets: What do we learn from the lab? *Journal of Economic Surveys, 27*(3), 515–535.

Friesen, L., and Gangadharan, L. (2013b). Designing self-reporting regimes to encourage truth telling: An experimental study. *Journal of Economic Behavior and Organization*, 13, 90–102.

Friesen, L., Gangadharan, L., Khezr, P., & Mackenzie, I. (2020). *Mind your Ps and Qs! Variable allowance supply in the US Regional Greenhouse Gas Initiative* (Discussion Paper 618). University of Queensland School of Economics.

Gilpatric, S., Vossler, C., & Liu, L. (2015). Using competition to stimulate regulatory compliance: A tournament-based dynamic targeting mechanism. *Journal of Economic Behavior and Organization*, 119, 182–196.

Gilpatric, S., Vossler, C., & McKee, M. (2011). Regulatory enforcement with competitive endogenous audit mechanisms. *RAND Journal of Economics*, 42(2), 292–312.

Gray, W., & Shimshack, J. (2011). The effectiveness of environmental monitoring and enforcement: A review of the empirical evidence. *Review of Environmental Economics and Policy*, 5, 3–24.

Harel, A., & Segal, U. (1999). Criminal law and behavioral law and economics: Observations on the neglected role of uncertainty in deterring crime. *American Law and Economics Review*, 1, 276–312.

Harrington, W. (1988). Enforcement leverage when penalties are restricted. *Journal of Public Economics*, 37, 29–53.

Ito, K., Ida, T., & Tanaka, M. (2018). The persistence of moral suasion and economic incentives: Field experimental evidence from energy demand. *American Economic Journal: Economic Policy*, 10(1), 240–67.

Khadjavi, M. (2014). On the interaction of deterrence and emotions. *The Journal of Law, Economics, and Organization*, 31(2), 287–318.

List, J. A., & Price, M. K. (2016). The use of field experiments in environmental and resource economics. *Review of Environmental Economics and Policy*, 10, 206–225.

Malik, A. S. (1990). Markets for pollution control when firms are noncompliant. *Journal of Environmental Economics and Management*, 18, 97–106.

Mazar, N., Amir, O., & Ariely, D. (2008). The dishonesty of honest people: A theory of self-concept maintenance. *Journal of Marketing Research*, 45, 633–644.

Montgomery, W. D. (1972). Markets in licenses and efficient pollution control programs. *Journal of Economic Theory*, 5, 395–418.

Murphy, J. J., & Stranlund, J. K. (2006). Direct and indirect effects of enforcing emissions trading programs: An experimental analysis. *Journal of Economic Behavior and Organization*, 61, 217–233.

Murphy, J. J., & Stranlund, J. K. (2007). A laboratory investigation of compliance behavior under tradable emissions rights: Implications for targeted enforcement. *Journal of Environmental Economics and Management*, 53, 196–212.

Oestreich, A. (2015). Firms' emissions and self-reporting under competitive audit mechanisms. *Environmental and Resource Economics*, 62, 949–978.

Perkis, D., Cason, T. N., & Tyner, W. (2016). An experimental investigation of hard and soft price ceilings in emissions permit markets. *Environmental and Resource Economics*, 63, 703–718.

Polinsky, A. M., & Shavell, S. (2000). The economic theory of public enforcement of law. *Journal of Economic Literature*, 38, 45–76.

Price, M. K. (2014). Using field experiments to address environmental externalities and resource scarcity: Major lessons learned and new directions for future research. *Oxford Review of Economic Policy*, 30, 621–638.

Raymond, L., & Cason, T. (2011). Can affirmative motivations improve compliance in emissions trading programs? *Policy Studies Journal*, 39, 659–678.

Salmon, T. C., & Shniderman, A. (2019). Ambiguity in criminal punishment. *Journal of Economic Behavior and Organization, 163,* 361–376.

Shen, P., Betz, R., Ortmann, A., & Gong, R. (2020). Improving truthful reporting of polluting firms by rotating inspectors: Experimental evidence from a bribery game. *Environmental and Resource Economics, 76,* 201–233.

Shimshack, J. P. (2014). The economics of environmental monitoring and enforcement. *Annual Review of Resource Economics, 6,* 339–360.

Slemrod, J. (2019). Tax compliance and enforcement. *Journal of Economic Literature, 57*(4), 904–954.

Stavins, R. (1995). Transactions costs and tradeable permits. *Journal of Environmental Economics and Management, 29,* 133–148.

Stranlund, J. K. (2017). The economics of enforcing emissions markets. *Review of Environmental Economics and Policy, 11,* 227–246.

Stranlund, J. K., Costello, C., & Chavez, C. A. (2005). Enforcing emissions trading when emissions permits are bankable. *Journal of Regulatory Economics, 28,* 181–204.

Stranlund, J. K., & Dhanda, K. K. (1999). Endogenous monitoring and enforcement of a transferable emissions permit system. *Journal of Environmental Economics and Management, 38,* 267–282.

Stranlund, J. K., & Moffitt, L. J. (2014). Enforcement and price controls in emissions trading. *Journal of Environmental Economics and Management, 67,* 20–38.

Stranlund, J. K., Murphy, J. J., & Spraggon, J. M. (2011). An experimental analysis of compliance in dynamic emissions markets. *Journal of Environmental Economics and Management, 62,* 414–429.

Stranlund, J. K., Murphy, J. J., & Spraggon, J. M. (2013). Imperfect enforcement of emissions trading and industry welfare: A laboratory investigation. In J. List & M. Price (Eds.), *Handbook on experimental economics and the environment* (pp. 265–288). Northampton, MA: Edward Elgar.

Stranlund, J. K., Murphy, J. J., & Spraggon, J. M. (2014). Price controls and banking in emissions trading: An experimental evaluation. *Journal of Environmental Economics and Management, 68,* 71–86.

Stranlund, J. K., Murphy, J. J., Spraggon, J. M., & Zirogiannis, N. (2019). Tying enforcement to prices in emissions markets: An experimental evaluation. *Journal of Environmental Economics and Management, 98,* 102246.

van Egteren, H., & Weber, M. (1996). Marketable permits, market power, and cheating. *Journal of Environmental Economics and Management, 30,* 161–73.

Zhang, Z. (2015). Carbon emissions trading in China: The evolution from pilots to a nationwide scheme. *Climate Policy, 15,* S104–S126.

5　Behavioural characteristics, stability of preferences and entrepreneurial success

Pushkar Maitra and Ananta Neelim

1.　Introduction

Behavioural characteristics of individuals, such as preferences towards risk, time, and competition, and non-cognitive traits, including confidence and perseverance, have significant influence on their economic decisions. Simultaneously, research has shown significant heterogeneity in these characteristics across countries (Heinrich et al., 2010; Falk et al., 2018). Not only do average risk, time, and social preferences vary considerably across countries, even within the set of developing nations, large heterogeneity exists in this regard. Falk et al. (2018) show that, at the country level, there are statistically significant correlations between these preferences and other presumably exogenous variables, such as agricultural suitability, religion, and language structure. Importantly though, variations in these behavioural preferences are significantly correlated with economic outcomes and behaviours. For example, social preferences have been shown to effect behavioural outcomes like pro-sociality, including trust and trustworthiness, that can have considerable influence on social and economic development. While Arrow (1972) argues that virtually every commercial transaction has within itself some elements of trust, these traits are of particular importance in environments where contracts may be incomplete, and where the rule of law and the ability of courts to enforce contracts is limited. Trust, or a lack thereof, can lead to a lack of social cohesion and ultimately to conflicts within society. A good example is the poor economic performance of many African nations, which are also characterised by a lack of trust in political institutions and leaders (see Nunn and Wantchekon, 2011, and Acemoglu and Robinson, 2012).

At the micro (individual) level, behavioural characteristics can affect different dimensions of individuals' lives in both developed and developing countries. For example, (1) risk preferences have significant effects on occupational choices, schooling decisions, technology adoption, and choosing to be enrolled in skills-training programs (e.g. Castillo et al., 2010; Belzil and Leonardi, 2009; Liu, 2013; Dasgupta et al., 2015), while (2) preference for competition has been shown to influence wage differences, educational choices, workplace choices, and to influence the evolution of gender differences in the workplace (Niederle and Vesterlund, 2007; Gneezy et al., 2009; Andersen et al., 2013; Flory et al., 2015; Buser et al., 2014). At the same time, research has shown that individual-level differences in non-cognitive traits are positively correlated with economic outcomes. For example, confidence is positively associated with wage rates (Fang and Moscarini, 2005), performance in financial markets (Biais et al., 2005), entrepreneurial behaviour (Cooper et al., 1988; Camerer and Lovallo, 1999; Bernardo and Welch, 2001; Koellinger et al., 2007), enrolment in programs that aid skill development (Dasgupta et al., 2015), and can explain the persistence of intergenerational inequality in income and education (Filippin and Paccagnella, 2012).

While behavioural characteristics can influence decision-making in many spheres of life, in this chapter, we focus on one such sphere, entrepreneurship. We explore entrepreneurship in developing countries where labour markets are characterised by low levels of formality and are generally associated with low productivity (La Porta and Shleifer, 2014). In such an environment, the formal employment sector often fails to provide enough jobs to meet the employment needs of the population. Further, returns to education and experience in the formal labour market are low in developing countries relative to their high-income counterparts (Lagakos et al., 2018), making entrepreneurship a lucrative employment option. According to the data from the International Labour Organization, in 2018, self-employment accounted for 75% of the total employment in low-income countries.[1] This is in stark contrast to high-income countries, where self-employment only accounts for 35% of the total. Indeed, the distribution of the share of self-employment is skewed to the right in developing countries (with the mass of the distribution at more than 80%), and it is skewed to the left in developed countries (with the mass of the distribution at less than 20%; ILO, 2020). All of this makes entrepreneurship a critical vehicle of economic growth in developing countries.[2]

We start by providing a brief review of the literature to identify the main behavioural preferences and non-cognitive traits of individuals that affect entrepreneurial choice and success. We utilise studies conducted in both developing and developed countries, though our primary focus is on those conducted in developing countries. Second, we provide a review of experimental studies from the development literature that examine the impact of standard interventions, including the provision of finance and business training in improving micro-enterprise performance. We show that the behavioural preferences and non-cognitive skills of entrepreneurs are often correlated with the successes and failures of these standard interventions conducted in the developing countries. Finally, we offer a discussion on the stability of behavioural preferences and examine whether individuals can be trained to alter these preferences with an aim to make them better.

2.   Who Becomes a Successful Entrepreneur?

Uncovering the behavioural differences between entrepreneurs and the rest of the population has been a long-standing focus of research in business and the social sciences. The starting point of any analysis is the assumption that the world of business venturing is riskier than paid work. Indeed, Åstebro et al. (2014), using data from the US, provide evidence of this assumption. They show that, of the businesses founded in 1996, around 50% of them failed, 10% achieved more than $1 million in sales, and less than 1% made sales of $10 million or higher by 2002. This suggests that entrepreneurship tends to be low-median but high-variance activity: a majority of entrepreneurs fail, while some are extremely successful.

Given the inherent risks associated with entrepreneurship, a plausible starting point is to examine whether individuals with lower levels of risk-aversion are more likely to engage in entrepreneurship. The seminal work by Kihlstrom and Laffont (1979) theorises that individuals who are most risk tolerant are more likely to be entrepreneurs, while the less risk-tolerant individuals are more likely to seek paid employment. Similarly, their work also predicts that individuals with higher risk tolerance are expected to be more successful once they enter entrepreneurship. A significant amount of research has been conducted to test these predictions.

2.1   Choosing to Become an Entrepreneur

Let us start by looking at studies that investigate the role of risk on entrepreneurial choice. These studies can be divided into three categories on the basis of how risk is measured. The first set of studies measure risk preference based on behaviour in other domains of life, and correlate it with the choice of self-employment (as a proxy for entrepreneurial choice). For example, Hvide and Panos (2014) use individual-level administrative data on stock market participation, fraction of wealth invested in stock markets, and type of stock portfolio to measure risk tolerance and show that this variable is correlated with choosing to be self-employed. The second set of studies compares entrepreneurial choice and hypothetical risk preferences measured later in life (longitudinal data) and finds a positive relationship between becoming self-employed and risk tolerance (Ahn, 2010; Cramer et al., 2002). While some of these works conclude a positive relationship between risk tolerance and enterprise choice, the literature overall is inconsistent (see Parker, 2009, for a discussion).

One of the problems with survey measures that elicit risk preferences is that they might pick up other dimensions of behaviour that are correlated with a person's risk preference in addition to the actual risk preference. For example, survey questions may ask an individual to indicate their self-perception of their risk across many dimensions of life. While answers to these questions are informative about risk preferences, they might not satisfy incentive compatibility conditions. Incentives provided in experimental elicitation of risk ensure that participants reveal their true preferences, thus reducing the noise associated with measurements. We discuss the relative advantages and disadvantages of risk preferences elicited using surveys versus experimental methods in Section 4.1.

In the entrepreneurship literature, there are a number of studies that utilise experimental tasks to elicit risk preferences to investigate whether these preferences differ across entrepreneurs and non-entrepreneurs. Holm et al. (2013) utilise a multiple price list technique to elicit risk aversion based on Holt and Laury (2002).[3] Their sample consists of 700 entrepreneurs and 200 non-entrepreneurs in China. They find that entrepreneurs are no more likely to have a higher tolerance for risk than are non-entrepreneurs. List and Mason (2011) elicit the risk preferences of 29 CEOs and 101 students in Costa Rica and show that risk preferences do not vary significantly across these two groups.

An alternative explanation for entrepreneurial choice is that individuals who choose to be entrepreneurs are more likely to be optimistic and/or overconfident than others. To test whether over-optimism is a factor in entrepreneurial choice, Puri and Robinson (2007) measure optimism by comparing a person's self-reported life expectancy to that of statistical tables. They show that optimists are more likely to believe that future economic conditions will improve. Further, they show that, relative to regular wage earners, entrepreneurs are more likely to be optimists. In contrast to optimism, overconfidence is a concept that has many facets, one of which is over-placement: specifically, how individuals rate their own ability relative to that of others. Camerer and Lovallo (1999) designed an experiment to measure over-placement. In this experiment, individuals were to enter a "market" where pay-offs depended on relative ranks amongst all entrants. In the control condition, individual ranks were given out randomly, and in the skill condition the ranking was based on performance in a trivia task. They showed that, relative to the control condition, market entry was higher in the skill condition. This was despite participants predicting excessive entry in the latter treatment. They conclude that participants must be biased about the superiority of their own skills, making the entry profitable in expected terms.

The higher entry in the skills condition, as in Camerer and Lovallo (1999), can also be driven by a simple preference for competition and not necessarily overconfidence (i.e. individuals get additional happiness from competing against others, irrespective of the outcome). To test whether entrepreneur choice is driven by overconfidence or a higher preference for competition, Holm et al. (2013) conducted an experiment with entrepreneurs and a relevant control group. Using a task similar to Camerer and Lovallo (1999), they found that entrepreneurs are significantly more likely to compete relative to the control group when overconfidence is controlled for. Similarly, using German subjects, Urbig et al. (2020) found that, controlling for other factors, entrepreneurs are more likely to enter competition for the sake of competition rather than the prospect of winning or personal development.

In summary, the results of studies examining the effect of individual preference for risk and competition, as well as related non-cognitive traits such as optimism and overconfidence, provide a more nuanced picture of entrepreneurial choice relative to the theoretical model of Kihlstrom and Laffont (1979). The studies highlight that it is not risk preferences, per se, but preferences for competition that drive entrepreneurial choice.

Other behavioural characteristics, such as time preference and trust in others, have also been investigated as being potentially different for entrepreneurs. Using a sample of Danish entrepreneurs, Andersen et al. (2014) found that entrepreneurs are more likely to be patient relative to the general population.[4] Fessler et al. (2004) compared trust and trustworthiness behaviour of CEOs and students in Costa Rica. They elicited trust using the standard Trust Game (Berg et al., 1995) and the gift-exchange game (Fehr et al., 1993).[5] Fehr and List (2004) found that CEOs are more trusting and exhibit more trustworthiness than students. Holm et al. (2013) also investigated the question of trust using Chinese entrepreneurs and non-entrepreneurs and found that entrepreneurs in their sample were significantly more trusting than non-entrepreneurs.[6]

Finally, studies have also investigated the role of other non-cognitive traits on choice of entrepreneurship. One of the broader measures of non-cognitive traits is personality traits, which are measured using the Big-5. Here, personality is defined on the basis of openness, conscientiousness, extraversion, agreeableness, and neuroticism. Zhao and Seibert (2006) conducted a meta-analysis of 27 studies and found significant differences between entrepreneurs and managers. Entrepreneurs scored higher on conscientiousness and openness to experience, and lower on neuroticism and agreeableness. Managers and entrepreneurs were not different in terms of extroversion. Other measures of personality traits, such as locus of control (LOC), have also been shown to influence entrepreneurial choice. For example, Caliendo et al. (2014) used a large German household panel to investigate whether and to what extent personality traits influence entry and exit decisions in self-employment. They find that internal LOC is one of the two personality traits that best predict entry into entrepreneurship.

2.2   Entrepreneurship Growth and Success

Now we turn to entrepreneurship growth and performance. In a meta-analysis of 60 studies, Zhao et al. (2010) showed that risk propensity is not related to entrepreneurial success. Similarly, Kessler et al. (2012), studying 227 nascent entrepreneurs, found that risk-taking preferences are not related to entrepreneurial survival. Using small-scale business owners in Tanzania, Berge et al. (2015a) found that risk preferences and time preference did not determine enterprise performance (profit and sales of firms). They also found that overconfidence did not affect enterprise performance. In fact, the only behavioural characteristic that appears to have a positive impact on entrepreneurial success is preference for competition. This view was corroborated by a later study, where Berge et al. (2015b) showed preferences for competition to be an important predictor for enterprise success.

Researchers have also investigated the role of personality traits on entrepreneurial performance. In a meta-study, Zhao et al. (2010) found that conscientiousness, openness to experience, emotional stability, and extraversion are positively related to entrepreneurial firm performance. Likewise, Rauch and Frese (2007) identified that innovativeness and LOC are positively correlated with entrepreneurial success. For a detailed review of the role of personality traits on entrepreneurial success we direct our readers to the reviews by Kerr et al. (2017) and Frese and Gielnik (2014).

3.   Constraints on Entrepreneurship

Given the importance of entrepreneurship in the economies of developing countries, a significant research effort has been expended recently to understand and improve micro-enterprise performance. In this section, we focus on recent research from development economics that investigates the effect of (1) access to capital and (2) business training on enterprise success. For a broader review of the literature looking at other dimensions that affect entrepreneurship, we refer the readers to Quinn and Woodruff (2019).

3.1   Access to Capital

As discussed in the introduction, self-employment in developing countries accounts for a much larger share of total employment relative to developed countries. This implies that developing countries typically have more entrepreneurs and, coupled with the underdeveloped nature of financial markets, potential entrepreneurs are likely to face larger capital constraints relative to entrepreneurs in the developed world. Thus, one of the main areas of research focus in recent development economics in enterprise development has been access to external finance for entrepreneurs. The working hypothesis of most of these studies is that entrepreneurs do not have access to capital, and relaxing constraints will lead to more enterprise success. These studies increase access to capital for enterprises by providing either grants or loans, and measure its effect on enterprise-level outcomes.

Generally, the results suggest that returns to grants (cash or in-kind) to microenterprises are high. For example, De Mel et al. (2008) show that providing microenterprises in Sri Lanka with $100–$200 grants led to an average return of 5.7% per month, which was much higher than the prevailing market interest rates. In a follow-up survey, they investigated the long-term effects of these grants and found that the firms that received grants were 10 percentage points more likely to survive (De Mel et al., 2012). McKenzie (2017) examined the effect of grants on survival for larger enterprises and found that these grants also led to increases in enterprise survival and in the likelihood of them hiring more workers. However, the positive effects of access to capital via grants on enterprise outcomes do not replicate when grants are replaced by microloans.

In a review of six randomised evaluations, Banerjee et al. (2015) concluded that microloans have modest positive, but not transformative, effects on business growth for the average borrower. According to a review by Quinn and Woodruff (2019), the discrepancy between behaviours under loans and grants can be related to sub-optimal choices made by borrowers who are faced with constraining repayment schedules or the terms under which microloans are made (e.g. group lending). Nevertheless, improving entrepreneurial success via grants is extremely capital intensive and, as a result, may be difficult for policymakers to fund. Given this reality, policymakers have investigated other ways to address the issue of enterprise development. One such way is training potential entrepreneurs to develop skills so that they can take advantage of financial opportunities (like loans) to become successful.

3.2   Access to Skills-Based Business Training

Identifying potential entrepreneurs is not an easy task. This is because many of the traits that are associated with successful entrepreneurship are unobservable. A way in which researchers have tried to tackle this issue is by providing training to potential entrepreneurs to build entrepreneurial skills. In a review article, McKenzie and Woodruff (2013) investigate the role of management practices (marketing, stock-keeping, record-keeping, and financial planning) in determining the performance of small firms in developing countries. They find that these practices can predict success across firms and that better business practices lead to higher survival rates and faster growth in sales.

A plausible starting point for training interventions is to provide potential entrepreneurs with management skills. A review of the evidence from 16 studies was carried out by McKenzie and Woodruff (2013); they found that classroom-based standard business training only had modest effects on enterprise performance. However, the effectiveness of training depends on its uptake. McKenzie and Woodruff (2013) show that training programs that had larger effects on management practices led to better enterprise performance. This is echoed by the study of Bjorvatn and Tungodden (2010), who show that participation rates in training programs are important in determining the successful translation of training to business knowledge. One way in which training can be made more lucrative is by providing more context to participants. A study conducted by Drexler et al. (2014) shows that, relative to a standard accounting training, a simplified rule-of-thumb training that taught basic financial heuristics led to improved financial practices and revenue for low-skilled micro-entrepreneurs.

4.   Stability of Preferences: Evidence from Economic Shocks

The decision to become an entrepreneur and entrepreneurial success are both moderated by behavioural preferences and non-cognitive traits. It is therefore plausible that individuals who possess certain preferences and traits are more likely choose to become entrepreneurs and be successful at it. They are also more likely to benefit from skills training by translating the new skills acquired to newer business opportunities. In a study conducted in Tanzania, Berge et al. (2015b) show that both male and female entrepreneurs translate their business training into better business practices. However, when business training is given in combination with access to capital (via grants), it is only male entrepreneurs who can translate them into profitable and productive investments. Female entrepreneurs appear to be unable to take advantage of the potential opportunities provided by the same human capital and financial capital interventions. The authors argue that the significant behavioural differences elicited by lab-in-the-field experiments between male and female entrepreneurs in risk and tolerance for competition can provide potential explanations for this gender difference.

Given the critically important role of behavioural preferences and non-cognitive traits on entrepreneurial choice and success, an important question is: Are behavioural preferences and personality traits malleable? If they are, appropriate interventions can be designed to train individuals to develop them, resulting in a better stock of potential entrepreneurs in the population via policy intervention. In the next two sections, to investigate malleability of behavioural preferences and personality traits, we first review the literature on preference stability in response to major life events (both positive and negative) in developed and developing countries, and second, we review recent studies that investigate whether or not individuals can be trained to develop personality traits that are important for entrepreneurship.

4.1   Shocks and Changes in Preferences

Traditional economic theory has typically assumed that preferences are stable over time. Indeed, without this assumption we are unable to relate changes in opportunity sets and changes in optimal choices. In particular, if preferences are themselves endogenous, they can be affected by policy choices and, hence, by changes in opportunity sets. While this assumption of stable preferences has been a given in neo-classical economics for more than a century, in recent years there is a developing strand of the literature that seeks to investigate the validity and plausibility of it. This literature has used life-changing events and the responses to them to understand whether preferences are stable or whether they are endogenous, mutable, and open to modifications.

Chuang and Schechter (2015) provide an excellent summary of the literature on stability of preferences (see Tables 1 and 2 in Chuang and Schechter, 2015, for a summary of the literature on stability of risk and time preferences, respectively). Using panel data from Paraguay, they examine the question using two approaches: a survey-based approach that uses a social preference survey, and one that uses experimental measures of risk and time preferences. They find that, although survey-based measures of social preferences are stable over long periods of time in the data, this is not so with the experimental measures. The lack of temporal correlation in the experimental measures of risk and time preference from developing-country samples (see Dohmen et al., 2011) could be driven by higher tendencies of developing-country subjects to exhibit behavioural biases due to less familiarity with computationally complex questions.

Overall, in the absence of changes in opportunity sets, there is no reason to believe that a rational, utility-maximising individual will exhibit temporal variation in preferences. Therefore, to understand whether preferences are stable, the literature has focused on the effect of shocks on preferences. Chuang and Schechter (2015) study the correlations between preferences and changes in incomes, thefts, and health in the past year. They do not find any systematic evidence of shocks being correlated with changes in preferences. Of course, given that the shocks considered are not exogenous, one needs to be careful in interpreting these results. In particular, the shocks could themselves be the consequence of the preferences of the individuals.

To examine whether changes in the economic environment affect preferences, the literature has increasingly used life-changing exogenous events. This has often taken the form of natural hazards and calamities. There are different ways in which natural disasters can affect individual preferences. For example, events like tsunamis, floods, earthquakes, cyclones, and hurricanes can make individuals more aware of these life-changing events and possibly reduce their life expectancy. In consequence, those experiencing such shocks can become less risk averse and more impatient. On the other hand, individuals affected by such shocks could benefit from the generosity of those around them, and this, in turn, could induce individuals to become more pro-social, more trusting, and more trustworthy. However, the mechanism through which this happens is not clear. The psychology literature argues that a particular type of emotion triggered by the negative shock can affect individuals' risk preferences (e.g.

Leith and Baumeister, 1996; Lerner and Keltner, 2001; Loewenstein et al., 2001).

Additionally, it is also not clear whether the effects are homogeneous by gender and the type of emotion. For example, it has been argued that anger makes males less risk averse, and disgust makes females more risk averse (Fessler et al., 2004). If shocks trigger different types of emotions in men and women, the effects of such shocks on preferences (in terms of both magnitude and direction) might also differ by gender.

4.1.1   Evidence from Developed Countries

The question of whether such natural hazards affect preferences is not restricted to developing countries. Indeed, some of earlier papers examined this question using data from developed countries. Eckel et al. (2009) examined the risk preferences of the victims of hurricane Katrina, one of the deadliest hurricanes to ever hit the US. Almost 2 000 people died as a direct consequence of the hurricane, and millions of others were left homeless in New Orleans and along the Gulf Coast. Many of the victims of the hurricane were evacuated and, in particular, many were provided accommodation in Houston. Eckel et al. (2009) consider three samples: recent evacuees to Houston, shortly after the hurricane (Wave 1); a similar sample of Katrina evacuees, one year after the event, when they were considerably less stressed (Wave 2); and finally, a sample of long-term residents of Houston matched in terms of observables, but not exposed to the traumatic conditions experienced by the Katrina evacuees (Wave 3). The last two groups participated one year after the event, with the Wave-3 subjects acting as a control group. The authors identified the evolution of risk attitudes among the three waves of post-hurricane refugees and, in particular, found that those in Wave 1 were less risk averse.[7] However, it is not clear that the results can be interpreted as a causal impact of the shock since the characteristics of the evacuees in Waves 1 and 2 were different; this could be a potential confounding factor in explaining the observed differences in risk attitudes between the two groups.

Page et al. (2014) examine the risk-taking behaviour of individuals who suffered from considerable losses arising from floods. Specifically, they use the Brisbane floods of January 2011 as the setting for their natural experiment. These floods resulted in significant damage and, in particular, caused substantial destruction to homes. The authors compare the risk-taking behaviour of individuals affected by the flood (homes below the flood line – what they call the treatment group) and those not affected by the flood (homes above the flood line – what they call the control group; see Page et al., 2014, Figure

1). These two groups are similar in terms of other observable characteristics, including house values and long-term flood risks (the last major flood in Brisbane was in 1974). Individuals sampled were offered the choice between a safe asset (a voucher worth $10) and a risky gamble (a lottery scratch card, potentially worth half a million dollars, but having a face value of $10) as a remuneration for taking part in the survey. Their results show that individuals who were affected by the flood were significantly more likely to accept the risky gamble compared to their unaffected neighbours. However unlikely, the risky gamble presents the possibility of breaking even by cancelling previous losses, and the findings are consistent with prospect theory predictions regarding the adoption of a risk-seeking attitude after a loss.

One potential criticism of the approach adopted by both Eckel et al. (2009) and Page et al. (2014) is that the data on preferences are available after the event and not before. This is especially the case for natural disasters because researchers cannot anticipate where natural disasters will occur. They use innovative methods to obtain control groups so that the effects of shocks on preferences can be interpreted as causal. However, evidence using data after the event is open to selection bias, arising from potential migration and attrition from the sample of individuals with specific characteristics: for example, it is feasible that individuals who are more risk averse might be excluded from the sample after the event. Hanaoka et al. (2018) examine whether individuals' risk preferences change after they have experienced a major shock – in this case, the 2011 Japan earthquake. Importantly, they use panel data from representative household surveys that measure preferences of the same individuals before, one year after, and five years after the earthquake. They examine whether individuals who live in regions where the intensity of the earthquake was greater report greater risk aversion or risk tolerance relative to those who live in regions where the intensity of the earthquake was lower.[8] Given the data available, they also examine whether the effects persist over time and the heterogeneity of effects by gender. Indeed, their results clearly show that gender matters. Men are less risk averse than women (pre-shock, consistent with the existing literature; Eckel and Grossman, 2008) and exhibit a stronger decline in risk aversion after the shock. The change in risk preferences for males are persistent: males who experience shocks of greater magnitude exhibit lower degrees of risk aversion, not just immediately after the earthquake, but also five years after. Risk preferences, as we know, have significant effects on economic behaviour (including occupational choices, schooling decisions, and technology adoption; see Section 1), and a natural shock, such as an earthquake, by altering an individual's risk preferences can have very fundamental effects on the economic outcomes of those affected.

4.1.2   Evidence from Developing Countries

Residents of developing countries are over ten times more likely to be affected (in terms of mortality and economic impacts) by natural calamities. Additionally, factors such as population pressures and infrastructure development in risk-prone areas have possibly increased the exposure risk and the risk of loss and damage due to natural disasters. Understanding how these shocks affect the preferences of individuals in developing countries is therefore of crucial importance. The environment in developing countries is unique, which makes it important to examine whether and how individuals are affected by these life-changing events (including natural disasters) in these countries.

In recent years, academic papers have examined the effects of life-changing events on preferences using lab-in-the-field experiments and surveys conducted in developing countries. While the use of experiments is open to the criticism that experimental results are affected by cognitive and behavioural biases (see Chuang and Schechter, 2015), the lack of systematic survey data on preferences targeted to answering this question means that lab-in-the field experiments are possibly the only way we can collect data on preferences.

The question of how exposure to natural disasters changes perceptions to risk is an important one. If exposure to natural disasters alters the perceptions of individuals towards the riskiness of their environment, then we might see individuals exhibiting greater risk aversion after experiencing a natural disaster. On the other hand, in the presence of migration, it is possible that those remaining in the geographical location after the disaster might be positively selected in terms of their risk preferences and exhibit greater tolerance for risk. Alternatively, those in the high-risk environment might be less concerned about smaller risks and thus exhibit behaviour consistent with greater tolerance for risk.

Cameron and Shah (2015) investigate the relationship between natural disasters and risk preferences using experimental data from Indonesia. They utilise geographical variation in the timing of natural disasters in a region that would be affected by a natural disaster (earthquakes and floods): while the exact timing of the occurrence of the shock cannot be predicted with certainty, the majority of locations they sample are likely to be exposed to some form of natural disaster. Subjects participate in a risk task (similar to Binswanger, 1980, and Barr and Genicot, 2008).[9] Their results show that participants from villages that experienced a flood or an earthquake in the three years previous exhibit a significantly higher degree of risk aversion relative to households residing in villages that have not experienced a natural disaster. They find that the effects are persistent: natural disasters affect risk attitudes beyond the year in which they occur. Importantly, the extent of the persistence of the effect appears to vary depending on the severity of the experience, and greater damage or trauma leave a deeper and longer lasting effect on the risk attitudes of individuals.

Turning to the mechanisms, Cameron and Shah (2015) argue that, while income loss is significant in explaining the increase in risk aversion, much of the explanation rests on how natural disasters affect beliefs: those recently experiencing a shock have a significantly higher belief of another similar shock happening soon. Given that beliefs and risk preferences can have significant effects on other dimensions of their lives, such shocks can therefore have long-term effects on the economic outcomes of individuals.

Brown et al. (2018) consider the aftermath of Cyclone Evan, which affected Fiji in 2012. They find that being struck by the extreme event changed both risk perceptions and beliefs about the frequency and magnitude of future shocks. They use both survey and experimental measures of willingness to take risks. The main outcome variable is average subjective annual expected losses from all natural disasters, which is derived from an experimental survey module that elicits a probability distribution over future losses. They also analyse the effects of being struck by Cyclone Evan on risk aversion by analysing individuals' willingness to take risks using an approach developed by Dohmen et al. (2011), where participants are asked to self-assess their general level of risk using a survey question.[10] Brown et al. (2018) find that being struck by an extreme event (like Cyclone Evan) results in significant changes in individuals' risk perceptions and also their beliefs about the frequency and magnitude of future shocks. However, they also find significant heterogeneity in results by ethnicity, with one ethnic group significantly more affected than the other. Brown et al. (2018) find that the effects were different across population groups. Indo-Fijians, but not the Indigenous Fijians (Indo-Fijians and Indigenous Fijians are the two main ethnic population groups), were affected by the shocks. This difference in risk perceptions along ethnic lines has the potential to exacerbate ethnic differences and inequalities.

In a recent paper, Islam et al. (2020), using a field experiment conducted in Bangladesh, examine how exposure to a natural disaster (in this case, Cyclone Aila, which affected large parts of India and Bangladesh) affects risk-sharing behaviour. In their analysis, villages that were hit with the storm surge are treatment villages, while neighbouring villages that were not affected by cyclone-related flooding are control villages. Participants first had to choose from a set of alternative lotteries in a standard risk-taking game (similar to the task used by Cameron and Shah, 2015, and Carvalhoa et al., 2016). They were then asked to form a risk-sharing group that pools and shares the gains from the group members' gambles. Finally, participants were assigned into one of the three information treatments, which varied with respect to the level of exogenous commitments that allowed individuals to defect, and whether such a defection was public or private information. They find that participants in disaster-affected areas are more risk loving, form smaller risk-sharing groups, and are less likely to defect in risk-sharing commitments, regardless of the level of exogenous commitment and information. This suggests a strengthening of the social norms supporting risk-sharing commitments in the wake of natural disasters.

Cassar et al. (2017) examine the effect of the Indian Ocean Tsunami of December 2004, which followed what is now known as the Sumatra-Andaman earthquake. Specifically, they focus on how exposure to the disaster can affect trust, risk, and time preferences. They conduct experiments in the province of Thailand that was the hardest hit by the tsunami, almost five years after the disaster. Their experimental subject pool consisted of individuals who were affected by the tsunami and those who were not: experimental sessions were conducted in villages that experienced severe damage, and with those in nearby villages that were largely spared (Cassar et al., 2017, Figure 1). The tsunami was largely unanticipated and, in terms of village-level characteristics pre-tsunami, villages that were affected by the tsunami were not significantly different from those that were affected by the tsunami. Subjects participated in a risk-elicitation task (Holt and Laury, 2002) that elicits preferences for time discounting (Andersen et al., 2008), and a task to elicit trust and trustworthi-ness (Berg et al., 1995). The risk results are consistent with the literature. As with Cameron and Shah (2015), Cassar et al. (2017) also find that residing in a tsunami village results in a statistically significant, 20% increase in risk aver-sion. Importantly, however, the change in behaviour is driven by exposure to the tsunami itself and not by how others around them respond to the tsunami. Similarly, residents in the tsunami-affected villages appear to discount the future more.

Turning to the results on social preferences, Cassar et al. (2017) find that individuals living in a tsunami village exhibit significantly higher trust. Importantly, they also examine the mechanisms behind this increase in trust and find that this is driven, to a considerable extent, by the positive experience of receiving help from others (both private and institutional). The authors also find that individuals who experienced financial damage are more trustworthy. These results highlight the role of social capital on how a natural disaster affects preferences.

The issue of change in pro-sociality as a result of exposure to the 2004 tsunami is also analysed by Becchetti et al. (2017), who rely on a sample of microfinance borrowers in Sri Lanka, seven years after the tsunami hit the villages. Their focus is on generosity, as measured by a dictator game (Forsythe et al., 1994). They find that being hit by the tsunami negatively affects generosity: those affected by the tsunami give less (and also expect less in return) than those not affected by the tsunami.

While the experimental evidence on changes in risk preferences in developing countries in response to extreme events is roughly consistent, the same cannot be said for patterns of other preferences. The same tsunami resulted in significant differences in pro-social behaviour in different countries and in different populations.

5.   Changing Preferences through Interventions

Not all life-changing events involve disasters. Indeed, any (randomised) intervention that exogenously changed the income opportunity set of participants can be viewed as a life-changing event. An exogenous shock of this kind can be effectively used to investigate stability of preferences. In this context, changes (or otherwise) of preferences can provide us with mechanisms to understand why certain programs/interventions are successful. We next evaluate each of these questions using a specific intervention conducted in Delhi, India (Dasgupta et al., 2015; Dasgupta et al., 2017; Maitra and Mani, 2017).

We start with some background on the specific intervention. Lack of skills (and, more broadly, human capital) acts as a significant barrier to the process of development, and the problem is particularly severe for women. There is now increased emphasis from policymakers from around the world on developing and encouraging participation in vocational training programs aimed at providing skills that are readily marketable. The idea is that skill training will ultimately lead to better life outcomes, including better economic outcomes. However, as we know from the fairly large literature on participation in programs that facilitate skill development, participants in such programs are not random. This leads to selection bias in the estimated effects of such programs. The solution is to randomly provide skills training to some individuals. Maitra and Mani (2017) consider the effects of participating in and completing a vocational education program. The intervention targeted women from low-income households residing in two regions of New Delhi, India. All women aged 18–39 with five or more completed grades of schooling and residing in these specific regions were invited to apply. A randomly selected set of applications was offered the 6-month-long training, with the remaining participants acting as the control group.

Indeed, Maitra and Mani (2017) found that participation in the program (assignment to the treatment group) resulted in significant and temporally non-decreasing effects on employment, hours worked, earnings, and entrepreneurship for women. They estimate that the vocational education program increased the monthly earnings of women in the treatment group by a statistically significant 140% (over the mean for the women in the control group) in the short run, and by a statistically significant 96% in the medium run. This is, however, only the direct effect and is possibly an underestimate of the total impact of the program, in that it does not include potential gains from network formation, access to information, and other related effects. Dasgupta et al. (2017) argue that the program resulted in an exogenous, salient, and significant change in the opportunity set for women assigned to the treatment group.

In addition to collecting data on labour-market outcomes, a random subset of all applicants to the program were invited to participate in a lab-in-the-field experiment both before and after the training program. The first round of experimental sessions (the pre-training session) was conducted after the application process was complete but before the outcome of the randomisation process that defined assignment to the program (treatment or control group) was revealed (i.e. participants in the experimental sessions did not know whether or not they had been assigned to the treatment group). This was done to avoid bias that could arise from knowing one's treatment status. Individuals who participated in these pre-training sessions (from both the treatment group and the control group) were invited to participate in a second round of lab-in-the-field sessions (post-training sessions) six months after the training program had finished. While there was attrition (of the 146 women who participated in the pre-intervention sessions, 121 participated in the post-intervention sessions), there is no statistically significant difference in the attrition rates between the treatment and control groups. In both sessions, individuals participated in a set of experimental tasks, which enabled the authors to obtain data on the competitiveness, risk preferences, and confidence of these women.

The data collected before and after the intervention, therefore, enable an examination of whether preferences are stable, given an exogenous change in the opportunity set. Indeed, Dasgupta et al. (2017) find that, after accounting for the change in the income opportunity set, the elicited preferences indeed appear to be temporally stable, providing support to a representative agent model of decision-making with temporally stable preferences.

Continuing with the intervention discussed above, one added advantage of lab-in-the-field experiments is that they can help understand the mechanisms as to why some programs are successful. Recall, as Maitra and Mani (2017) show, training resulted in significantly improved labour-market outcomes. The question is: what drove this improvement? Was it skills (as one would like to believe), or was it changes in other intrinsic characteristics that could potentially contaminate the impacts of training? These are important questions because we otherwise obtain biased estimates of the program.

Maitra and Mani (2017) consider the effects of program participation (assignment to the treatment group) on four behavioural characteristics: risk preferences, competitiveness, self-confidence, and relative rank. They find that training does not result in any changes in any of the behavioural outcomes considered, a result that is consistent with Dasgupta et al. (2017). These results suggest that changes in skills as opposed to changes in preference drive the program effects.

While the goal of the above-mentioned research was not to change preferences per se, a set of recent papers has investigated the question of changing preferences through mindset interventions. These interventions typically involve training individuals to develop mindsets that are associated with career or entrepreneurial success. One example includes work by Campos et al. (2017), who train individuals in taking personal initiatives (defined as a self-starting, future-oriented, and persistent proactive mindset), and measure its impact on enterprise success. In a trial conducted with 1 500 microenterprises in Togo, Campos et al. (2017) show that personal-initiative training led to a 30% increase in profits two years after the intervention was administered. This was significantly higher than a statistically non-significant 11% increase in profits due to traditional class-based training. More generally, there is now a growing body of literature that shows that teaching individuals non-cognitive interpersonal traits can lead to better outcomes. For example, Ashraf et al. (2020) show that training schoolgirls in Zambia to negotiate allows them to attain better school outcomes for themselves by strategically cooperating with their parents.

While training in non-cognitive skills and mindset can lead to better outcomes, randomised controlled trials (RCTs) often do not explicitly examine the behavioural channels through which changes occur. This is where lab-in-the-field experiments can be very useful. Given the importance of behavioural characteristics in explaining selection into entrepreneurship and success therein, experimental tasks can be used to elicit whether mindset training indeed affects individual preferences. A template for using experiments to elicit preferences before and after an intervention is provided by Dasgupta et al. (2017) and is discussed in detail in Section 4. Further, more novel tasks can be built to measure changes in personality traits that mindset trainings try to address. For example, Alan et al. (2019) administer grit training for schoolchildren in Turkey. Grit (see Duckworth et al., 2007; Duckworth, 2018) is a non-cognitive skill that measures a person's ability to bounce back from failure. It has been shown to be highly predictive of achievement. Alan et al. (2019) design a novel experiment using two real-effort tasks where one was more difficult than the other. Lack of grit is measured by the propensity to switch to the easier task in response to failure in completing the harder task. To examine whether grit training actually worked, the authors investigated the behaviour of individuals in their control and treatment groups. They found that children in their treatment group were less likely to switch to the easy task than were children in the control group. Further, using follow-up administrative data, they show that grit training led to students achieving higher math test scores.

6.   Conclusion

It is now well accepted that the behavioural characteristics and preferences of individuals can affect decisions in many spheres of life. In this chapter, we focused on one such sphere, entrepreneurship, and discussed how behavioural preferences and non-cognitive traits affect choices to become an entrepreneur and enterprise success. We discussed the stability of preferences in response to negative and positive economic shocks, and we show that, under certain circumstances, individual preferences are malleable. Most importantly, we show that individuals can be trained to develop mindsets or change preferences that allow them to achieve better outcomes in their careers or businesses. Finally, we provide examples of how lab-in-the-field experiments can complement training interventions to explicitly examine the behavioural channels through which changes occur.

Acknowledgments

We thank Ananish Chaudhuri, Robert Hoffman and Minhaj Mahmud for comments on a previous version of the paper. We remain responsible for errors and omissions.

Notes

1. Self-employed workers are those who, working on their own account or with one or a few partners or in a cooperative, hold the type of jobs defined as "self-employment jobs" (i.e. jobs where the remuneration is directly dependent upon the profits derived from the goods and services produced). Self-employed workers include three sub-categories of employers: own-account workers, members of producers' cooperatives, and contributing family workers.
2. See Kerr et al. (2017) and Frese and Gielnik (2014) for a discussion of the role of non-cognitive traits in the entrepreneurial process, and Åstebro et al. (2014) for a longer discussion of the behavioural economics roots of entrepreneurship.
3. Holt and Laury (2002) use a multiple price list format where participants are presented with a list of ten decisions. In each decision, they are asked to choose between two paired gambles (Option A and Option B) of different relative risk. The two gambles for each decision are stacked in rows. Across the ten decisions, the payoffs associated with each of the gambles remain the same; the only thing that varies is the probabilities associated with each of the payoffs within the gambles. In the first row, there is only a 10% chance of getting the high payoff for each gamble, and the expected payoff of the gamble in Option A is greater than that in Option B. Thus, only a very risk-seeking individual would choose Option B in the first decision row. As we move down the rows, the probability of the high payoff increases for each of the gambles, and by the last decision the choice is between a smaller amount with certainty in Option A and a larger amount with certainty in Option B. Assuming rationality, the participants should be choosing Option B in this decision irrespective of risk preferences. Generally, most people will start choosing Option A and switch to Option B as we move down the list. The switch point is used as a measure of the individual's risk preference.
4. Time preferences are elicited using the approach developed in Andersen et al. (2008). Participants are provided with pay-off tables at symmetric intervals. In each interval participants are provided with two options to choose from: Option A pays out an amount immediately, and Option B pays out an amount with an additional rate of return between 5% and 50% in the future.
5. The Trust Game (Berg et al., 1995) is a two-person game. One person is the sender (or the first mover), the other is the receiver (or the second mover). The sender is provided with an endowment from which they can transfer an amount to the second player. The amount transferred is tripled by the experimenter (i.e. for every $1 transferred, the receiver, or second mover, receives $3). The receiver then decides how much of the amount transferred they want to return. The choice of the first player is interpreted as a measure of trust, and the choice of the second

player is interpreted as a measure of trustworthiness. The gift exchange task (Fehr et al., 1993) is also a two-person game and is often used to capture reciprocity in labour-market relations. The two players are often categorized as the employer and the employee. The first mover (employer) has to decide, first, whether to award a higher salary. Then, the decision of the second mover (employee) about putting in extra effort follows. Gift-exchange games are also used to study reciprocity.

6.   To elicit trust in this study, each participant is presented with ten choice tasks using a multiple price list format. In each task, participants are asked to choose between a socially risky option (payoff determined by the choice of another player) and a risky option (payoff determined by a standard lottery). Across the ten options, the relative attractiveness of the socially risky option vis-à-vis the risky option is systematically varied, and the switching point at which the participant prefers the risky option over the socially risky option is used to measure their trust in others.

7.   Participants are presented with a set of six gambles (or lottery choices) that involve a 50/50 chance of winning a low prize or a high prize. The gambles are designed so that they increase in expected payoff and risk (standard deviation), and the rela-tionship between expected payoff and risk is linear for all but the last gamble. See Figure 5 in Eckel et al. (2009) for the payoffs associated with the six lottery choices.

8.   The measure of risk preferences is elicited from a hypothetical lottery question in the Japan Household Panel Survey on Consumer Preferences and Satisfaction (JHPS-CPS), the main data set used in the paper. Respondents were asked about their willingness to pay for a hypothetical lottery with a 50% chance of winning JPY 100 000 (US$1 000) or nothing otherwise.

9.   Subjects had to choose from six lotteries (termed gamble choices) that varied in terms of both average return and riskiness. See Figure 1 in Barr and Genicot (2008) for the payoffs associated with the six lotteries.

10.   To measure risk preferences, Dohmen et al. (2011) utilize a survey item that asks individuals about a judgment of their own willingness to take risks. They establish the validity of this self-assessment instrument by comparing it with behaviour in paid real-stakes lotteries using a representative sample of adults in Germany.

References

Acemoglu, D., and Robinson, J. (2012). *Why Nations Fail*. Random House.

Ahn, T. (2010). Attitudes toward Risk and Self-Employment of Young Workers. *Labour Economics*, 17, 434–442.

Alan, S., Boneva, T., and Ertac, S. (2019). Ever Failed, Try Again, Succeed Better: Results from a Randomized Educational Intervention on Grit. *Quarterly Journal of Economics*, 134, 1121–1162.

Andersen, S., Di Girolamo, A., Harrison, G., and Lau, M. (2014). Risk and Time Preferences of Entrepreneurs: Evidence from a Danish Field Experiment. *Theory and Decision*, 77, 341–357.

Andersen, S., Ertac, S., Gneezy, U., List, J., and Maximiano, S. (2013). Gender, Competitiveness and Socialization at a Young Age: Evidence from a Matrilineal and a Patriarchal Society. *Review of Economics and Statistics*, 95, 24–30.

Andersen, S., Harrison, G., Lau, M., and Rutstrom, E. (2008). Eliciting Risk and Time Preferences. *Econometrica*, 76, 583–618.

Arrow, K. (1972). Gifts and Exchanges. *Philosophy and Public Affairs*, 1, 340–362.

Ashraf, N., Bau, B., Low, C., and McGinn, K. (2020). Negotiating a Better Future: How Interpersonal Skills Facilitate Intergenerational Investment. *Quarterly Journal of Economics*, 135, 1095–1151.

Åstebro, T., Herz, H., Nanda, R., and Weber, R. (2014). Seeking the Roots of Entrepreneurship: Insights from Behavioral Economics. *Journal of Economic Perspectives*, 28, 49–70.

Banerjee, A., Karlan, D., and Zinman, J. (2015). Six Randomized Evaluations of Microcredit: Introduction and Further Steps. *American Economic Journal: Applied Economics*, 7, 1–21.

Barr, A., and Genicot, G. (2008). Risk Sharing, Commitment, and Information: An Experimental Analysis. *Journal of the European Economic Association*, 6, 1151–1185.

Becchetti, L., Castriota, S., and Conzo, P. (2017). Disaster, Aid, and Preferences: The Long-Run Impact of the Tsunami on Giving in Sri Lanka. *World Development*, 94, 157–173.

Belzil, C., and Leonardi, M. (2009). Risk Aversion and Schooling Decisions. Ecole Polytechnique. Working Paper #2009-028.

Berg, J., Dickhaut, J., and McCabe, K. (1995). Trust, Reciprocity, and Social History. *Games and Economic Behavior*, 10, 122–142.

Berge, L., Bjorvatn, K., Pires, A., and Tungodden, B. (2015a). Competitive in the Lab, Successful in the Field? *Journal of Economic Behavior & Organization*, 118, 303–317.

Berge, L., Bjorvatn, K., Pires, A., and Tungodden, B. (2015b). Human and Financial Capital for Microenterprise Development: Evidence from a Field and Lab Experiment. *Management Science*, 61, 707–722.

Bernardo, A., and Welch, I. (2001). On the Evolution of Overconfidence and Entrepreneurs. *Journal of Economic and Management Strategy*, 10, 301–330.

Biais, B., Hilton, D., Mazurier, K., and Pouget, S. (2005). Judgemental Overconfidence, Self-Monitoring, and Trading Performance in an Experimental Financial Market. *Review of Economic Studies*, 72, 287–312.

Binswanger, H. P. (1980). Attitudes toward Risk: Experimental Measurement in Rural India. *American Journal of Agricultural Economics*, 62, 395–407.

Bjorvatn, K., and Tungodden, B. (2010). Teaching Business in Tanzania: Evaluating Participation and Performance. *Journal of the European Economic Association*, 8, 561–570.

Brown, P., Daigneault, A., Tjersonström, E., and Zou, W. (2018). Natural Disasters, Social Protection, and Risk Perceptions. *World Development*, 104, 310–325.

Buser, T., Niederle, M., and Oosterbeek, H. (2014). Gender, Competitiveness and Career Choices. *Quarterly Journal of Economics*, 129, 1409–1447.

Caliendo, M., Fossen, F., and Kritikos, A. (2014). Personality Characteristics and the Decisions to Become and Stay Self-Employed. *Small Business Economics*, 42, 787–814.

Camerer, C., and Lovallo, D. (1999). Overconfidence and Excess Entry: An Experimental Approach. *American Economic Review*, 89, 306–318.

Cameron, L., and Shah, M. (2015). Risk Taking Behavior in the Wake of Natural Disasters. *Journal of Human Resources*, 50, 484–515.

Campos, F., Frese, M., Goldstein, M., Iacovone, L., Johnson, H., McKenzie, D., and Mensmann, M. (2017). Teaching Personal Initiative Beats Traditional Training in Boosting Small Business in West Africa. *Science*, 357, 1287–1290.

Carvalhoa, L., Prinab, S. and Sydnor, J. (2016). The Effect of Saving on Risk Attitudes and Intertemporal Choices. *Journal of Development Economics*, 120, 41–52.

Cassar, A., Healey, A., and von Kessler, C. (2017). Trust, Risk, and Time Preferences after a Natural Disaster: Experimental Evidence from Thailand. *World Development*, 94, 90–105.

Castillo, M., Petrie, R., and Torero, M. (2010). On the Preferences of Principals and Agents. *Economic Inquiry*, 48, 266–273.

Chuang, Y., and Schechter, L. (2015). Stability of Experimental and Survey Measures of Risk, Time, and Social Preferences: A Review and Some New Results. *Journal of Development Economics*, 117, 151–170.

Cooper, A. C., Woo, A., and Dunkelberg, W. (1988). Entrepreneurs Perceived Chances for Success. *Journal of Business Ventures*, 3, 97–109.

Cramer, J. S., Hartog, J., Jonker, N., and van Praag, C. M. V. (2002). Low Risk Aversion Encourages the Choice for Entrepreneurship: An Empirical Test of a Truism. *Journal of Economic Behavior & Organization*, 48, 29–36.

Dasgupta, U., Gangadharan, L., Maitra, P., and Mani, S. (2017). Searching for Preference Stability in a State Dependent World. *Journal of Economic Psychology*, 62, 17–32.

Dasgupta, U., Gangadharan, L., Maitra, P., Mani. S., and Subramanian, S. (2015). Choosing to Be Trained: Do Behavioral Traits Matter? *Journal of Economic Behavior and Organization*, 110, 145–159.

De Mel, S., McKenzie, D., and Woodruff, C. (2008). Returns to Capital in Microenterprises: Evidence from a Field Experiment. *Quarterly Journal of Economics*, 123, 1329–1372.

De Mel, S., McKenzie, D., and Woodruff, C. (2012). One-Time Transfers of Cash or Capital Have Long-Lasting Effects on Microenterprises in Sri Lanka. *Science*, 335, 962–966.

Dohmen, T., Falk, A., Huffman, D., Sunde, U., Schupp, J., and Wagner G. G. (2011). Individual Risk Attitudes: Measurement, Determinants, and Behavioral Consequences. *Journal of the European Economic Association*, 9, 522–550.

Drexler, A., Fischer, G., and Schoar, A. (2014). Keeping It Simple: Financial Literacy and Rules of Thumb. *American Economic Journal: Applied Economics*, 6, 1–31.

Duckworth, A. L. (2018). *Grit: The Power of Passion and Perseverance*. Scribner.

Duckworth, A. L., Peterson, D., Matthews, M. D., and Kelly, R. D. (2007). Grit: Perseverance and Passion for Long-Term Goals. *Journal of Personality and Social Psychology*, 92, 1087–1101.

Eckel, C., El-Gamal, A., and Wilson, R. (2009). Risk Loving after the Storm: A Bayesian-Network Study of Hurricane Katrina Evacuees. *Journal of Economic Behavior and Organization*, 69, 110–124.

Eckel, C., and Grossman, P. (2008). Men, Women and Risk Aversion: Experimental Evidence, in Plott, C., Smith V. (Eds.). *Handbook of Experimental Economics Results*, Vol. 1, 1061–1073. North-Holland.

Falk, A., Becker, A., Dohmen, T., Enke, B., Huffman, D., and Sunde, U. (2018). Global Evidence on Economic Preferences. *Quarterly Journal of Economics*, 133, 1645–1692.

Fang, H., and Moscarini, G. (2005). Morale Hazard. *Journal of Monetary Economics*, 52, 749–777.

Fehr, E., Kirchsteiger, G., and Riedl, A. (1993). Does Fairness Prevent Market Clearing? An Experimental Investigation. *Quarterly Journal of Economics*, 58, 437–460.

Fehr, E., & List, J. A. (2004). The hidden costs and returns of incentives – Trust and trustworthiness among CEOs. *Journal of the European Economic Association*, 2(5), 743-771.

Fessler, D. M. T., Pillsworth, E. G., and Flamson, T. J. (2004). Angry Men and Disgusted Women: An Evolutionary Approach to the Influence of Emotions on Risk Taking. *Organizational Behavior and Human Decision Processes*, 95, 107–123.

Filippin, A., and Paccagnella, M. (2012). Family Background, Self-Confidence and Economic Outcomes. *Economics of Education Review*, 31, 824–834.

Flory, J. A., Leibbrandt, A., and List, J. (2015). Do Competitive Workplaces Deter Female Workers? A Large-Scale Natural Field Experiment on Job Entry Decisions. *Review of Economic Studies*, 82, 122–155.

Forsythe, R., Horowitz, J. L., Savin, N. E., and Sefton, M. (1994). Fairness in Simple Bargaining Experiments. *Games and Economic Behavior*, 6, 347–369.

Frese, M., and Gielnik, M. M. (2014). The Psychology of Entrepreneurship. *Annual Review of Organizational Psychology and Organizational Behavior*, 1, 413–438.

Gneezy, U., Leonard, K., and List, J. (2009). Gender Differences in Competition: Evidence from a Matrilineal and Patriarchal Society. *Econometrica*, 77, 1637–1664.

Hanaoka, C., Shigeoka, H., and Watanabe, Y. (2018). Do Risk Preferences Change? Evidence from the Great East Japan Earthquake. *American Economic Journal: Applied Economics*, 10, 298–330.

Heinrich, J., Heine, S. J., and Noranzayan, A. (2010). Beyond Weird: Towards a Broad-Based Behavioral Science. *Behavioral and Brain Sciences*, 33, 111.

Holm, S. J., Opper, S., and Nee, V. (2013). Entrepreneurs under Uncertainty: An Economic Experiment in China. *Management Science*, 59, 1671–1687.

Holt, C., and Laury, S. K. (2002). Risk Aversion and Incentive Effects. *American Economic Review*, 92, 1644–1655.

Hvide, H. K., and Panos, G. A. (2014). Risk Tolerance and Entrepreneurship. *Journal of Financial Economics*, 111, 200–223.

ILO (2020). International Labour Organization, Ilostat Database.

Islam, A., Leister, C. M., Mahmud, M., and Raschky, P. A. (2020). Natural Disaster and Risk-Sharing Behavior: Evidence from Rural Bangladesh. *Journal of Risk and Uncertainty*, 61, 67–99.

Kerr, S. P., Kerr, W. R., and Xu. T. (2017). Personality Traits of Entrepreneurs: A Review of Recent Literature. NBER Working Paper #w24097.

Kessler, A., Korunka, C., Frank, H., and Lueger, M. (2012). Predicting Founding Success and New Venture Survival: A Longitudinal Nascent Entrepreneurship Approach. *Journal of Enterprising Culture*, 20, 25–55.

Kihlstrom, R. E., and Laffont, J. J. (1979). A General Equilibrium Entrepreneurial Theory of Firm Formation Based on Risk Aversion. *Journal of Political Economy*, 87, 719–748.

Koellinger, P., Minniti, M., and Schade, C. (2007). "I Think I Can, I Think I Can": Overconfidence and Entrepreneurial Behavior. *Journal of Economic Psychology*, 28, 502–527.

La Porta, R., and Shleifer, A. (2014). Informality and Development. *Journal of Economic Perspectives*, 28(3), 109–126.

Lagakos, D., Moll, B., Porzio, T., Qian, N., and Schoellman, T. (2018). Life Cycle Wage Growth across Countries. *Journal of Political Economy*, 126, 797–849.

Leith, K. P., and Baumeister, R. F. (1996). Why Do Bad Moods Increase Self-Defeating Behavior? Emotion, Risk Taking, and Self-Regulation. *Journal of Personality and Social Psychology*, 71, 1250–1267.

Lerner, J. S., and Keltner, D. (2001). Fear, Anger, and Risk. *Journal of Personality and Social Psychology*, 81, 146–159.

List, J., and Mason, C. F. (2011). Are CEOs Expected Utility Maximizers? *Journal of Econometrics*, 162, 114–123.

Liu, E. (2013). Time to Change What to Sow: Risk Preferences and Technology Adoption Decisions of Cotton Farmers in China. *Review of Economics and Statistics*, 95, 1386–1403.

Loewenstein, G. F., Weber, E. U., Hsee, C. K., and Welch, N. (2001). Risk as Feelings. *Psychological Bulletin*, 127, 267–286.

Maitra, P., and Mani, S. (2017). Learning and Earning: Evidence from a Randomized Evaluation in India. *Labour Economics*, 45, 116–130.

McKenzie, D. (2017). Identifying and Spurring High-Growth Entrepreneurship: Experimental Evidence from a Business Plan Competition. *American Economic Review*, 107, 2278–2307.

McKenzie, D., and Woodruff, C. (2013). What Are We Learning from Business Training and Entrepreneurship Evaluations around the Developing World? *World Bank Research Observer*, 29, 48–82.

Niederle, M., and Vesterlund, L. (2007). Do Women Shy Away from Competition? Do Men Compete Too Much? *Quarterly Journal of Economics*, 122, 1067–1101.

Nunn, N., and Wantchekon, L. (2011). The Slave Trade and the Origins of Mistrust in Africa. *American Economic Review*, 101, 3221–3252.

Page, L., Savage, D., and Torgler, B. (2014). Variation in Risk Seeking Behaviour Following Large Losses: A Natural Experiment. *European Economic Review*, 71, 121–131.

Parker, S. (2009). *The Economics of Entrepreneurship*. Cambridge University Press.

Puri, M., and Robinson, D. T. (2007). Optimism and Economic Choice. *Journal of Financial Economics*, 86, 71–99.

Quinn, S., and Woodruff, C. (2019). Experiments and Entrepreneurship in Developing Countries. *Annual Review of Economics*, 11, 225–248.

Rauch, A., and Frese, M. (2007). Let's Put the Person Back into Entrepreneurship Research: A Meta-Analysis on the Relationship between Business Owners' Personality Traits, Business Creation, and Success. *European Journal of Work and Organizational Psychology*, 16, 353–385.

Urbig, D., Bönte, W., Procher, V.D., and Lombardo, S. (2020). Entrepreneurs Embrace Competition: Evidence from a Lab-in-the-Field Study. *Small Business Economics*, 55, 193–214.

Zhao, H., and Seibert, S. E. (2006). The Big Five Personality Dimensions and Entrepreneurial Status: A Meta-Analytical Review. *Journal of Applied Psychology*, 91, 259–271.

Zhao, H., Seibert, S. E., and Lumpkin, G. T. (2010). The Relationship of Personality to Entrepreneurial Intentions and Performance: A Meta-Analytic Review. *Journal of Management*, 36(2), 381–404.

6 Experimental evidence on behavioural nudges in health

John Gibson

1. Introduction

In comparison to many areas of applied economics, the experimental agenda has made less progress in health economics research. One reason is that health-related studies already made widespread use of the term "experiment", but they used it to refer to research designs where the subjects do not face real consequences for their stated choices. That the term "experiment" was used in a very different way to how it is used in experimental economics is reflective of the fact that developments in health economics – and even more so in public health research that overlaps with economics (such as studies of consumer responses to potential taxes on unhealthy foods) – have occurred with very little overlap with the experimental economics agenda. Indeed, writing in an introduction to a special issue of the journal *Health Economics* that was devoted to behavioural experiments in health, Galizzi and Wiesen (2017) noted that the two research communities – of behavioural and experimental economists on the one hand, and health economists on the other – "were at the moment quite disconnected" (p. 3).

Moreover, despite efforts to connect these two research communities, such as the journal special issue noted above, the use of the term "experiment" in behavioural health studies to refer to research designs that are not incentive compatible continues even now. Indeed, much of the research carried out in this area by public health scholars is explicit in divorcing any compensation that is given to research subjects from the choices they make, in stark contrast to the typical design of economics laboratory experiments. For example, Waterlander et al. (2019) recruited subjects to shop in an online virtual supermarket where the layout and design aimed to replicate the in-store environment of a leading New Zealand supermarket brand, but with prices that were varied to examine the effects of potential health-related food taxes and subsidies. However, despite the authors using the word "experiment" in the title of their study, they explicitly note that: "Unlike online shopping, participants did not receive the purchases they made" (p. e396) and, instead, all of the participants were simply given a $10 voucher after their first virtual shopping episode, irrespective of their choices, and another $30 voucher if they made up to five visits to the virtual shopping platform. As a consequence of this design, the choices reported by this study remain entirely hypothetical, which is a feature of many other public health studies that examine similar issues within the online environment (see, for example, Blake et al., 2019, who attempt to simulate the physical environment of a convenience store, but again without any consequences for choices made by the participants).

The second reason for a lack of progress stems, paradoxically, from what may be seen as a success, which is the growing interest of policymakers in applying what can be thought of as insights from behavioural economics to policy decisions in the health context. Good coverage of this so-called "behavioural public policy" is provided by Oliver (2013), while a focus particularly on health is discussed by Loewenstein et al. (2012). Indicators of this policy interest include the development of the Nudge Unit in the Cabinet Office of the United Kingdom (Halpern, 2015) and the acclaim given by politicians, such as Leigh (2018), to the policy guidance that can come from randomized experiments. Yet, with this success has come potential confusion about whether the distinguishing feature of behavioural public policy is the method used to gather the evidence (such as randomized designs versus observational studies) or the content of and the insights gained from such evidence (Galizzi, 2014).

This chapter focusses particularly on evidence obtained from research designs where subjects bear real consequences for the choices they make. A good summary of the attributes that make evidence relevant for the review comes from Galizzi and Wiesen (2017), in their explanation of what constitutes a behavioural experiment:

> Common to experimental social and behavioural sciences, moreover, the outcomes of behavioural experiments in health are "behavioural", that is, they consist of directly observable and measurable behavioural responses rather than self-reported statements. Typically, subjects in behavioural experiments in health are directly observed in field situations or face real consequences for their stated choices or behaviours through aligned monetary and non-monetary incentives. Behaviours and decisions of participants in a behavioural experiment in health are thus typically (whenever possible) "incentive compatible", in the usual experimental economics sense that participants bear real behavioural consequences for their choices in the experiment. (p. 4)

2.   "Experiment" Means Different Things in Different Literatures

To provide some evidence on the comparative immaturity of the experimental agenda in health economics, a search was made of the IDEAS/RePEc repository of economic literature in June 2020, restricting attention to articles but otherwise putting no limit on date, language, and so forth. Searching for "experiment" and "health economics" yielded 83 articles, which were divided into various types of research designs, as summarized in Table 1. The most common type of study that uses the term "experiment" is not the focus of this chapter and is not consistent with what Galizzi and Wiesen (2017) lay out as the agenda for behavioural experiments in health. Instead, the most common type of study uses non-incentivized stated preferences, typically modelled in a discrete-choice or choice-modelling framework. Almost half of the studies that were uncovered in this literature search were of this "discrete choice experiment" (DCE) genre, where there are no consequences for the statements made by participants.

An interesting set of semantic questions in the history of ideas is when, why and how the literature that relies on these stated-preference questionnaires elevated them to the status of "experiments" rather than calling them hypothetical valuation questionnaires. A typical description of these stated-preference studies comes from a widely cited primer on carrying them out in low-income countries: a DCE "is a quantitative technique for eliciting individual preferences. It allows researchers to uncover how individuals value selected attributes of a programme, product or service by asking them to state their choice over different hypothetical alternatives" (Mangham et al., 2009, p. 151). These DCE approaches have no mechanisms to induce behavioural consequences for the stated preferences of the subjects, and in this manner they deviate substantially from the economics laboratory experimental methodology where monetary rewards are used. As noted by Smith (1994), using such research designs that are based on statements without consequences, in situations where subjects are faced by hypothetical choices that do not take into account their self-interested nature, should not be expected to provide data that inform about real-world decisions: "if subjects care less about getting it right when there are zero or low rewards, and decision is costly, this is because it is in their interest to care less" (p. 127).

About one-quarter of the studies from the RePEc search are either randomized field experiments or quasi- or natural experiments (at least as styled by their authors). In some cases, these studies rely on quasi-randomization induced

Table 6.1   A scan of the literature on experiments and health economics

Type of study	Share of all studies	Title and author of a typical study
DCEs, a.k.a. stated-preference studies (non-incentivized)	47%	"Valuing health at the end of life: A stated preference discrete choice experiment", Shah et al. (2015)
Randomized field experiment	12%	"Encouraging health insurance for the informal sector: A cluster randomized experiment in Vietnam", Wagstaff et al. (2016)
Natural or quasi-natural experiment	13%	"Introduction of a national minimum wage reduced depressive symptoms in low-wage workers: A quasi-natural experiment in the UK", Reeves et al. (2017)
Laboratory, artefactual or framed field experiment (incentivized)	17%	"Incentivizing cost-effective reductions in hospital readmission rates", Cox et al. (2016)
Reviews/other types of studies	11%	"The economics of credence goods – A survey of recent lab and field experiments", Kerschbamer and Sutter (2017)

Notes: The reported results are based on a search of articles listed in IDEAS/RePEc using the keywords "experiment" and "health economics" on 18 June 2020.

by policy changes, and use administrative data, while others randomize explicitly as part of their study protocol, and then rely on either measured or self-reported indicators of various health outcomes.

It is puzzling that studies based on explicit randomization, such as the field experiments, make up such a small share of the health economics literature. It was health economics that was home to one of the earliest and largest randomized interventions in rich countries, the RAND Health Insurance Experiment that began in the 1970s (Aron-Dine et al., 2013). Yet, if one thinks of randomized controlled trials (RCTs) in economics today, they are typically found in disciplines such as development economics, where there has been huge growth in the last two decades in the number of RCTs focussed on development economics questions (Bouguen et al., 2019; Ravallion, 2020). Undoubtedly many of these RCTs in developing countries examine some impacts on health, but evidently the use of randomized experiments in the health literature per se remains somewhat limited.

About one-sixth of the articles found through the RePEc search are based on incentive-compatible research designs that are implemented in economics laboratories or in artefactual or framed field-experiment settings. This is a surprisingly small share of the literature, given that the search was restricted to a focus on experiments. In other words, the point made by Galizzi and Wiesen (2017) that health economists have been disconnected from behavioural and experimental economists appears to be supported by these search results.

3.   Areas of Focus

The health-related studies that rely on methods where subjects bear real consequences for their choices cover a variety of topics. In this section I provide an overview for four of these topics. A particular emphasis in the review is on ways that the research designs could be improved upon or on questions that remain hard to answer with the research designs that have been used thus far.

3.1   Measuring Preferences

The decisions that individuals make about health-related behaviours, such as diet, drinking, and smoking, are affected by their discount rates and risk preferences, amongst other things. Consequently, there is considerable interest in measuring preferences and relating these preferences to risky health behaviour, with over two decades of research in this area (see Barsky et al., 1997, as a key early study). One debate in this literature is the question of whether data obtained using hypothetical scenarios ("statements without consequences") are a useful guide to predicting behaviour in real-world settings. For example, several studies find that measured risk preferences are not stable across elicitation methods; specifically, when the same subjects are given survey questions about hypothetical risks and also play games with actual stakes where the choices made in these games can reveal risk preferences, the two types of elicited data on their preferences are not aligned (Anderson & Mellor, 2009; Gibson et al., 2019).

In light of these differences in apparent preferences depending on the elicitation mechanism, there is considerable interest in the literature in using economics laboratory methods to measure discount rates and risk preferences. This can be done using incentive-compatible tests where there are real consequences (typically in terms of money) for the choices that subjects make (Holt & Laury, 2002). Some examples of applications to health include Borghans and Golsteyn (2006), who relate experimentally measured time preferences to the body mass index (BMI) of their subjects, while Anderson and Mellor (2008) relate risk aversion (using the lottery-choice approach pioneered by Holt and Laury, 2002) to whether subjects are overweight or obese, and also to their likelihood of cigarette smoking, heavy drinking, and not using seat belts. In contrast, some other studies find no association between experimentally elicited measures of risk aversion and the smoking behaviour of their subjects (Harrison et al., 2010; Szrek et al., 2012).

Even for studies that do find that the experimentally elicited preferences are related to health behaviour, the stability of these preferences remains an unresolved question. Many of the studies are one shot, where the subjects are in the economics laboratory on just one occasion rather than having their preferences elicited repeatedly over time. Consequently, it is difficult to assess the stability of the elicited preferences, so researchers must rely on either drawing different samples from the same population (but at different times so as not to rule out that events that might affect preferences could have occurred in the interim) or using between-subjects designs where some subjects have experienced larger shocks than others.

For example, studies have used experimental methods to show that there are changes in risk preferences after negative shocks. Eckel et al. (2009) found that Hurricane Katrina evacuees exhibited more risk-loving behaviour in the immediate aftermath of the disaster than was exhibited by a different sample drawn from the same population one year later. Conversely, Cameron and Shah (2015) found that individuals who had recently experienced either a flood or an earthquake exhibited more risk aversion than was exhibited by others in their sample who did not experience these shocks. Thus, it is perhaps unsurprising that a review study by Chuang and Schechter (2015) notes that, even for these sorts of extreme negative events, the literature does not seem to give a consistent set of results regarding preference stability.

The review also notes that, for less extreme shocks such as changes in income, unemployment, health status, and family composition, many studies find no shifts in risk or time preferences as a result of these changes. Along these lines, Gibson et al. (2019) study a migration lottery program and find no difference in experimentally elicited risk preferences between ballot-selected migrants and would-be migrants who stayed in their home country; moreover, both groups were similar in terms of their observable attributes and their unobservable characteristics, given that a random ballot is used for selection in the migration lottery program. This stability remains despite migration increasing migrants' incomes more than threefold, and increasing financial wealth by even more, while also bringing about large changes in diet and health-related behaviours like smoking.

3.2   Information Interventions

The idea of providing more information to consumers so that they can improve their decision-making is a popular type of intervention. The graphic health warnings on cigarette packets are one of the earliest examples, and there is some evidence that such warnings have promoted smoking cessation and discouraged youth uptake (Hammond, 2011). This type of health messaging has also been copied for interventions that aim to improve the quality of diets, such as the "5+ a day" messages for increasing fruit and vegetable consumption, or regulations that require posting calorie information on food labels and menus.

Much of the public health literature that considers the impact of such interventions is based on stated preferences over hypothetical choices, where data on these choices may be obtained from online surveys. Thus, even though some authors call these studies "randomized controlled trials" (e.g. Billich et al., 2018) or "experimental studies" (e.g. Bollard et al., 2016), there are no behavioural consequences for the statements made by the participants. Indeed, a feature of this type of research is that, often, more attention is paid to what could be termed the "virtual reality" aspects of the study – to make the appearance of the online setting correspond to something that subjects may have experienced first-hand, such as creating an online interface to mimic a hypothetical vending machine (VanEpps & Roberto, 2016) – than to the most relevant feature of the real world – that the choices made by consumers have consequences. Given that this evidence is not elicited from research designs that use incentive-compatible tests, it is unclear what weight should be placed on it.

However, there is a smaller part of the literature that does rely on changing the information environment in real-world settings. One approach uses what could be thought of as an interrupted time-series design, where sales are observed in certain locations for a baseline period and then information is introduced to consumers in those locations, with the impact of that information intervention then measured as the difference between the sales after the information was provided versus before. For example, Bleich et al. (2014) posted signs on soft drink display cases located in convenience stores, where the signs had different types of caloric information about sugar-sweetened beverages (the total calories in a bottle, the equivalent teaspoons of sugar and the amount of time spent running or walking needed to work off the calories). After this information was posted, the records from the outlets showed a one-third drop in the rate of regular soda sales, while the sales of diet soda and water rose significantly; these effects persisted for some weeks after the signs were removed.

A similar interrupted time-series research design was used by Jue et al. (2012), who displayed posters and signs in the cafeterias and convenience shops of three hospitals; these signs advertised the health benefits of switching to zero-calorie drinks. The researchers then obtained the daily sales data for the zero-calorie and sugar-sweetened beverages sold by the cafeterias and convenience shops over the next three months. Unexpectedly, they found that the sales of the sugared beverages increased by 7%, while there was no change in sales of the zero-calorie beverages.

These time-series approaches may be affected by uncontrolled outside factors that affect the comparisons between the pre-intervention and post-intervention environments. For example, the Jue et al. (2012) study ran from winter until late spring, with the pre-intervention phase carried out when the weather was colder (the sites were all in cold-weather cities, such as Detroit and Philadelphia), while the post-intervention phase occurred when the weather was warmer. The consumption of sugar-sweetened soft drinks is typically higher in summer months, so the unexpected rise in sales after the information campaign may have simply reflected these seasonal consumption patterns that the investigators were not able to control.

One way for researchers to have more control over potentially confounding factors is to introduce between-subject variation within the same time and place setting. For example, Wisdom et al. (2010) designed an intervention for a sample of more than 600 lunch-time customers who were surveyed when entering a fast-food sandwich restaurant and were offered a free meal for participating in the survey. The researchers randomized over three dimensions: whether a daily calorie recommendation was provided or not; whether calorie information for items on the menu was provided or not; and by inducing a marginal increase in the convenience of selecting a healthy sandwich option. The results suggest that providing calorie information for each menu item caused subjects to order lower-calorie options, while providing the information in the form of an overall daily calorie recommendation only had this effect for the individuals who were not overweight (i.e. this treatment did not work for the target group). A nudge to make the healthy sandwich choices more convenient reduced the calories ordered in the form of sandwiches; however, this effect was partly undermined by compensatory choices of higher calorie drinks and side orders.

There are several other nudge-like studies that conduct various subtle manipulations in natural settings that are designed to make it easier to obtain healthier foods while making unhealthier foods less convenient. These studies often take place in school lunchrooms, where it is argued that simple innovations, such as pre-ordering, could lead to healthier choices. The argument for pre-ordering is that it may pre-empt some hunger-based spontaneous menu selections that could be driven by sensory cues from the evocative sights and smells of the food if the student orders at the time of eating (and presumably while hungry). These spontaneous menu selections are argued to be especially drawn from the less healthy menu choices (Hanks et al., 2013).

However, several of these studies, including the Hanks et al. (2013) one noted above, were co-authored by the former Cornell University researcher Brian Wansink who thus far has had 18 papers retracted, 7 others issued with expressions of concern and a further 15 corrected, with Cornell determining that he had committed scientific misconduct and removing him from research activities in late 2018. Several of these retracted papers involved manipulation of the food environment in natural settings (e.g. at a pizza restaurant, a Super Bowl party and in school lunchrooms), so there is now a question mark over some of these findings. Thus, it is unclear whether this part of the literature about the apparent effectiveness of small nudges to make healthy options more convenient is still as influential as it seemed to be a few years ago.

Even more control over potential confounding effects can come from conducting information interventions within the confines of an economics laboratory experiment. In particular, within-subjects research designs can be used, where subjects make various incentive-compatible choices and then the information environment is changed to see how their choices shift in response to new information. For example, Gibson, Tucker, and Boe-Gibson (2019) conducted an experiment with soft drink purchases, for 14 items (energy drinks, colas and lemonades) under various pricing environments and with real consequences for the choices made (purchases made in one randomly chosen round comprised part of the payment to subjects). A video presentation by the celebrity chef Jamie Oliver that highlighted some of the adverse health consequences of sugary drinks consumption was then watched (in private) and the choice tasks were repeated. The within-subject change in demand due to the information intervention resulted in an overall 25% reduction in purchases, with one sugar-free option, Diet Coke, experiencing a demand increase of 36%. The effects of the information intervention were larger for those who (self-reportedly) spend more on soft drinks and usually ignore the sugar content when making purchases. However, the challenge with this sort of research design is to evaluate the persistence of the effects, which is difficult to do in the laboratory setting due to limits on follow-up observation (Dolan et al., 2015).

3.3   Price-Based Interventions

Several studies have manipulated the prices faced by subjects to inform debates about policies to tax unhealthy food and drink (e.g. fat taxes or soda taxes) or to subsidize fruits and vegetables. The economic argument behind such policies is that they are an externality, so food prices need to be shifted to reflect the social (especially health) costs of unhealthy diets. The key question that experiments can help to answer involves the magnitude of the response to potential tax and subsidy changes, and especially whether or not small price changes, such as abolishing value-added tax on healthy foods, nudge consumers into eating a healthier diet.

Some of these studies take place in experimental economics laboratories, while others are set in supermarkets, cafeterias or restaurants (Giesen et al., 2011; Velema et al., 2017). A selective review is provided by Wilson et al. (2016). Typically the studies involve price manipulation, sometimes in conjunction with information interventions. For example, Streletskaya et al. (2014) consider treatments of a 20% unhealthy food tax or a 20% subsidy on healthy foods, in the context of lunch-time menu choices in a university cafeteria, and in conjunction with a healthy food advertising treatment. Chen et al. (2015) consider similar sized price changes in the same setting, but with the prices either displayed as tax inclusive or tax exclusive. For both treatments, subjects were informed that there was a 20% excise tax on unhealthy food items.

An important limitation of these studies is that subjects are not allowed to keep the unspent portions of the meal vouchers that they are given as part of the compensation for their participation in the experiment, so there is no opportunity cost for their purchase decisions. For example, subjects in the experiment by Chen et al. (2015) received a $10 voucher and a $20 participation fee, and it is noted by these authors that, "Subjects were informed that if they spent less than $10 on the drawn menu, they would not receive the excess in cash" (p. 15). This is the same set-up used by Streletskaya et al. (2014), except that the latter's participation fee was only $15. Thus, for any items selected whose costs added up to less than $10, the price was effectively free, so there was no reason for subjects to choose wisely.

However, there is an even more pernicious effect of the decision to not let subjects keep the unspent portion of their endowment due to two other factors: any spending above $10 is taken out of the participation fee, and the menu prices that are used for the lunch items are from two to five times as expensive as prices in other outlets. Consequently, the demand response to a 20% tax on unhealthy lunch items (one of the treatments used by Streletskaya et al., 2014, with a 20% subsidy on healthy items as another) is greatly overstated. This was explained by Fischer (2014) in his critical comments on this design. The price at the margin does not change by 20% when taxed or subsidized but rather changes from zero to a price that is double or more the ordinary retail price. The magnitude of the recorded dietary changes in response to what the experimenters treat as a 20% unhealthy food tax will therefore be greatly overstated because the effective price change that the subjects face is far larger than the 20% change expected, given the design of the experiment.

3.4   Supply-Side Issues: Payments Systems

While many studies focus on nudges on the demand side, to alter the behaviour of consumers, an important literature focusses on the supply side. In particular, both laboratory and artefactual field experiments have been used to understand how physicians respond to incentives from payment schemes. A typical contrast is between fee-for-service payments, which vary according to the provider's estimate of the costs, and capitation payments, where a fixed amount per patient or per unit of time is paid in advance to the physician for the delivery of health care services. Hennig-Schmidt et al. (2011) use an experiment to find that patients are over-served with the fee-for-service payment scheme and under-served with capitation. Brosig-Koch et al. (2016) extend these comparisons using medical students, nonmedical students, and physicians as their experimental subjects, and find that more medical services are provided under fee-for-service arrangements, but the intensity by which subjects respond to incentives differs by subject pool (the physicians respond to the incentives less than the students do). A further refinement is to consider mixed payment systems, which are the subject of a laboratory experiment used by Brosig-Koch et al. (2017).

4.   Conclusions

Many studies by health economists and public health researchers are called experiments, but few of them are based on research designs where subjects face real consequences for their choices. This lack of incentive compatibility reflects a disconnect between behavioural and experimental economists on the one hand, and researchers in the health area, on the other. Nevertheless, there is an emerging literature at the intersection of these two distinct traditions, and the review here has covered four topics within this area: measuring preferences, information interventions, price-based interventions and payments systems. Some of the experiments carried out in these areas could be improved upon, particularly in terms of ensuring that subjects face the opportunity costs of their choices. There are also unanswered questions, such as the persistence of effects that are measured in the experimental environment where it is rare to see the same subjects repeatedly over time.

One implication of the comparative immaturity of the experimental economics agenda in health economics is that very little attention is paid to what can be considered "second-generation" features of experimental economics. These features include adjusting for multiple hypothesis tests (List et al., 2019), encouraging systematic replication to improve the quality of research (Camerer et al., 2019) and using pre-analysis plans (Olken, 2015). All of these features can serve to limit data-mining problems that are the outcome of what is now often known as "p-hacking". Other reviews of the interface between experimental economics and health have also noted that very few studies in behavioural health economics have issued pre-analysis plans or public protocols that set out how the data will be analyzed (including the particular health behaviours that will be studied) in advance of the researchers either seeing the data or collecting the data (Galizzi & Wiesen, 2018). I have already noted the retraction of a large number of studies by Wansink that involved manipulation of the food environment in natural settings as a way to provide evidence on the health effects of small behavioural nudges. The fact that these studies had to be retracted partly reflects a failure to use any of these second-generation features, such as pre-analysis plans, which might have limited the likelihood (or suspicion by others) that apparently statistically significant results were due to the use of p-hacking.

One recommendation for future behavioural experiments in health is to be more transparent, in terms of using pre-analysis plans and facilitating replicability. There are also important design features to pay attention to, such as ensuring that subjects do face the opportunity costs of their choices. In that way, the responses observed in the experimental environment can be a better guide to what should happen in the real world.

References

Anderson, L. R., & Mellor, J. M. (2008). Predicting health behaviors with an experimental measure of risk preference. *Journal of Health Economics*, *27*(5), 1260–1274.

Anderson, L. R., & Mellor, J. M. (2009). Are risk preferences stable? Comparing an experimental measure with a validated survey-based measure. *Journal of Risk and Uncertainty, 39*(2), 137–160.

Aron-Dine, A., Einav, L., & Finkelstein, A. (2013). The RAND health insurance experiment, three decades later. *Journal of Economic Perspectives, 27*(1), 197–222.

Barsky, R.B., Juster, F.T., Kimball, M.S., & Shapiro, M.D. (1997). Preference parameters and behavioral heterogeneity: An experimental approach in the health and retirement study. *The Quarterly Journal of Economics, 112*(2), 537–579.

Billich, N., Blake, M. R., Backholer, K., Cobcroft, M., Li, V., & Peeters, A. (2018). The effect of sugar-sweetened beverage front-of-pack labels on drink selection, health knowledge and awareness: An online randomised controlled trial. *Appetite, 128*, 233–241.

Blake, M. R., Lancsar, E., Peeters, A., & Backholer, K. (2019). Sugar-sweetened beverage price elasticities in a hypothetical convenience store. *Social Science & Medicine, 225*(1), 98–107.

Bleich, S. N., Barry, C. L., Gary-Webb, T. L., & Herring, B. J. (2014). Reducing sugar-sweetened beverage consumption by providing caloric information: How black adolescents alter their purchases and whether the effects persist. *American Journal of Public Health, 104*(12), 2417–2424.

Bollard, T., Maubach, N., Walker, N., & Mhurchu, C. N. (2016). Effects of plain packaging, warning labels, and taxes on young people's predicted sugar-sweetened beverage preferences: An experimental study. *International Journal of Behavioral Nutrition and Physical Activity, 13*(1), 95.

Borghans, L., & Golsteyn, B. H. (2006). Time discounting and the body mass index: Evidence from the Netherlands. *Economics & Human Biology, 4*(1), 39–61.

Bouguen, A., Huang, Y., Kremer, M., & Miguel, E. (2019). Using randomized controlled trials to estimate long-run impacts in development economics. *Annual Review of Economics, 11*(1), 523–561.

Brosig-Koch, J., Hennig-Schmidt, H., Kairies-Schwarz, N., & Wiesen, D. (2016). Using artefactual field and lab experiments to investigate how fee-for-service and capitation affect medical service provision. *Journal of Economic Behavior & Organization, 131*, 17–23.

Brosig-Koch, J., Hennig-Schmidt, H., Kairies-Schwarz, N., & Wiesen, D. (2017). The effects of introducing mixed payment systems for physicians: Experimental evidence. *Health Economics, 26*(2), 243–262.

Camerer, C. F., Dreber, A., & Johannesson, M. (2019). Replication and other practices for improving scientific quality in experimental economics. In A. Schram & A. Ule (Eds.), *Handbook of research methods and applications in experimental economics* (pp. 83–102). Edward Elgar Publishing.

Cameron, L., & Shah, M. (2015). Risk-taking behaviour in the wake of natural disasters. *Journal of Human Resources, 50*(2), 484–515.

Chen, X., Kaiser, H. M., & Rickard, B. J. (2015). The impacts of inclusive and exclusive taxes on healthy eating: An experimental study. *Food Policy, 56*(1), 13–24.

Chuang, Y., & Schechter, L. (2015). Stability of experimental and survey measures of risk, time, and social preferences: A review and some new results. *Journal of Development Economics, 117*(1), 151–170.

Cox, J. C., Sadiraj, V., Schnier, K. E., & Sweeney, J. F. (2016). Incentivizing cost-effective reductions in hospital readmission rates. *Journal of Economic Behavior & Organization, 131*(1), 24–35.

Dolan, P., Galizzi, M. M., & Navarro-Martinez, D. (2015). Paying people to eat or not to eat? Carryover effects of monetary incentives on eating behaviour. *Social Science & Medicine, 133*(1), 153–158.

Eckel, C. C., El-Gamal, M. A., & Wilson, R. K. (2009). Risk loving after the storm: A Bayesian-network study of Hurricane Katrina evacuees. *Journal of Economic Behavior & Organization, 69*(2), 110–124.

Fischer, A. J. (2014). Some comments on "Taxes, subsidies, and advertising efficacy in changing eating behavior: An experimental study." *Applied Economic Perspectives and Policy, 36*(4), 717–721.

Galizzi, M. M. (2014). What is really behavioral in behavioral health policy? And does it work? *Applied Economic Perspectives and Policy, 36*(1), 25–60.

Galizzi, M. M., & Wiesen, D. (2017). Behavioural experiments in health: An introduction. *Health Economics, 26*(S3), 3–5.

Galizzi, M. M., & Wiesen, D. (2018). Behavioral experiments in health economics. In A. Dixit, S. Edwards, & K. Judd (Eds.), *Oxford research encyclopedia of economics and finance.* https://oxfordre.com/economics/view/10.1093/acrefore/9780190625979.001.0001/acrefore-9780190625979-e-244

Gibson, J., McKenzie, D., Rohorua, H., & Stillman, S. (2019). The long-term impact of international migration on economic decision-making: Evidence from a migration lottery and lab-in-the-field experiments. *Journal of Development Economics, 138,* 99–115.

Gibson, J., Tucker, S., & Boe-Gibson, G. (2019). *Testing an information intervention: Experimental evidence on the effect of Jamie Oliver on fizzy drinks demand.* (MPRA Working Paper No. 94182). Munich: Munich Personal RePEc Archive. https://mpra.ub.uni-muenchen.de/94182/

Giesen, J., Payne, C., Havermans, R., & Jansen, A. (2011). Exploring how calorie information and taxes on high-calorie foods influence lunch decisions. *American Journal of Clinical Nutrition, 93*(4), 689–694.

Halpern, D. (2015). *Inside the nudge unit: How small changes can make a big difference.* Random House.

Hammond, D. (2011). Health warning messages on tobacco products: A review. *Tobacco Control, 20*(5), 327–337.

Hanks, A. S., Just, D. R., & Wansink, B. (2013). Preordering school lunch encourages better food choices by children. *JAMA Pediatrics, 167*(7), 673–674.

Harrison, G. W., Lau, M. I., & Rutström, E. E. (2010). Individual discount rates and smoking: Evidence from a field experiment in Denmark. *Journal of Health Economics, 29*(5), 708–717.

Hennig-Schmidt, H., Selten, R., & Wiesen, D. (2011). How payment systems affect physicians' provision behaviour—An experimental investigation. *Journal of Health Economics, 30*(4), 637–646.

Holt, C. A., & Laury, S. K. (2002). Risk aversion and incentive effects. *American Economic Review, 92*(5), 1644–1655.

Jue, J. S., Press, M. J., McDonald, D., Volpp, K. G., Asch, D. A., Mitra, N., Stanowski, A. C., & Loewenstein, G. (2012). The impact of price discounts and calorie messaging on beverage consumption: A multi-site field study. *Preventive Medicine, 55*(6), 629–633.

Kerschbamer, R., & Sutter, M. (2017). The economics of credence goods–A survey of recent lab and field experiments. *CESifo Economic Studies, 63*(1), 1–23.

Leigh, A. (2018). *Randomistas: How radical researchers are changing our world.* Yale University Press.

List, J. A., Shaikh, A. M., & Xu, Y. (2019). Multiple hypothesis testing in experimental economics. *Experimental Economics, 22*(4), 773–793.

Loewenstein, G., Asch, D. A., Friedman, J. Y., Melichar, L. A., & Volpp, K. G. (2012). Can behavioural economics make us healthier? *BMJ, 344*, e3482.

Mangham, L. J., Hanson, K., & McPake, B. (2009). How to do (or not to do) … Designing a discrete choice experiment for application in a low-income country. *Health Policy and Planning, 24*(2), 151–158.

Oliver, A. (Ed.). (2013). *Behavioural public policy.* Cambridge University Press.

Olken, B. A. (2015). Promises and perils of pre-analysis plans. *Journal of Economic Perspectives, 29*(3), 61–80.

Ravallion, M. (2020). *Should the randomistas (continue to) rule?* (Working Paper w27554). Cambridge, MA: National Bureau of Economic Research.

Reeves, A., McKee, M., Mackenbach, J., Whitehead, M., & Stuckler, D. (2017). Introduction of a national minimum wage reduced depressive symptoms in low-wage workers: A quasi-natural experiment in the UK. *Health Economics, 26*(5), 639–655.

Shah, K. K., Tsuchiya, A., & Wailoo, A. J. (2015). Valuing health at the end of life: A stated preference discrete choice experiment. *Social Science & Medicine, 124*(1), 48–56.

Smith, V. L. (1994). Economics in the laboratory. *Journal of Economic Perspectives, 8*(1), 113–131.

Streletskaya, N. A., Rusmevichientong, P., Amatyakul, W., & Kaiser, H. M. (2014). Taxes, subsidies, and advertising efficacy in changing eating behavior: An experimental study. *Applied Economic Perspectives and Policy, 36*(1), 146–174.

Szrek, H., Chao, L. W., Ramlagan, S., & Peltzer, K. (2012). Predicting (un) healthy behavior: A comparison of risk-taking propensity measures. *Judgment and Decision-Making, 7*(6), 716–727.

VanEpps, E. M., & Roberto, C. A. (2016). The influence of sugar-sweetened beverage warnings: A randomized trial of adolescents' choices and beliefs. *American Journal of Preventive Medicine, 51*(5), 664–672.

Velema, E., Vyth, E., & Steenhuis, I. (2017). Using nudging and social marketing techniques to create healthy worksite cafeterias in the Netherlands: Intervention development and study design. *BMC Public Health, 17*(1), 63.

Wagstaff, A., Nguyen, H. T. H., Dao, H., & Bales, S. (2016). Encouraging health insurance for the informal sector: A cluster randomized experiment in Vietnam. *Health Economics, 25*(6), 663–674.

Waterlander, W. E., Jiang, Y., Nghiem, N., Eyles, H., Wilson, N., Cleghorn, C., Genc, M., Swinburn, B., Ni Mhurchu, C., & Blakely, T. (2019). The effect of food price changes on consumer purchases: A randomised experiment. *The Lancet Public Health, 4*(8), e394–e405.

Wilson, A., Buckley, E., Buckley, J., & Bogomolova, S. (2016). Nudging healthier food and beverage choices through salience and priming. Evidence from a systematic review. *Food Quality and Preference, 51*(1), 47–64.

Wisdom, J., Downs, J. S., & Loewenstein, G. (2010). Promoting healthy choices: Information versus convenience. *American Economic Journal: Applied Economics, 2*(2), 164–178.

PART II

7 The gender leadership gap: insights from experiments

Catherine Eckel, Lata Gangadharan, Philip J. Grossman, and Nina Xue

1. Introduction

Differences in the economic decisions and labor market outcomes of women and men are widely documented. Women have lower earnings, work in different occupations, and invest in lower-risk retirement portfolios. They are less likely to be found in leadership positions, and, when leading, may be evaluated and rewarded differently. Women's underrepresentation in leadership positions may arise from several sources. First, women might choose differently (i.e., women may be less likely to prefer a leadership role). Second, women may be less likely to be selected for a leadership position. Third, women's effectiveness may be perceived and evaluated differently from men's, jeopardizing their success as leaders.

Considerable evidence documents gender differences in preferences and attitudes, showing that women are, on average, more risk averse and altruistic, and less competitive and confident than men (Niederle, 2015).[1] In turn, many studies show that preferences impact labor market outcomes; for example, individuals who are more averse to risk select professions with lower earnings risk, such as those in the public sector, and more altruistic individuals select low-paying "care" occupations, such as education or health care (Shurchkov and Eckel, 2018). Evidence also indicates that women are reluctant to volunteer for or accept a leadership position; this is found even for those who are at least as competitive and risk tolerant as their male counterparts. These differences in preferences or attitudes might explain why women, on average, would be less willing to choose to become leaders.

Women may also be less likely to be selected as leaders. This could be due to stereotypes, beliefs about preferences or ability, or discrimination. For example, opportunities for women to be hired into risky positions could be constrained by employers' beliefs, effectively barring women from some professions or leadership positions. Traditional gender roles may leave potential employers with a belief that women are simply not suitable for leadership.

Finally, leaders do not exist in a vacuum: social interactions and norms affect perceptions of leader performance. The evaluations of leaders may also be shaped by gender-based stereotypes and beliefs. It is often said that a woman has to be twice as good at her job as a man to be seen as equally competent. Social interactions, with decision-makers in the leader-selection process and with potential followers, are therefore important to the success of a leader. Environments that are male-dominated or generally considered to be masculine (such as STEM fields) are especially susceptible to stereotypes that fuel negative reactions to female candidates and contribute to women's reluctance to assume leadership roles. These factors may explain the underrepresentation of women in leadership roles, as well as the mixed success of interventions and policies that aim to correct for historical inequalities by providing more opportunities for women.

Most of the research on gender and the labor market relies on observational data to document and explore the underlying causes of gender differences (Blau and Kahn, 2017), but it can be difficult or impossible to disentangle potential causal relationships or to obtain appropriate counterfactuals using these data. Looking only at the outcomes of the decision process, it is impossible to identify the causal effects of preferences, or to separate preferences from the effects of stereotypes or discrimination. Research using experimental methods provides a way to examine gender differences, isolating preferences from constraints. Preferences can be elicited one at a time, and ways in which women are treated can be observed without confounds, such as performance and candidate quality.

Experimental research is useful in testing potential remedies for differences in outcomes. Lab experiments provide a low-cost "wind tunnel" option for pre-testing responses to specific interventions. Both lab and field experiments have been designed to test the effectiveness of interventions aimed at improving gender equality. Interventions may attempt to change preferences by making women more risk tolerant or competitive, or they may implement new institutions, such as hiring or personnel-evaluation practices. Experiments also can be designed to shed light on the mechanisms underlying an intervention's success or failure.

In this chapter, we offer a review of experimental research that we see as relevant for understanding the gender gap in leadership. Our primary focus is on lab experiments and lab-in-the-field experiments (Eckel and Candelo, 2020).[2] This research area is large and growing, and our space is limited; necessarily, our review omits many important and interesting papers. Some of the papers we include examine factors that affect differences in labor market outcomes more generally, while others focus more closely on leadership, per se. Our purpose is to highlight studies that help us understand the gender gap in leadership, and the potential effectiveness of measures that might close that gap.

The chapter proceeds as follows. Section 2 focuses on women's willingness to lead. We address gender differences in preferences, summarizing the most common experimental findings and their relevance for the gender leadership gap. Section 3 examines the selection of women as leaders, and reviews work that explores differences in perceptions, beliefs, and behavior that may contribute to the leadership gap. We discuss stereotypes, which play an important role, not just in this section, but in all aspects of the gender leadership gap. We also discuss evidence of discrimination in the selection of leaders. Section 4 discusses the ways in which male and female leaders may differ in how they are evaluated as well as in their effectiveness as leaders. The focus of Section 5 is on interventions and their effectiveness in terms of improving outcomes for women. The final section discusses policy directions (e.g., affirmative action and leader selection methods) and future research.

2.   Women's Decision to Lead

Not everyone has what it takes to be a leader. The role of leader requires specific talents and a level of confidence in one's ability. Even if a person has the required talents and confidence, the desire to take on the role may be lacking. The process of becoming a leader is often competitive, and leaders are expected to take risks for their group or organization, to take responsibility for their own decisions and their group's success, and to be willing to sacrifice for the team when needed. Not everyone wishes to put themselves under this strain. As such, preferences are likely to influence both the decision to pursue leadership and the decisions made as leaders. In this section, we review the research on gender differences in relevant preferences, confidence, and the desire to lead.

2.1   Preferences: Risk Aversion, Competitiveness, Altruism

Research on gender differences in preferences in a leadership context has largely focused on differences in risk aversion, competitiveness, and other-regarding preferences, including altruism, inequality aversion, and cooperation (Croson and Gneezy, 2009; Niederle, 2015).

Incentivized and survey risk-elicitation measures find consistent evidence that women are more risk averse, though the magnitude of the difference varies depending on the method and target population (Byrnes et al., 1999; Eckel and Grossman, 2008).[3] Greater risk tolerance is associated with the choice of STEM fields by high-school students (Buser et al., 2017), selection of riskier investment portfolios (Jianakoplos and Bernasek, 1998), and the choice of riskier occupations (Bonin et al., 2007). Even among CEOs, women select less risky compensation packages, with a smaller proportion of their incomes based on firm performance (Chauvin and Ash, 1994). In the lab, women choose less risky real-effort tasks to determine their earnings, with a resulting loss in earnings (Jung et al., 2018).

Entrepreneurship is another manifestation of leadership that is related to preferences. Jiang and Capra (2018) find that women are less likely to be entrepreneurs, but do not observe a connection between risk tolerance and entrepreneurship.[4] However, in a sample of small business managers in Peru, Castillo et al. (2010) find that entrepreneurs have greater risk tolerance than do hired managers. Since women are, on average, more risk averse, this may help explain their underrepresentation among entrepreneurs.

A preference for competition has implications for the decision to lead. Rising through the ranks of an organization is a competitive process not unlike participating in a winner-take-all tournament. To assess gender differences in competitiveness, Niederle and Vesterlund (2007) developed a multistage experimental paradigm that first asks subjects to complete a task for a piece rate, then to complete the same task under a tournament (competitive) setting, and finally to choose which they prefer for a third round of the task. This study has been replicated numerous times with different populations, and most results support the finding that women are less competitive (Niederle, 2015, 2017).[5] A preference for competition is associated with choice of occupation and earnings and, like risk tolerance, also predicts selection of math-intensive education tracks (Buser et al., 2014, 2017). For MBA students, differences in competitiveness are associated with industry choice and starting salaries after graduation (Reuben et al., 2015).

The relationship between cooperation and altruism and the decision to become a leader has at least two facets. On one hand, we may not typically associate cooperation and altruism with leaders. On the other hand, a good leader puts the welfare of the group ahead of personal well-being. Leadership can involve taking on a task for the benefit of a group, such as chairing a committee or accepting a departmental administrative position, and altruism might play an important part in this kind of leadership role. Babcock et al. (2017) show that women are more likely to volunteer for thankless tasks (i.e., women are more willing to "take one for the team" by performing a sacrifice that benefits the other members of the group). Their result can be reinterpreted as evidence that women are more likely to volunteer to take on a particular type of leadership role. While this argument was not explicitly tested in their study, this kind of sacrifice is often expected of leaders in a group.[6]

Women's greater altruism may contribute to their career choices and to their lower earnings.[7] With respect to other-regarding preferences, as measured in the simple setting of a dictator game, women are typically more generous, giving more to an anonymous counterpart than do men; the difference is even more pronounced when the recipient is a needy individual or a charitable organization (see Bilén et al., 2020, for a meta-analysis). In this game, women are also observed to be more inequality averse, and men are more concerned with maximizing efficiency (Andreoni and Vesterlund, 2001). Altruistic decisions in the dictator game have been shown to predict the choice of public-sector occupations (Tonin and Vlassopoulos, 2015; Banuri and Keefer, 2016). Altruism is also higher for workers in care-work sectors (England et al., 2002; Folbre, 2012).

2.2   Confidence and the Decision to Lead

The literature on gender and leadership generally shows that women are less likely to want to take on a leadership role in many contexts, including investment (Ertac and Gurdal 2012), public goods (Arbak and Villeval 2013), politics (Preece and Stoddard, 2015; Kanthak and Woon, 2015), and in a competition (Reuben et al., 2012; Erkal et al., 2019). While this may be partially explained by preferences, that may not be the full story. Even women with a preference for leadership roles may lack confidence in their ability to be successful leaders.

Women may be less likely to consider themselves qualified for a leadership position. In male-typed domains, women are shown to be more reluctant to contribute ideas to group discussions (Bordalo et al., 2019), indicating a lack of confidence in putting themselves forward. Gender stereotypes can influence women's self-assessments of how qualified they are to lead in particular fields

(Coffman, Collis, and Kulkarni, 2020). Coffman (2014) argues that an individual's decision to contribute ideas is a function of ability, gender, and the gender stereotype associated with the domain. If a domain is stereotypically outside their gender's domain, the individual is less willing to contribute. The author's design allows her to infer that this behavior reflects self-assessment differences, not a fear of discrimination.

This gender confidence gap is also observed by Niederle and Vesterlund (2007), who assess confidence as a possible reason for women's lower competitiveness by asking participants to make incentivized guesses about their own performance in the tournament relative to others. While both genders are overconfident regarding their abilities, men are more overconfident than women. Controlling for actual performance, women are significantly less confident than men about their relative ranks. Beyer (1990) reports an overestimation of ability by men on masculine and neutral tasks, while women are more likely to underestimate their performances in masculine tasks.[8]

Exley and Kessler (2019) show that gender differences in self-assessment drive a substantial gender gap in self-promotion. Even though women slightly outperform men in a commonly used test of ability (the Armed Services Vocational Aptitude Battery), their self-assessments show the opposite pattern: women report less favorable evaluations of their own performance despite performing slightly better than men. This gap in self-promotion persists even after accurate information is provided about absolute and relative past performance. This difference in the willingness to self-promote offers a key insight into the underrepresentation of women in leadership positions, as many leadership selection processes rely on a candidate's self-evaluation of performance and ability.[9]

Gender stereotypes, while applicable to the perceptions and evaluations of others may also be applied to one's own performance. Inzlicht and Ben-Zeev (2000) observe that women's performance in a math test declines with the number of men in their group. Since mathematics is typically considered to be a male domain, they propose that the presence of male team members strengthens the salience of the stereotype, thus creating a "stereotype threat" (Aronson and Steele, 1995). While stereotypes may offer an exaggeration of real differences, stereotypes themselves may be strengthened by environmental factors, such as a group's gender composition. Kamas and Preston (2018) measure the taste for competition and confidence of college seniors and then track their labor market experiences in the years following graduation. They find that a preference for competition and confidence are positively correlated with compensation for women, but not for men. Competitive and confident women earn more than other women and just as much as men.

2.3   Willingness to Accept the Role of Leader

A consequence of the differences in preferences and the confidence gap is seen in the reluctance of women even to accept the role of leader. Grossman et al. (2015) and Li et al. (2020) find that women are less willing to lead, particularly in situations in which the leader's gender is revealed to group members, with female leaders most willing to lead in all female groups. Similarly, Born et al. (2019) find that women's willingness to lead is greatest in female majority groups. Subjects participate in two framed survival tasks, both individually and in a group of four (either three men/one woman or one man/three women). Individuals indicate their willingness to lead their groups (i.e., make the final decisions based on members' suggestions). Men are more willing to be the leader, and are even more willing to lead in female-majority groups. Men are more confident, have more influence, and are ranked higher than equally performing women.

Chen and Houser (2019) manipulate the salience of gender stereotypes to test whether a group's gender mix affects the willingness to become a leader. Participants are randomly assigned to groups with varying gender compositions, and are then asked to report their willingness to answer general knowledge questions for their groups. Women in same-gender groups are twice as willing to accept a leadership role as those in mixed-gender groups, and the result is explained by a change in confidence levels. This suggests that women's confidence is particularly likely to suffer in male-dominated fields.

Ertac and Gurdal (2012) show that women are less willing to lead in a simple risky environment, that is, deciding how much of a fixed endowment to invest in a risky asset. When placed in groups of five, women are more likely to refuse to make a decision on behalf of their group. Ertac et al. (2019) assess how much individuals are willing to pay either to obtain the authority to make a risky decision for themselves, or to avoid the responsibility of making the decision by deferring it to the leader. Subjects are randomly allocated to the decision-maker role, but then can pay to change the situation. The experiment elicits the leader's willingness to pay to avoid the leadership position (demand to avoid responsibility, DAR), and the follower's willingness to pay to make their own decision (demand for autonomy, DFA). Someone who prefers to be a leader has negative DAR and positive DFA. Women are substantially less likely to fall into this category than are men (25.5% of women and 43.3% of men). This study also shows a negative relationship between other-regarding preferences and the preference to be a leader.

Chakraborty and Serra (2019) design an experiment that mimics corporate decision-making, where the leader faces the possibility of angry messages from subordinates. They show that "backlash aversion" can play an important role in women's decision not to pursue a leadership role. Propp (1995) argues that a reluctance to take on leadership roles may also be due to an inability to exert influence. Attempts by women to exert influence are often resisted or ignored, men have more influence than women in mixed groups, and the contributions of men, relative to the same contribution by women, receive more attention from other group members (Carli, 2001; Gangadharan et al., 2016). We discuss the evaluation of male and female leaders further in Section 4.

Leaders are often elected, or chosen, through some other process. Women's under-representation among candidates for political office is often decried in the popular press. Kanthak and Woon (2015) investigate why women do not run for office, and find that women are averse to elections. They rule out differences in preferences or confidence as reasons why women do not run, and suggest another possibility. When elections are completely truthful – that is, no one has the scope to make unwarranted claims about their qualifications – women are as likely as men to put themselves forward. Women are averse to competing in an environment in which qualifications are not verifiable, and in which exaggeration of candidates' own qualifications and false doubt about others' claims play a role.

In sum, gender differences in risk-taking, aversion to competition, altruism, confidence in own ability, self-promotion, and willingness to lead offer possible explanations for the gender gap in leadership, but the underrepresentation of women in leadership roles is not fully explained by these factors.

3.   Perceptions, Beliefs, and the Selection of Leaders

In this section, we consider the beliefs and perceptions of those involved in appointing leaders and those of potential followers regarding female leaders, as well as how this affects the selection of women as leaders. Even if women possess the same preferences, attitudes, qualities, and talents as their male counterparts, gender-based perceptions or beliefs can persist. If women are perceived to be less risk tolerant and/or less competitive, this could influence their selection for a competitive task. Indeed, there is evidence that, to be perceived as effective, women may be held to different standards than men, and may need to show that they are simultaneously sensitive (other-regarding) as well as strong (risk-taking and competitive; Johnson et al., 2008).

3.1   Gender Stereotypes

Gender stereotypes about preferences can play an important part in leader selection. Considerable evidence supports the presence of stereotypes that exaggerate underlying true differences. For example, Eckel and Grossman (2002) show that women are stereotyped as more risk averse than men; beliefs about gender differences are greater than actual gender differences in risk aversion. Similarly, Cason et al. (2020) find that men and women both believe that women are more community minded and more likely to make pro-social choices and inflate the underlying difference.

Another area in which stereotypes matter is confidence. Confidence affects women's willingness to become leaders (discussed in Section 2.2), but stereotypes about confidence also are likely to affect women's selection as leaders. Bordalo et al. (2019) argue that men's overconfidence may be based in part on the exaggeration of true underlying differences, and in part on an overestimation of own ability. They confirm that stereotypes exaggerate the performance gap. Both men and women are influenced by stereotypes: in male- (female-) oriented domains, both men and women underestimate (overestimate) the ability of women relative to men.

3.2   Discrimination

Discrimination against women in the selection of leaders can be based on differences in beliefs about women and men, including gender stereotypes and statistical discrimination, or can be taste based. While the evidence of gender stereotyping is fairly conclusive, its impact on the selection of female leaders is discussed in this section.

In general, considerable evidence documents gender differences in the selection of workers. In labor markets, women are less likely to be hired into male-dominated domains, and women's credentials are often discounted.[10] Blau and Kahn (2017) survey the evidence on gender discrimination in hiring, including the pathbreaking study by Goldin and Rouse (2000) showing that implementing blind auditions for orchestras substantially increased the hiring of women.

Gender discrimination can also be seen in studies focusing on the selection of leaders. For example, Moss-Racusin et al. (2012) submitted identical applications, differing only in the gender of the applicant, for a lab manager position. Both male and female employers exhibited a preference for male applicants for this leadership position; women with identical qualifications were perceived as less qualified than male candidates.

Coffman, Exley, and Niederle (2020) focus on distinguishing between belief and taste-based gender discrimination. They conducted an experiment in which employers select workers to complete tasks in male-stereotyped domains (math and sports). The researchers pretested their subjects' performance in a math and a sports quiz. Employers then selected among available workers. In one treatment, workers were identified by gender; the control condition was cleverly designed by allocating the same set of workers into two groups depending on whether someone was born in an odd or even birth month (all male workers and all female workers, respectively), a categorization about which there are no differences in beliefs. Their design isolates the gender-specific, taste-based component of discrimination. Their clever design includes women born in even months and men born in odd months. When the labelling is changed from gender to birth month, but the same information is given about the groups, employers discriminate against even-month workers. The design creates the same set of beliefs in the two treatments, and similar behavior is observed in both. This allows the authors to conclude that the discrimination is belief-based and not taste-based.[11]

3.3   Negotiation

Even if women are willing to take on leadership roles, a further roadblock lies in the negotiation process. The process of becoming a leader often involves some form of negotiation (such as negotiating for a promotion). Hernandez-Arenaz and Iriberri (2019a) provide an extensive survey of the literature on gender differences in negotiation.

There is substantial evidence that women are more reluctant to enter into negotiations than men (Babcock and Laschever, 2009; Eriksson and Sandberg, 2012), and this has been studied extensively in the context of wage negotiations (Dittrich et al., 2014). Gender stereotypes can be especially harmful to women during the negotiation process. When women do enter negotiations, Amanatullah and Morris (2010) find that women take a less aggressive approach in anticipation of backlash for violating gender stereotypes. In a series of experiments, Bowles et al. (2007) examine willingness to negotiate and the treatment of men and women who attempt to negotiate. Female candidates who initiate wage negotiations are penalized more than male candidates, and this effect appears to be driven by male evaluators.

Eckel et al. (2008) survey negotiation experiments in the simple environments of dictator and ultimatum games. They note that differences in negotiation outcomes can result from differences in the behavior of women and men, or differences in how women and men are perceived and treated. While women have a stronger preference for fair outcomes than men, this difference in behavior is small compared to the difference in expectations about how men and women behave. They also offer evidence that women may be more sensitive to the negotiation context. Small et al. (2007) report a gender difference due to the bargaining context. If the interaction is framed as a negotiation for higher earnings, women are less willing to negotiate. Reframing the interaction as an opportunity to "ask" for higher pay appears to eliminate gender differences.[12]

On balance, stereotypes have an important and persistent influence on perceptions of others' preferences and abilities. Stereotypes can also lead to discrimination and gender differences in negotiation outcomes contributing to the leadership gap.

4.   Leader Evaluation and Effectiveness

Gender stereotypes play a key role in the selection of female leaders, but also in the assessment of leaders and their effectiveness. Not only do these factors contribute to an ability to lead effectively, and to be seen as such, they can also bias the negotiation process (for wages or promotions), which, as discussed in Section 3.3, is often biased against women. In this section, we discuss research on the evaluation of leaders and leader effectiveness.

4.1   Gender and the Evaluation of Leaders

Gender stereotypes can bias the evaluation of women as leaders. This may be especially detrimental to female leaders when qualities that are desirable for a leader (such as assertiveness) are incongruent with stereotypes about women. Observationally, women appear to be evaluated differently in many domains, from teaching evaluations (Boring, 2017) to candidates running for office (Murray, 2008). We discuss experiments that test whether male and female leaders are indeed evaluated differently.

Grossman et al. (2019) employ a repeated weakest-link coordination game to address gender differences in leader effectiveness and followers' perceptions of leaders' effectiveness. The leader's intervention is a short, semi-scripted speech advising followers on how to maximize earnings. The advantage of their design is that there can be no difference in leader ability or quality, removing these as explanations for variations in evaluations. Followers evaluate their leaders' effectiveness and may reward their leaders with a bonus. While followers are influenced equally by the advice of male and female leaders, female leaders are assessed less positively and rewarded less generously than are equally effective male leaders. Using a similar design, Li et al. (2020, discussed in Section 2.3) also observe no difference in followers' responses to the messages of male and female leaders.

Similar to Grossman et al. (2019), Brooks et al. (2014) find that both professional investors and nonprofessional evaluators prefer entrepreneurial pitches presented by male as compared to female entrepreneurs, even when the content of the pitch is the same. Using tenure decisions of academic economists and evidence from experiments, Sarsons et al. (2020) explore gender differences in credit for group work. They find that women receive less credit for group work when employers cannot perfectly observe their contributions. Women are therefore less likely to receive tenure the more they coauthor, and these differences are explained mainly by stereotypes and biases.

Erkal et al. (2020) examine whether gender contributes to biased belief formation about the leader's outcomes. They find that gender distorts perceptions of outcomes in risky environments. Relative to unbiased Bayesian updating, good outcomes of women are attributed more to luck, and bad outcomes of men more to effort. In treatments in which members can offer bonuses or impose penalties on decision-makers (leaders), female leaders receive lower bonuses than their male counterparts. The authors identify channels underlying bonus payments and find that, while outcome matters for both men and women, beliefs about intentions only matter for men. Hence, good outcomes are necessary for women to get a bonus, but men can get a high bonus for bad outcomes as long as evaluators hold them in high regard.

4.2   Leader Effectiveness

Closely related to how leaders are evaluated is the effectiveness of leaders in rallying support from their followers to achieve certain goals. Gender differences in leader effectiveness have been studied in two distinct ways: first, by inducing leadership roles in the laboratory, and second, by examining the performance of incumbent leaders in the corporate or political arena.[13]

Andreoni and Petrie (2008) find that their laboratory subjects are more willing to follow the lead of generous men in a linear public goods game with sequential contributions. When the first mover is male and his contribution is known with certainty, subsequent movers make more generous contributions than when a similar contribution is made by a woman. This effect increases with the proportion of men in the group. Reuben and Timko (2018) compare the effectiveness of elected leaders and randomly selected leaders of groups playing a coordination game. Elected leaders are more effective, but teams selecting a male leader have higher performance than teams that elect a female leader, mostly because male leaders are more likely to be followed when they request the highest effort level. The difference disappears over time, as high-performing leaders are more likely to be re-elected.

Grossman et al. (2015) conduct a collective-action experiment with asymmetrical information in which free-riding and coordination failures can prevent efficient group cooperation. Randomly selected leaders, knowing the value of the project assigned to their groups, decide first whether they want to contribute to the projects. Uninformed followers observe the leader's decision, then simultaneously decide whether to invest. There are three treatments: single-gender groups, mixed-gender groups with no leader gender signaling, and mixed-gender groups with leader gender signaling. While there are significant differences by gender in the behavior of leaders (discussed in Section 2.3), Grossman et al. (2015) report that, contingent on their leader investing, followers are as likely to invest regardless of the gender of the leader.

Comparing the effectiveness of incumbent female leaders with male leaders is often difficult to do, as female leadership is rarely observed.[14] To circumvent this problem, researchers have used conditions created by natural policy experiments that mandate women be considered for leadership positions (for example, Norway, where publicly listed firms were mandated to have at least 40% woman directors, and India, where leadership positions were randomly reserved for women).[15]

Gangadharan et al. (2016) and Gangadharan et al. (2019) are examples of how researchers can combine natural variations caused by policy (the Indian policy of reserving randomly determined village leadership roles for women) with experimental methods. Using a lab-in-the-field experiment, the two papers explore gender differences in leaders' behavior and followers' behavior toward male and female leaders. Villagers in both reserved and non-reserved villages take part in a Public Good with Leadership experiment. They find that female leaders are more likely to contribute less than what they propose, compared to men in similar positions. This negative deviation from proposals is pronounced when the leader's gender is revealed. Men contribute significantly less to the public good when the group leader is revealed to be a woman.

In summary, the studies show mixed evidence of gender differences in both the evaluation of leaders and leader effectiveness. A pattern that emerges across the papers, however, is that perceptions of legitimacy and the social environment can be critical to facilitate the effectiveness of female leaders.

5.   Interventions to Address the Gender Gap in Leadership

Despite improvements over the past decades, gender differences are evident in the workplace in terms of fewer opportunities for career advancements and lower wages for women. Decision-makers in the public and private sectors have considered several approaches to accelerate progress toward gender parity. These include initiating diversity and leadership programs to encourage women to take up senior positions, programs to reduce unconscious biases of managers, and more explicit legislative policies, such as mandatory affirmative action.

Our focus in this section is on three broad types of interventions. First, an obvious solution to the problem of the underrepresentation of women in leadership is to simply increase female representation through mandatory affirmative action. However, such top-down measures may invite backlash, especially in the absence of wide-ranging support from peers and followers. Second, we discuss interventions aimed at addressing the willingness of women to become leaders by encouraging them to "lean in" (Sandberg, 2013). Third, we consider proposed changes to institutions that aim to reduce biased beliefs and the role of gender stereotypes for female candidates.

5.1   Interventions to Regulate Increases in Female Representation

The main purpose of affirmative action is to establish access to educational or employment opportunities for underrepresented groups, in this case, women. Several policy interventions have been initiated to close the gender gap (corporate board membership and directorships in California, McGreevy, 2018; gender-based quotas in the political arenas in Europe, Casas-Arce and Saiz, 2015; and the policies adopted in India and Norway, see Section 4.2). One of the arguments against affirmative action is that these policies prevent the allocation of jobs to the best available candidate. Testing the empirical validity of this argument using observational data is difficult as important variables, such as merit and candidate quality, can be hard for researchers to observe and quantify.

Over the last decade, several studies have used the Niederle and Vesterlund (2007) paradigm to examine the effectiveness of affirmative action policies to enhance entry into competition. Niederle et al. (2013) explore whether affirmative action can encourage applications from female candidates who would otherwise fail to apply for positions for which they are qualified. They find that this policy leads to a large increase in tournament entry by women and a decrease in entry by men. The magnitude of this change is beyond what might be expected from only the changes in the probability of winning for men and women. The authors argue that the large effect on women could be explained by a reduction in the gender differences in beliefs about relative performance and by a reduction in the gender difference in the willingness to compete. They show that, while some high-performing men fail to enter the competition, many more high-performing women do enter, hence the overall number of high-performing people in the pool is unaffected.

Balafoutas and Sutter (2012) examine four policy interventions compared to a no-intervention control scenario. The policies include: 1) quotas that require a minimum fraction of winners to be women; 2) a weak preferential treatment scheme in which a tie-breaking rule favors women in situations in which men and women have equal performance; 3) a strong preferential treatment scheme in which each woman receives a head start; and finally, 4) repeating the competition until a critical threshold of women has been reached. They find that the gender gap in the willingness to enter competition, observed in the control, is reduced with the policy interventions. The strong preferential treatment is the most effective in encouraging women to compete. The weak preferential treatment and quotas have a similar effect, and the repetition of competition generates the weakest incentives for entry. The policies influence women's behavior and do not have a significant impact on men's behavior. Importantly, they also find that the policies do not lead to efficiency losses, either in terms of the selection of winners or in terms of earnings in a post-competition coordination game.

Balafoutas et al. (2016) examine whether or not individuals are willing to support quotas, and how the endogenous implementation of these policies affects performance and efficiency. An important aspect of their design is that the quota can either favor women or a completely arbitrary subgroup (defined by color: pink versus green). Subjects can vote for or against the policy, or abstain. When quotas are based on color instead of gender, performance becomes skewed; members in the advantaged (disadvantaged) color group significantly increased (decreased) their performance. The authors conclude that if there is justification for one group to receive preferential treatment, as in the case of quotas for women, but not in the case of quotas based on color, then this policy does not reduce performance or efficiency. Similarly, Ip et al. (2020) find that the effectiveness of affirmative action can depend significantly on the acceptability of the underlying reason for the initial disadvantage.

Maggian et al. (2020) ask, at which stage would quotas be most effective, at the entry level or for more senior positions? They find that quotas introduced at the final stage of the competition, or at both the entry and the final stages, helped increase women's willingness to compete. They find that introducing a quota only at the top is as effective as introducing quotas at all stages. The interventions do not lead to any efficiency loss, as measured by the performance of winning subjects and the overall earnings. However, only entry-level quotas have the perverse effect of discouraging women from competing at higher levels due to the stereotype threat (Aronson and Steele, 1995).

While affirmative action may increase the proportion of women in leadership positions, simply enforcing gender-based quotas may have little (or even a negative) effect on the acceptance of female leaders. Leibbrandt et al. (2018) address how affirmative action policies interact with other institutional features of organizations, such as a peer-review process, or the social environment. They introduce two treatment dimensions, one in which an affirmative action policy is initiated and another in which subjects peer-review others' performances. Introducing peer review provides an opportunity for sabotage; subjects can choose to misreport the performances of others and hence reduce others' earnings. They find that in treatments with no peer review, quotas are effective in encouraging women to compete. In the presence of peer review, however, the quota both fails to encourage women to compete and, for those women who do compete, there is significant backlash (i.e., sabotage).

Gangadharan et al. (2016, discussed in Section 4.2) report evidence of male backlash in their lab-in the-field experiments in India. This backlash is considerably stronger in villages that were exposed to female leaders due to the affirmative action policy. Male backlash is explained by a perceived transgression of gender norms regarding greater male authority. When women become leaders, men believe their identity is violated and their behavior reflects this resentment.[16]

Taken together, the findings from Leibbrandt et al. (2018) and Gangadharan et al. (2016) raise concerns about the effectiveness of strong policy interventions, such as gender-based quotas, and indicate that these may lead to perverse outcomes in some situations. On the other hand, Beaman et al. (2009) report a positive effect of the gender quotas imposed on Indian village councils. Extended exposure to female leaders resulted in electoral gains for women. In villages required to have a female leader in the prior two elections, women were more likely to run and win elected council positions. The authors argue that this exposure weakened gender stereotypes and improved the perception of female leader effectiveness. In a follow-up paper, Beaman et al. (2012) report that this policy had the added effect of raising the career aspirations and educational attainment of adolescent girls in quota villages relative to non-quota villages.

5.2   Interventions to Change Women's Preferences

Given the reluctance of women to be considered for leadership roles, a seemingly straightforward solution is to encourage women to "lean in." However, as discussed in Section 3.2, gender stereotypes can be especially harmful to female candidates who ask for more. Bowles et al. (2007, discussed in Section 3.3) posit that women are punished for diverging from their gender stereotype of not being greedy and not being too assertive, raising doubts about the notion that women need only to ask.

Exley et al. (2020) build on the idea that simply encouraging women to lean in to negotiations may neglect the fact that society is not always accepting of women who do so. The authors take advantage of the ability to isolate mechanisms in laboratory experiments by controlling for factors that are known to contribute to the gender gap. These include the fear of backlash, ambiguity in the negotiation environment, and differences in confidence. By exogenously varying whether participants can opt out or must always enter negotiations, they compare financial gains when women choose to enter negotiations with gains when negotiation is mandated. The results suggest that, when given a choice, women tend to avoid negotiations that would have resulted in negative profits and generally make positive profits when they do enter, thus revealing a subtle nuance in the importance of knowing when to lean in. A key implication of these findings is that lean-in policies that are aimed at women may backfire in certain contexts, particularly if women face similar levels of pushback from their negotiating counterparts. It is therefore important to also examine the ways in which the social environment might be made more favorable to female candidates.

5.3 Interventions to Change Institutions

Moving away from changing women's preferences and addressing instead how institutions can be changed has also emerged as an approach to reducing gender gaps (Bohnet, 2016). Erkal et al. (2019) is a step in this direction. They start with the premise that leadership selection in most organizations often requires candidates to actively express their interest. They compare such an opt-in mechanism with an opt-out mechanism in which everyone qualified for the position is in the candidate pool by default, but individuals can choose to opt out of the selection process. They find that conventional opt-in mechanisms contribute to a gender gap in participation decisions, which strikingly remains even when individuals know that they are the top performers in their group. In contrast, under the opt-out mechanism, women are more likely to choose to be a leader. They argue that by changing the selection default, an opt-out mechanism may make being in a leadership position appear more acceptable for women. Also, participating under the opt-out mechanism does not necessarily convey the same image of competitiveness or aggressiveness, since one does not need to actively choose to participate. Hence, debiasing the institution by simply changing the default from an opt-in to an opt-out mechanism, can be fruitful in closing the gender gap. He et al. (2019) find a similar result in the context of choosing to enter competition. In the opt-out system, both women and men choose to compete at the same rate as men in the opt-in system, and the opt-out system has the additional advantage that it does not lead to penalties from evaluators making decisions about whom to hire.

Hernandez-Arenaz and Iriberri (2019b) also highlight the important role of institutions in enhancing or diminishing gender biases. In their experiment, participants completed a real-effort task and then negotiated over how the earnings should be shared in either a symmetric environment or an asymmetric environment, in which a fair split is not possible. The findings indicate that women obtain worse outcomes only in the asymmetric environment, suggesting that gender stereotypes are more likely to be activated in the absence of an institution with clear decision rules (such as a sharing rule).

The provision of direct information has been proposed as another means to the same end of debiasing beliefs. However, the evidence is not positive. Two studies ask whether direct information about risk preferences can diminish gender stereotypes. In Grossman and Lugovvsky (2011), subjects predict the lottery choice made by their fellow subjects based on visual gender-revealing clues, responses to a risk-based survey, or both. They find that, without survey information, subjects apply the gender stereotype. Survey responses alone shape guesses, but when both are provided, gender stereotypes again dominate. Grossman (2013) further explores the sequencing of information, and finds that both types of information initially affect predictions, but the gender stereotype is strong when visual cues are available, regardless of the sequence.

6.   Conclusion and Discussion

The experimental literature has shown that both preferences and beliefs play a role in explaining the gender gap in leadership. While differences do exist between the sexes with respect to risk aversion, competitiveness, altruism, and willingness to lead, these differences tend to be amplified in the beliefs and perceptions about female candidates and leaders. Gender stereotypes throw crucial fuel on the flame of discrimination against women in the leader-selection process. For instance, the expectation that women should not be demanding can hurt them in the process of negotiating for a promotion. Perceptions that are negatively biased by stereotypes can then feed into the evaluation of women as leaders. Being perceived as less effective can in fact be self-fulfilling if others are less likely to follow and work alongside female leaders. Investigating the conditions under which women are more reluctant to become leaders as well as the differences in the evaluation of male and female leaders offer interesting avenues for future work.

From a policy perspective, interventions directed at changing women's preferences or encouraging more women to lead neglect the other side of the problem, namely, beliefs that may be biased against female leaders. Without a corresponding change in general attitudes, these attempts may be ineffective at best, and at worst, women may become the targets of backlash and resentment. Greater acceptance of women in leadership roles and a greater willingness of women to participate may be aided by structural changes, such as clear rules and procedures to prevent harmful stereotypes from being activated in the first place. These are promising areas for future research.

Acknowledgement

The authors gratefully acknowledge research assistance provided by Evelina Onopriyenko.

Notes

1. Falk and Hermle (2018) report evidence suggesting that gender differences in preferences are positively related to economic development and gender equality.
2. We also consider particularly relevant field experiments.
3. For examples of commonly used incentivized elicitation measures, see Gneezy and Potters (1997), Holt and Laury (2002), and Eckel and Grossman (2002). Studies using the Holt and Laury (2002) elicitation task typically find no gender difference (Filippin and Crosetto, 2016). Booth and Nolan (2012b) report that girls who attended same-sex schools were not more risk averse than boys. Many studies have assessed the external validity of risk aversion measures, correlating them with a variety of real-world, high-stakes decisions as discussed in the main text.
4. However, their sample included only participants in entrepreneurship-related conferences and courses, and showed a high degree of risk tolerance overall.
5. In some settings, women are not less competitive, including when competing against their own past performance (Apicella et al., 2017, Carpenter et al., 2018); when the reward is high enough (Petrie and Segal, 2015); when looking at a stereotypically female task (Dreber et al., 2014); and when competing for the benefit of their children (Cassar et al., 2016). In matriarchal societies, girls are observed to be as competitive as boys (Gneezy et al., 2009). Girls who attended same-sex schools are also observed to be as competitive as boys (Booth and Nolan, 2012a).
6. O'Gorman et al. (2008) find that leaders with punishment powers in public goods games sacrifice their own earnings and use their power to increase group cooperation, while Gillet et al. (2011) report that leaders (i.e., first movers) in coordination games are less selfish and more altruistic, earning less than their followers.
7. Women have been shown to be more cooperative than men in the prisoners' dilemma game (Ortmann and Tichy, 1999).
8. Lower confidence is not innocuous with respect to performance. For example, women are less willing to guess on multiple-choice tests, which may reflect their lower confidence level, or perhaps greater risk aversion, depending on the grading scheme (Baldiga, 2014). This difference can account for much of the gender difference in scores on standardized tests.
9. De Paola et al. (2017) document a similar pattern in the willingness of female Italian academics to put themselves up for promotion. In fields with more "objective" productivity measurement, this tendency is less likely to be observed.
10. For a review of field experiments on this topic, see Bertrand and Duflo (2017).
11. Statistical discrimination is a subset of belief-based discrimination. The distinction is where the beliefs are accurate (Bertrand and Duflo, 2017).
12. Leibbrandt and List (2015) report similar results from a natural field experiment in which job seekers are randomly assigned to a job advertisement that either explicitly stated that wages are negotiable or did not mention that wages are negotiable.
13. The early psychology literature on gender differences in leader effectiveness provides a rich context to these studies (Eagly et al., 1995; Ridgeway et al., 1994; Ridgeway, 2001).
14. In recent experience, countries led by women appear to be more proactive and successful in enacting measures to combat COVID-19 (Taub, 2020). Though it is difficult to draw causal conclusions, this suggests that different situations may require different leadership styles.

15. See, for example: Norway (Ahern and Dittmar, 2012; Bertrand et al., 2019); India (Chattopadhyay and Duflo, 2004; Beaman et al., 2009). See Section 5.1.
16. Increased exposure to female leaders reduces male bias against female leaders to some extent.

References

Ahern, K.R. and Dittmar, A.K. 2012. The changing of the boards: The impact on firm valuation of mandated female board representation. *The Quarterly Journal of Economics* 127, 137–197.

Amanatullah, E.T. and Morris, M.W. 2010. Negotiating gender roles: Gender differences in assertive negotiating are mediated by women's fear of backlash and attenuated when negotiating on behalf of others. *Journal of Personality and Social Psychology* 98, 256.

Andreoni, J. and Petrie, R. 2008. Beauty, gender and stereotypes: Evidence from laboratory experiments. *Journal of Economic Psychology* 29, 73–93.

Andreoni, J. and Vesterlund, L. 2001. Which is the fair sex? Gender differences in altruism. *The Quarterly Journal of Economics* 116, 293–312.

Apicella, C.L., Demiral, E.E., and Mollerstrom, J. 2017. No gender difference in willingness to compete when competing against self. *American Economic Review* 107, 136–140.

Arbak, E. and Villeval, M.C. 2013. Voluntary leadership: Motivation and influence. *Social Choice and Welfare* 40, 635–662.

Aronson, J. and Steele, C.M. 1995. Stereotype threat and the intellectual test performance of African Americans. *Journal of Personality and Social Psychology* 69, 797–811.

Babcock, L. and Laschever, S. 2009. *Women don't ask: Negotiation and the gender divide.* Princeton, NJ: Princeton University Press.

Babcock, L., Recalde, M.P., Vesterlund, L., and Weingart, L. 2017. Gender differences in accepting and receiving requests for tasks with low promotability. *American Economic Review* 107, 714–747.

Balafoutas, L., Davis, B.J., and Sutter, M. (2016). Affirmative action or just discrimination? A study on the endogenous emergence of quotas. *Journal of Economic Behavior and Organization* 127, 87–98.

Balafoutas, L. and Sutter, M. 2012. Affirmative action policies promote women and do not harm efficiency in the laboratory. *Science* 335, 579–582.

Baldiga, K. 2014. Gender differences in willingness to guess. *Management Science* 60, 434–448.

Banuri, S. and Keefer, P. 2016. Pro-social motivation, effort and the call to public service. *European Economic Review* 83, 139–164.

Beaman, L., Chattopadhyay, R., Duflo, E., Pande, R., and Topalova, P. 2009. Powerful women: Does exposure reduce bias? *The Quarterly Journal of Economics* 124, 1497–1540.

Beaman, L., Duflo, E., Pande, R., and Topalova, P. 2012. Female leadership raises aspirations and educational attainment for girls: A policy experiment in India. *Science* 335, 582–586.

Bertrand, M., Black, S.E., Jensen, S., and Lleras-Muney, A. 2019. Breaking the glass ceiling? The effect of board quotas on female labour market outcomes in Norway. *The Review of Economic Studies* 86, 191–239.

Bertrand, M. and Duflo, E. 2017. Field experiments on discrimination. In E. Duflo and A. Banerjee (Eds.), *Handbook of field experiments* (Vol. 1). Amsterdam: North-Holland, 309–393.

Beyer, S. 1990. Gender differences in the accuracy of self-evaluations of performance. *Journal of Personality and Social Psychology* 59, 960.

Bilén, D., Dreber, A., and Johannesson, M. 2020. Are women more generous than men? A meta-analysis. Available at SSRN: http://dx.doi.org/10.2139/ssrn.3578038

Blau, F.D. and Kahn, L.M. 2017. The gender wage gap: Extent, trends, and explanations. *Journal of Economic Literature* 55, 789–865.

Bohnet, I. 2016. *What works: Gender equality by design.* Cambridge, MA: Harvard University Press.

Bonin, H., Dohmen, T., Falk, A., Huffman, D., and Sunde, U. 2007. Cross-sectional earnings risk and occupational sorting: The role of risk attitudes. *Labour Economics* 14, 926–937.

Booth, A. and Nolen, P. 2012a. Choosing to compete: How different are girls and boys? *Journal of Economic Behavior and Organization* 81, 542–555.

Booth, A. and Nolen, P. 2012b. Gender differences in risk behavior: Does nurture matter? *Economic Journal* 122, F56–F78.

Bordalo, P., Coffman, K., Glennaiolli, N., and Shleifer, A. 2019. Beliefs about gender. *American Economic Review* 109, 739–773.

Boring, A. 2017. Gender biases in student evaluations of teaching. *Journal of Public Economics* 145, 27–41.

Born, A., Ranehill, E., and Sandberg, A. 2019. A man's world? The impact of a male dominated environment on female leadership. University of Gothenburg, Working Paper in Economics No. 744.

Bowles, H.R., Babcock, L., and Lai, L. 2007. Social incentives for gender differences in the propensity to initiate negotiations: Sometimes it does hurt to ask. *Organizational Behavior and Human Decision Processes* 103, 84–103.

Brooks, A.W., Huang, L., Kearney, S.W., and Murray, F.E. 2014. Investors prefer entrepreneurial ventures pitched by attractive men. *Proceedings of the National Academy of Sciences* 11, 4427–4431.

Buser, T., Niederle, M., and Oosterbeek, H. 2014. Gender, competitiveness, and career choices. *The Quarterly Journal of Economics* 129, 1409–1447.

Buser, T., Peter, N., and Wolter, S.C. 2017. Gender, competitiveness, and study choices in high school: Evidence from Switzerland. *American Economic Review* 107, 125–130.

Byrnes, J.P., Miller, D.C., and Schafer, W.D. 1999. Gender differences in risk taking: A meta-analysis. *Psychological Bulletin* 125, 367.

Carli, L.L. 2001. Gender and social influence. *Journal of Social Issues* 57, 725–741.

Carpenter, J., Frank, R., and Huet-Vaughn, E. 2018. Gender differences in interpersonal and intrapersonal competitive behavior. *Journal of Behavioral and Experimental Economics* 77, 170–176.

Casas-Arce, P. and Saiz, A. 2015. Women and power: Unpopular, unwilling, or held back? *Journal of Political Economy* 123, 641–669.

Cason, T., Gangadharan, L., and Grossman, P.J. 2020. Gender, beliefs, and coordination with externalities. Monash University, working paper.

Cassar, A., Wordofa, F., and Zhang, Y.J. 2016. Competing for the benefit of offspring eliminates the gender gap in competitiveness. *Proceedings of the National Academy of Sciences* 113, 5201–5205.

Castillo, M., Petrie, R., and Torero, M. 2010. On the preferences of principals and agents. *Economic Inquiry* 48, 266–273.

Chakraborty, P. and Serra, D. 2019. Gender differences in top leadership roles: Does worker backlash matter? Department of Economics, Southern Methodist University, working paper.

Chattopadhyay, R. and Duflo, E. 2004. Women as policy makers: Evidence from a ran-domized policy experiment in India. *Econometrica* 72, 1409–1443.

Chauvin, K.W. and Ash, R.A. 1994. Gender earnings differentials in total pay, base pay, and contingent pay. *ILR Review* 47, 634–649.

Chen, J. and Houser, D. 2019. When are women willing to lead? The effect of team gender composition and gendered tasks. *Leadership Quarterly* 30, 101340.

Coffman, K.B. 2014. Evidence on self-stereotyping and the contribution of ideas. *The Quarterly Journal of Economics* 129, 1625–1660.

Coffman, K.B., Collis, M., and Kulkarni, L. 2020. When to apply? Harvard Business School working paper.

Coffman, K.B., Exley, C.L., and Niederle, M. 2020. The role of beliefs in driving gender discrimination. Harvard Business School, Working Paper No. 18-054.

Croson, R. and Gneezy, U. 2009. Gender differences in preferences. *Journal of Economic Literature* 47, 448–74.

De Paola, M., Ponzo, M., and Scoppa, V. 2017. Gender differences in the propensity to apply for promotion: Evidence from the Italian Scientific Qualification. *Oxford Economic Papers* 69, 986–1009.

Dittrich, M., Knabe, A., and Leipold, K. 2014. Gender differences in experimental wage negotiations. *Economic Inquiry* 52, 862–873.

Dreber, A., von Essen, E., and Ranehill, E. 2014. Gender and competition in adoles-cence: Task matters. *Experimental Economics* 17, 154–172.

Eagly, A.H., Karau, S.J., and Makhijani, M.G. 1995. Gender and the effectiveness of leaders: A meta-analysis. *Psychological Bulletin* 117, 125–145.

Eckel, C. and Candelo, N. 2020. How to tame lab-in-the-field experiments. In J.N. Druckman and D.P. Green (Eds.), *Advances in experimental political science.* Cambridge, UK: Cambridge University Press, 79–102.

Eckel, C., de Oliveira, A.C.M., and Grossman, P.J. 2008. Gender and negotiation in the small: Are women (perceived to be) more cooperative than men? *Negotiation Journal* 24, 429–445.

Eckel, C.C. and Grossman, P.J. 2002. Sex differences and statistical stereotyping in attitudes toward financial risk. *Evolution and Human Behavior* 23, 281–295.

Eckel, C.C. and Grossman, P.J. 2008. Men, women and risk aversion: Experimental evidence. In C.R. Plott and V.L. Smith (Eds.), *Handbook of experimental economics results.* Amsterdam: North Holland/Elsevier Press, 1061–1073.

England, P., Budig, M., and Folbre, N. 2002. Wages of virtue: The relative pay of care work. *Social Problems* 49, 455–473.

Eriksson, K.H. and Sandberg, A. 2012. Gender differences in initiation of negotiation: Does the gender of the negotiation counterpart matter? *Negotiation Journal* 28, 407–428.

Erkal, N., Gangadharan, L., and Koh, B.H. 2020. Gender biases and performance evaluation: Do outcomes matter more than intentions? Monash University, working paper.

Erkal, N., Gangadharan, L., and Xiao, E. 2019. Leadership selection: Can changing the default break the glass ceiling? Monash University, working paper.

Ertac, S., Gumren, M., and Gurdal, M.Y. 2019. Demand for decision autonomy and the desire to avoid responsibility in risky environments: Experimental evidence. *Journal of Economic Psychology*, 102200.

Ertac, S. and Gurdal, M.Y. 2012. Deciding to decide: Gender, leadership and risk-taking in groups. *Journal of Economic Behavior and Organization* 83, 24–30.

Exley, C.L. and Kessler, J. 2019. The gender gap in self-promotion. NBER, Working Paper No. w26345.

Exley, C.L., Niederle, M., and Vesterlund, L. 2020. Knowing when to ask: The cost of leaning in. *Journal of Political Economy* 128, 816–854.

Falk, A. and Hermle, J. 2018. Relationship of gender differences in preferences to economic development and gender equality. *Science* 362, 6412.

Filippin, A. and Crosetto, P. 2016. A reconsideration of gender differences in risk attitudes. *Management Science* 62, 3138–3160.

Folbre, N. (Ed.). 2012. *For love or money: Care provision in the United States*. New York: Russell Sage Foundation.

Gangadharan, L., Jain, T., Maitra, P., and Vecci, J. 2016. Social identity and governance: The behavioral response to female leaders. *European Economic Review* 90, 302–325.

Gangadharan, L., Jain, T., Maitra, P., and Vecci, J. 2019. Female leaders and their response to the social environment. *Journal of Economic Behavior and Organization* 164, 256–272.

Gillet, J., Cartwright, E., and Van Vugt, M. 2011. Selfish or servant leadership? Evolutionary predictions on leadership personalities in coordination games. *Personality and Individual Differences* 51, 231–236.

Gneezy, U., Leonard, K.L., and List, J.A. 2009. Gender differences in competition: Evidence from a matrilineal and patriarchal society. *Econometrica* 77, 1637–1664.

Gneezy, U. and Potters, J. 1997. An experiment on risk taking and evaluation periods. *The Quarterly Journal of Economics* 112, 631–645.

Goldin, C. and Rouse, C. 2000. Orchestrating impartiality: The impact of "blind" auditions on female musicians. *American Economic Review* 90, 715–741.

Grossman, P.J. 2013. Holding fast: The persistence and dominance of gender stereotypes. *Economic Inquiry* 51, 747–763.

Grossman, P.J., Eckel, C., Komai, M. and Zhan, W. 2019. It pays to be a man: Rewards for leaders in a coordination game. *Journal of Economic Behavior and Organization* 161, 197–215.

Grossman, P.J., Komai, M., and Jensen, J.E. 2015. Leadership and gender in groups: An experiment. *Canadian Journal of Economics/Revue canadienne d'économique* 48, 368–388.

Grossman, P.J. and Lugovskyy, O. 2011. An experimental test of the persistence of gender-based stereotypes. *Economic Inquiry* 49, 598–611.

He, J., Kang, S., and Lacetera, N. 2019. Leaning in or not leaning out? Opt-out choice framing attenuates gender differences in the decision to compete. NBER, Working Paper No. 26484.

Hernandez-Arenaz, I. and Iriberri, N. 2019a. A review of gender differences in negotiation. *Oxford research encyclopedia of economics and finance*. https://oxfordre.com/economics/view/10.1093/acrefore/9780190625979.001.0001/acrefore-9780190625979-e-464

Hernandez-Arenaz, I. and Iriberri, N. 2019b. Gender differences in alternating-offer bargaining: An experimental study. Retrieved from https://www.socialscien ceregistry.org/trials/

Holt, C.A. and Laury, S.K. 2002. Risk aversion and incentive effects. *American Economic Review* 92, 1644–1655.

Inzlicht, M. and Ben-Zeev, T. 2000. A threatening intellectual environment: Why females are susceptible to experiencing problem-solving deficits in the presence of males. *Psychological Science* 11, 365–371.

Ip, E., Leibbrandt, A., and Vecci, J. 2020. How do gender quotas affect workplace relationships? Complementary evidence from a representative survey and labor market experiments. *Management Science* 66, 805–822.

Jianakoplos, N.A. and Bernasek, A. 1998. Are women more risk averse? *Economic Inquiry* 36, 620–630.

Jiang, B. and Capra, C.M. 2018. Are (active) entrepreneurs a different breed? *Managerial and Decision Economics* 39, 613–628.

Johnson, S.K., Murphy, S.E., Zewdie, S., and Reichard, R.J. 2008. The strong, sensitive type: Effects of gender stereotypes and leadership prototypes on the evaluation of male and female leaders. *Organizational Behavior and Human Decision Processes* 106, 39–60.

Jung, S., Choe, C., and Oaxaca, R.L. 2018. Gender wage gaps and risky vs. secure employment: An experimental analysis. *Labour Economics* 52, 112–121.

Kamas, L. and Preston, A. 2018. Competing with confidence: The ticket to labor market success for college-educated women. *Journal of Economic Behavior and Organization* 155, 231–252.

Kanthak, K. and Woon, J. 2015. Women don't run? Election aversion and candidate entry. *American Journal of Political Science* 59, 595–612.

Leibbrandt, A., and List, J.A. 2015. Do women avoid salary negotiations? Evidence from a large-scale natural field experiment. *Management Science* 61, 2016–2024.

Leibbrandt, A., Wang, L.C., and Foo, C. 2018. Gender quotas, competitions, and peer review: Experimental evidence on the backlash against women. *Management Science* 64, 3501–3516.

Li, S., Chaudhuri, A., and Sbai, E. 2020. (Un)Willing to lead? Men, women and the leadership gap. University of Auckland, working paper.

Maggian, V., Montinari, N., and Nicolò, A. (2020). Do quotas help women to climb the career ladder? A laboratory experiment. *European Economic Review* 123, 103390.

McGreevy, P. 2018, September 30. Gov. Jerry Brown signs bill requiring California corporate boards to include women. *Los Angeles Times*. Retrieved from https://www .latimes.com/politics/la-pol-ca-governor-women-corporate-boards-20180930-story .html

Moss-Racusin, C.A., Dovidio, J.F., Brescoll, V.L., Graham, M.J., and Handelsman, J. 2012. Science faculty's subtle gender biases favor male students. *Proceedings of the National Academy of Science* 109, 16474–16479.

Murray, R. 2008. The power of sex and incumbency: A longitudinal study of electoral performance in France. *Party Politics* 14, 539–554.

Niederle, M. 2015. Gender. In J.H. Kagel and A.E. Roth (Eds.), *The handbook of experimental economics* (Vol. 2). Princeton, NJ: Princeton University Press, 481–562.

Niederle, M. 2017. A gender agenda: A progress report on competitiveness. *American Economic Review: Papers and Proceedings* 107, 115–119.

Niederle, M., Segal, C., and Vesterlund, L. 2013. How costly is diversity? Affirmative action in light of gender differences in competitiveness. *Management Science* 59, 1–16.

Niederle, M. and Vesterlund, L. 2007. Do women shy away from competition? Do men compete too much? *The Quarterly Journal of Economics* 122, 1067–1101.

O'Gorman, R., Henrich, J., and Van Vugt, M. 2008. Constraining free riding in public goods games: designated solitary punishers can sustain human cooperation. *Proceedings of the Royal Society of London B: Biological Sciences* 276, 323–329.

Ortmann, A. and Tichy, L.K. 1999. Gender differences in the laboratory: evidence from prisoner's dilemma games. *Journal of Economic Behavior and Organization* 39, 327–339.

Petrie, R. and Segal, C. 2015. Gender differences in competitiveness: The role of prizes. Retrieved from https://papers.ssrn.com/sol3/Data_Integrity_Notice.cfm?abid=2520052

Preece, J. and Stoddard, O. 2015. Why women don't run: Experimental evidence on gender differences in political competition aversion. *Journal of Economic Behavior and Organization* 117, 296–308.

Propp, K.M. 1995. An experimental examination of biological sex as a status cue in decision-making groups and its influence on information use. *Small Group Research* 26, 451–474.

Reuben, E., Rey-Biel, P., Sapienza, P., and Zingales, L. 2012. The emergence of male leadership in competitive environments. *Journal of Economic Behavior and Organization* 83, 111–117.

Reuben, E., Sapienza, P., and Zingales, L. 2015. Taste for competition and the gender gap among young business professionals. NBER, Working Paper No. w21695.

Reuben, E. and Timko, K. 2018. On the effectiveness of elected male and female leaders and team coordination. *Journal of the Economic Science Association* 4, 123–135.

Ridgeway, C.L. 2001. Gender, status, and leadership. *Journal of Social Issues* 57, 637–55.

Ridgeway, C.L., Johnson, C., and Diekema, D. 1994. External status, legitimacy, and compliance in male and female groups. *Social Forces* 72, 1051–1077.

Sandberg, S. 2013. *Lean in: Women, work and the will to lead*. London: W.H. Allen.

Sarsons, H., Gerxhani, K., Reuben, E., and Schram, A. 2020. Gender differences in recognition for group work. *Journal of Political Economy* 129, 101–147.

Shurchkov, O. and Eckel, C.C. 2018. Gender differences in behavioral traits and labor market outcomes. In S.L. Averett, L.M. Argys, and S.D. Hoffman (Eds.), *The Oxford handbook of women and the economy*. Oxford: Oxford University Press, 481–512.

Small, D.A., Gelfand, M., Babcock, L., and Gettman, H. 2007. Who goes to the bargaining table? The influence of gender and framing on the initiation of negotiation. *Journal of Personality and Social Psychology* 93, 600–613.

Taub, A. 2020. Why are women-led nations doing better with COVID-19? *New York Times*. Retrieved from https://www.nytimes.com/2020/05/15/world/coronavirus-women-leaders.html

Tonin, M. and Vlassopoulos, M. 2015. Are public sector workers different? Cross-European evidence from elderly workers and retirees. *IZA Journal of Labor Economics* 4, 11.

8 Experiments in political psychology

Kyle Fischer, Quentin D. Atkinson, and Ananish Chaudhuri

1.   Introduction

The political scientist Harold Lasswell famously described politics as the process of deciding "who gets what, when, and how". This suggests that the subject should be amenable to being studied with the aid of incentivised experiments where participants can earn real money based on the decisions they make. However, while commonplace in social psychology, the use of such experiments is still relatively rare in political psychology, with scholars largely relying on survey questions. While surveys can certainly be useful for understanding issues in political psychology, they also suffer from drawbacks. For example, surveys may not always reveal private preferences that participants would display in the absence of real-world social and cultural constraints (Pisor et al., 2020). In contrast, the presence of real monetary incentives in predominantly abstract and anonymous economic games can reveal true preferences, such as the willingness to share. Consequently, behavioural economists tend to stress the value and importance of incentivised experiments (Chaudhuri, 2009; Smith, 1976, 1982).

Increasingly, researchers across a wide range of disciplines are turning towards experiments as a validated means of testing theoretical predictions. In this chapter, we provide an overview of the use of incentivised experiments in political psychology, with an emphasis on the intertwined set of political beliefs, values, and attitudes that may be collectively referred to as political ideology. In doing so, we hope to facilitate a fruitful dialogue with researchers in political psychology who may wish to explore the use of economic experiments (conceivably in conjunction with survey instruments) to study the basic dispositional antecedents of political ideology.

Traditionally, political scientists have tended to take a unidimensional view of political ideology, placing people along a liberal–conservative (left–right) spectrum. Liberals are generally more open to novelty, more egalitarian, and more supportive of redistributive policies, while conservatives are more concerned with preserving and enforcing traditional values, group conformity, and justifying existing hierarchies (e.g. Jost et al., 2003). However, scholars across diverse disciplines have repeatedly and independently found two primary dimensions of political ideology, often referred to as economic conservatism (vs. economic progressivism), and social conservatism (vs. social progressivism; see Claessens, Fischer et al., 2020, for details).

Recently, Claessens, Fischer et al. (2020) showed that there is a striking concordance between these dual dimensions of ideology and independent evidence for two key shifts in the evolution of human group living. First, humans began to cooperate more widely. Second, humans became more group minded, conforming to and enforcing social norms in culturally marked groups. Claessens, Fischer et al. (2020) propose that fitness trade-offs and environmental pressures have maintained variation in these tendencies to cooperate and conform, naturally giving rise to the two dimensions of political ideology. We begin our overview by looking at experimental studies that take a unidimensional view of politics. We then discuss studies that use incentivised experiments to explore the dual foundations of political ideology. Finally, we conclude with some thoughts on what we found in this chapter.

2. Experimental Studies of Unidimensional Political Ideology

In this section, we provide an overview of experimental studies that adopt a unidimensional view of political ideology along a single left–right continuum. We divide our discussion into two subsections: one looking at pro-sociality, referring to cooperation, compassion, trust, reciprocity, altruism, generosity, and egalitarianism in both individual and group contexts, and a second that focusses on compliance with established norms and punishment of norm-violators.

2.1 Pro-Sociality

Anderson et al. (2004) recruited a small sample of undergraduates in the US to play multiple rounds of trust and public goods games,[1] and found that Democrats or self-described liberals were no more pro-social than were

Republicans or self-described conservatives. Liberals were, however, more pro-social in the trust game when the experimenters induced inequality by giving some participants a higher endowment than others, suggesting that liberals' pro-sociality is connected to an aversion to inequality.

In another US study with a larger, more representative sample, there was no significant relationship between political ideology (self-described and measured with a Wilson–Patterson Inventory of Attitudes) and pro-sociality in the ultimatum game and a common-pool resource extraction game (Alford & Hibbing, 2007). Similarly, recent studies with relatively large samples have found no significant differences in pro-sociality between self-described left- and right-leaning people in public goods games in Germany (Kistler et al., 2017), dictator games in the Netherlands (Thomsson & Vostroknutov, 2017), and prisoner's dilemmas in the US (Balliet et al., 2018). Moreover, Müller (2019) found that neither self-described left- nor right-leaning people displayed in-group-biased cooperation in a study using a dictator game and the "minimal group paradigm" (in this case, assigning participants to groups based on their artistic taste).

Interestingly, the Balliet et al. (2018) study referred to above also varied whether participants were playing with Democrats or Republicans in two-person prisoner's dilemmas, and found that both Democrats and Republicans displayed in-group-biased cooperation mediated by trust that co-partisans would reciprocate. Other studies also found that partisans on both sides of the left–right spectrum, especially those who strongly identify with their party, gave more to co-partisans in the dictator game in the US, the UK, Canada, and Sweden (Dawes et al., 2012; Fowler & Kam, 2007), and this tendency was more pronounced among left-wing partisans (Dawes et al., 2012).

Given the political polarisation in the West, it is not surprising that both liberals and conservatives show in-group bias in games where political groups are salient. What is less intuitive is that both liberals and conservatives who are more politically engaged/extreme/partisan (Dawes et al., 2011; Fehr et al., 2003; Fowler & Kam, 2007; Müller & Renes, 2020; Smirnov et al., 2010) tend to be more pro-social in economic games devoid of political content. This may be partly explained by the fact that the very act of engaging in political activities is a collective action problem, and those who become so engaged on both sides are likely to be more pro-social to begin with.

However, a number of more recent studies, including several based on large sample sizes, provide evidence in favour of greater pro-social tendencies on the political left. Recent German studies found that: (1) left-leaning players in a modified dictator game were more pro-social (n = 116; Müller, 2019); (2) people in large, diverse samples on the political left (self-described and determined by political party support) were more inclined to be egalitarian when playing as "third-party" allocators (n = 2 189; Müller & Renes, 2020), and (3) left-leaning people were likely to be characterised by benevolent traits, like altruism and advantageous inequity aversion (a dislike of having more than others) in two-person games, whereas right-leaning people were likely to be characterised as "selfish", "spiteful", and "envious" (n = 2 794; Kerschbamer & Müller, 2020); (4) left-leaning people (self-described and measured by political party support) displayed more pro-social behaviour in public goods and trust games (n = 454; Grünhage & Reuter, 2020). In addition, people who reported voting for the left-wing coalition government in Norway were more generous in dictator games (Cappelen et al., 2017), and in Denmark, Fosgaard et al. (2019) undertook a study with 1 926 participants and found that, in a public goods game, self-described left-leaning people contributed slightly (albeit not statistically significantly) more than self-described right-leaning people, but this difference reached statistical significance when the game was framed as taking from the public good. It is possible that the latter framing, which essentially turns the game into a common-pool resource extraction game, elicits greater cooperation from left-leaning participants given their proclivity for being more environmentally conscious.

The greater pro-sociality of liberals is not limited to Europe. In an ambitious cross-country study, Dawes et al. (2012) recruited over 5 000 participants from the US, the UK, Canada, and Sweden to play a dictator game. Self-described left-leaning (vs. right-leaning) people were more generous in the US, the UK, and Sweden (left–right ideology was not measured in Canada), and people who voted for left-wing (vs. right-wing) parties in Canada and Sweden were more generous. However, in the US, there were no differences between Democrats and Republicans, and in the UK, supporters of the left-wing Labour party were less generous than were Tories and Liberal Democrats, who tend to be more right leaning.

Finally, studies conducted in the US, Italy, and the Netherlands (n = 3 314) relying on the Social Value Orientation (SVO) measure of pro-sociality (involving non-incentivised decomposed prisoner's dilemmas) and measuring unidimensional political ideology with self-placement, attitude scales, and/or party support, reveal that left-leaning people are more likely to be classified as pro-social, while the right-leaning tend to be pro-self (Balliet et al., 2018; Chirumbolo et al., 2016; Sheldon & Nichols, 2009; van Lange et al., 2012).

2.2 Norm Compliance and Punishment of Norm Violators

To our knowledge, only three studies have looked at the role of political ideology in terms of norm compliance and punishment of norm violations. In a recently developed computerised Rule Following Task, participants drag and drop balls into two buckets where every ball put in Bucket A yields, for example, $0.10, and every ball put in Bucket B yields half that amount. Participants are explicitly instructed that the rule is to put the balls in Bucket B. Therefore, the task measures willingness to pay a cost to follow an explicit rule, which is interpreted as social norm compliance (Kimbrough & Vostroknutov, 2018). A study using the Rule Following Task found no difference between political liberals and conservatives in rule-following behaviour (Thomsson & Vostroknutov, 2017). Interestingly, this study also investigated the norms that left- and right-leaning individuals held about giving in a dictator game, and found that, while giving behaviour did not differ between left- and right-leaning people, their motives for giving did – right-leaning people seemed more concerned about their reputations as norm followers in the eyes of the recipients.

Putterman et al. (2011) measured political attitudes of 80 undergraduates in the US and examined whether, in a public goods game, they would vote for efficient centralised sanctioning schemes to punish free-riding and encourage their groupmates to contribute. The authors report that political conservatives were less likely to vote for centralised punishments, a finding that may be related to the right's preference for greater self-reliance and smaller bureaucracies (at least in the US).

Using student participants (n = 120), Smirnov et al. (2010) examined whether partisans (those who explicitly identify as Democrat/Republican or strong Democrat/Republican) would display both cooperative and punitive behaviour in public goods and random income games with the option of decentralised punishments. Both Republican and Democratic partisans were more likely than non-partisans to punish high-income players in the random income game and low-contributing players in the public goods game. That is, partisans on both sides of the left–right political spectrum seem inclined to engage in costly norm enforcement. One of the evolutionary functions of norm-enforcement is thought to be the facilitation of group cooperation and cohesion, especially during intergroup competition. Given the intense political polarisation prevalent in the West (i.e. the tribalism on, and competition between, the political left and right), it is not surprising that norm enforcers are prevalent on both sides.

2.3   Summary

Taken together, the previous literature shows that political liberals tend to be more pro-social compared to political conservatives in economic games, but – going against the hypothesis that conservatives are more group minded and conformist (Jost, 2017) – there tend to be no significant differences between liberals and conservatives in terms of in-group bias, norm-following, and norm-enforcing behaviours (except one study showing that conservatives are less likely to vote for strict centralised sanctioning schemes). However, as we note above, this unidimensional view of political ideology is, if not incorrect, at least incomplete. We now turn to studies that acknowledge the two distinct dimensions of political ideology.

3.   Experimental Studies of Two-Dimensional Political Ideology and Related Variables

According to the Dual-Process Model of political ideology (Duckitt & Sibley, 2009, 2017), economic conservatism – widely measured with the Social Dominance Orientation (SDO) scale – sees the world as a competitive jungle and reflects hierarchy-enhancing views. This economic dimension of ideology is associated (either positively or negatively) with constructs such as the "individualising" (i.e. "care" and "fairness") moral foundations (Nilsson & Erlandsson, 2015; Federico et al., 2013), empathic concern and compassion (Chiao et al., 2009; Hirsh et al., 2010; Osborne et al., 2013), scores on Dark Triad scales (narcissism, Machiavellianism, and psychopathy; Jones & Figueredo, 2013), HEXACO honesty-humility (Duckitt & Sibley, 2017), justice sensitivity (i.e. inequality aversion and social justice activism; Reese et al., 2014), and even physical formidability, with physically stronger males more likely to be economic conservatives (Petersen & Laustsen, 2019). For example, those who score higher on the SDO scale are typically less empathic and more comfortable with social hierarchies and economic inequality.

Social conservatism – often measured with the right-wing authoritarianism (RWA) scale – sees the world as a dangerous place and reflects conformity- and cohesion-enhancing views that aim to conserve and enforce existing group norms (e.g. religious family values). This social dimension of ideology is positively correlated with dispositional variables related to group mindedness, such as a need for security, certainty, and conformity (Duckitt & Sibley, 2009; Federico & Malka, 2018); sensitivity to threats in the environment, such as terrorism and pandemics (Shaffer & Duckitt, 2013; Fischer, Chaudhuri, &

Atkinson, 2020); and neurobiological variables related to threat sensitivity, like a greater eyeblink startle response (Oxley et al., 2008).

Recently, Claessens, Fischer et al. (2020) provided an evolutionary account of how these two dimensions of political ideology came about as a response to the essential challenges of human group living. These authors point out two key shifts (Tomasello et al., 2012). The first of these required humans to cooperate more across wider interdependent networks and share the spoils of cooperation more evenly. This resulted in a human mind that was sensitive to the benefits of cooperative interactions with others and could extend cooperation beyond immediate genetic kin. However, cooperation is a collective action problem that is vulnerable to free-riding from opportunists. Thus, in a second key shift, as group sizes and intergroup competition increased, humans became more group minded, conforming to social norms in culturally marked groups and punishing norm-violators, thereby facilitating group cohesion and long-term group viability. Claessens, Fischer et al. (2020) argue that behavioural plasticity and the fitness trade-offs between cooperation and self-interested competition, on the one hand, and between conformity and individualism, on the other, maintain variation between individuals in human groups in terms of motivations to cooperate and conform. These individual differences in cooperativeness and conformity manifest in contemporary human populations as individual differences along the economic and social dimensions of political ideology, respectively.

Below, we review studies that focus on the dual foundations of political ideology by looking separately at the economic and social dimensions. Given that this is a new and emerging area of research, the literature here is not voluminous, with many open research questions providing avenues for further studies. In many instances, researchers have undertaken studies that imply one or both of these dual dimensions without explicitly referring to them as such. We have categorised these studies and results as systematically as possible using the dual foundations schema developed above.

3.1 Experimental Studies of Economic Conservatism/ Progressivism

3.1.1 Pro-Sociality

Little work has examined the behaviour of people with economically conservative vs. economically progressive[2] policy preferences, but there is some evidence that the latter tend to be more pro-social. Those who support increasing taxes to help the worse off (an economically progressive position) display cooperative behaviour across a battery of games (Peysakhovich et al., 2014), and compared to economic conservatives, economic progressives are more pro-social in dictator games in the US and UK (Dawes et al., 2012), and in two-person games in Germany (Kerschbamer & Müller, 2020).

A number of studies have looked at the relation between economic conservatism/progressivism measured with the SDO scale and pro-sociality. In two studies with undergraduate students in Belgium, SDO was negatively correlated with pro-sociality in many, but not all, economic games (Haesevoets et al., 2015, 2018). In the first study, it was significantly negatively related to pro-sociality in the dictator, commons dilemma, and one-shot public goods games, but it was not in the prisoner's dilemma, ultimatum, trust, stag hunt, and iterative public goods games. In the second study, SDO was significantly negatively related to pro-sociality across payoff structures in prisoner's dilemma games. The patterns across these studies were similar for RWA in that it negatively predicted pro-sociality in a subset of games.

One reason why SDO does not correlate with pro-sociality across all games could be that not all the games measure pro-sociality to the same extent (e.g. the dictator game is arguably a cleaner measure of pro-sociality, while for social dilemmas, the notion of pro-sociality may be intermingled with other strategic considerations and beliefs about others' actions). Another potential confound is that studies do not control for RWA (SDO) when exploring SDO's (RWA's) relationship with pro-sociality. This is important because RWA and SDO, or social and economic conservatism, are reliably correlated in the West and suppress each other's effects on external variables (see Costello & Lilienfeld, 2020). Claessens, Sibley et al. (2020) accounted for this and recruited a much larger, representative sample (n = 926) in New Zealand to examine whether SDO and RWA, controlling for demographic variables, differentially predicted cooperative and punitive latent variables (behavioural phenotypes) across a battery of economic games. They found that SDO (not RWA) significantly negatively predicted pro-sociality across the dictator, trust, ultimatum, public goods, stag hunt, and other games. Unlike Haesevoets et al. (2015, 2018), this shows that individual differences in a general cooperative phenotype that applies across games with different payoff structures predict individual differences in SDO, and not RWA.

Claessens, Sibley et al. (2020) also looked at Schwartz's values, which correspond to the two dimensions of political ideology, with "self-enhancement" vs. "self-transcendence" values reflecting economic conservatism vs. economic progressivism, and "conservation" vs. "openness" values reflecting social conservatism vs. social progressivism. They found that, controlling for demographics, self-enhancement (self-transcendence) significantly negatively (positively) predicted the cooperative phenotype, while conservation and openness values were unrelated to this. Evidence from earlier work generally supports this, with self-enhancement values tending to be positively associated with selfish behaviour, self-transcendent values with pro-sociality, and conservation and openness values tending to be unrelated to pro-sociality in different games (Gärling, 1999; Sagiv et al., 2011).

A recent meta-analysis confirms that SDO is significantly negatively correlated with pro-social behaviour aggregated across a number of economic games (Thielmann et al., 2020). Moreover, variables positively associated with SDO – like the Dark Triad, competitiveness, and power – as well as negatively associated with SDO – such as concern for others, inequity-aversion, agreeableness, honesty-humility, and empathy – are significantly related to pro-sociality (Thielmann et al., 2020). A recent German study not included in the meta-analysis above also shows that SDO mediated the relationship between left–right political affiliation and pro-social behaviour in a public goods game, while RWA mediated this relationship for a trust game (Grünhage & Reuter, 2020). Moreover, studies using the SVO measure of pro-sociality show that SDO tends to be more strongly and consistently negatively correlated with pro-sociality than is RWA (Balliet et al., 2018; Chirumbolo et al., 2016; Haesevoets et al., 2015, 2018).

Another noteworthy set of studies looks at the connection between pro-sociality and environmentalism. Given that environmental problems like climate change represent social dilemmas – a conflict between self-interest and cooperation – we expect economic conservatives, compared to economic progressives, to be less willing to make sacrifices for the environment. Indeed, environmentalism is more strongly negatively associated with SDO than RWA (Häkkinen & Akrami, 2014; Milfont et al., 2013, 2018; Stanley et al., 2019), and is positively associated with pro-social behaviour in economic games (Barclay & Barker, 2020; Kaiser & Byrka, 2011; Thielmann et al., 2020).

Finally, and in keeping with the concept of behavioural plasticity elucidated in the dual evolutionary foundations model of political ideology, pro-social behaviour is often influenced by situational cues. People low in honesty-humility, who tend to be high in SDO (Duckitt & Sibley, 2017), cooperate more in public goods games when they face the possibility of punishment by their peers (Hilbig et al., 2012). Moreover, high-SDO individuals are particularly competitive and display increased greed, effort, and rule breaking in situations of resource scarcity (Cozzolino & Snyder, 2008). However, people in general tend to become more cooperative with resource abundance (Nettle et al., 2011) and when dominance hierarchies based on self-interest or effort/ skill are removed or replaced with hierarchies based on altruism (Antonioni et al., 2018; Cronin et al., 2015); this may apply to high-SDO individuals as well.

3.1.2   Inequality

A major facet of the economic dimension of political ideology is inequality aversion, including redistributive preferences. Esarey et al. (2012) under-took a study where undergraduates could earn money by completing a multiple-choice spelling test, and then vote for different redistributive tax schemes. The money earned for the task was based on effort and skill (the task was difficult, tedious, performed under deadline pressure, and some people were better at it). There were also different conditions, a fair one (everyone got the same amount/penalty per correctly/incorrectly spelled word), one with inequality based on luck (subjects were randomly assigned to get a low or high pay rate), and one with inequality based on effort/skill in the task (after the first two periods, the top 50% of spellers got a higher pay rate than the bottom 50%). The results revealed that, regardless of condition, everyone tended to be self-interested, voting for higher taxes when they were poor and lower taxes when they were rich, but economic conservatives tended to be more self-interested than were economic progressives.

While the Esarey et al. (2012) study supports the view that economic conserv-atives tend to be more pro-self, it does not find differences between economic conservatives and economic progressives in terms of redistributive preferences. Since redistribution preferences are a defining feature of the economic dimen-sion of ideology, future experiments should study this by varying aspects of the social situation (e.g. wealth can be based on effort, skill, or luck, and redistri-bution can be based on equality or need). There is already suggestive evidence that such an approach will be fruitful. While Pratto et al. (1999) examined allocation decisions in hypothetical scenarios as opposed to economic games, they found that high-SDO individuals believe that fairness involves rewarding the meritorious, and they allocate more resources to meritorious parties; in contrast, low-SDO individuals believe that fairness involves helping the needy, and they allocate more resources to needy parties. Furthermore, social justice activism – a well-known correlate of economic progressivism – predicts giving mostly to recipients from disadvantaged groups in modified dictator games (Fietzer et al., 2016).

Other fruitful approaches seem to be the use of two-person games wherein participants are presented with various binary choices and must decide how to allocate points between themselves and another person, as well as third-party games. Recent studies with large, diverse samples in Germany found that people with economically progressive views (such as endorsing increased income tax or government intervention to reduce inequality) tend to display egalitarian behaviour in such two-person games (Kerschbamer & Müller, 2020) as well as when acting as impartial third-party allocators (Müller & Renes, 2020). Moreover, recent research using a third-party punishment game shows that people high in "dominance value orientation" (a composite of Individual Dominance Orientation, i.e. the degree to which a person values hierarchical relations between individuals, and SDO) seem to want to uphold inequalities between others by punishing people who make egalitarian offers to others (Bergh & Sidanius, 2020). In contrast, people low in dominance value orientation tend to punish people who make selfish offers to others. Finally, in third-party games where the participants witness one player financially harming another and can then help the victim or punish the perpetrator, well-known correlates of economic progressivism (justice sensitivity, empathic concern, compassion, and the fairness moral foundation) are related to helping victims but not consistently related to punishing perpetrators (Baumert et al., 2014; Weng et al., 2015; Leliveld et al., 2012; Zhao et al., 2017), perhaps because this relationship depends on the relative status of victim and perpetrator (Mattan et al., 2020).

Overall, existing evidence suggests that economic conservatives tend to be more pro-self and tolerant of inequality (but may be happy with redistributing resources based on merit). In contrast, economic progressives tend to be more egalitarian and inclined to redistribute resources to help the disadvantaged and punish the privileged and/or exploitative.

3.1.3   Within- and Between-Group Competition

SDO can be conceptualised as reflecting views that enhance both individual- and group-level hierarchy. On the individual level, this should manifest as self-interested competitiveness, and on the group level, it should manifest as a desire to dominate out-groups. In experimental studies, researchers have tried to tease out intergroup preferences by having participants choose between two or more of the following options in modified social dilemma games: (1) self-interest, where the individual keeps their money and so does not make a personal sacrifice for their in-group, (2) "in-group love", where the individual sacrifices money to benefit the in-group but does not affect the out-group, (3) "out-group hate", where the individual sacrifices money to benefit the in-group and harm the out-group, and (4) universalism, where the individual sacrifices money to benefit both in-group and out-group members (Aaldering & Böhm, 2020; Fischer, Claessens, Chaudhuri et al., 2021; Halali et al., 2018). In such studies, group identity is either based on real groups (e.g. Jews vs. Palestinians) or manipulated via the minimal group paradigm (Tajfel & Turner, 1979).

Taken together, the results suggest that SDO is positively related to self-interest and out-group hate, unrelated to in-group love, and negatively related to universalism. Along similar lines, a study measuring vertical individualism, a competitive, status-seeking type of individualism related to economic conservatism (Claessens, Fischer et al., 2020), finds that given a choice between self-interest and in-group love, vertical individualists choose the former; in contrast, given a choice between self-interest and out-group hate, they choose the latter (Probst et al., 1999). Finally, Halevy et al. (2012) show that self-interest and out-group hate increase perceptions of dominance, while universalism decreases this.

3.2   Experimental Studies of Social Conservatism/Progressivism

3.2.1   Trust

In Section 3.1.1, we found that economic rather than social conservatism is consistently negatively related to pro-sociality in general (Claessens, Sibley et al., 2020; Thielmann et al., 2020), but it seems that social conservatism is more consistently negatively related to one specific kind of pro-sociality: trusting strangers. Early research using the "Fascism" scale to measure authoritarianism found that it was significantly negatively correlated with trusting behaviour in a two-person, non-zero-sum game (Deutsch, 1960). And more recently, many studies show that, compared to SDO, RWA is more reliably negatively related to trusting behaviour (Grünhage & Reuter, 2020; Haesevoets et al., 2015; Ponsi et al., 2017, but see Claessens, Sibley et al., 2020). In fact, a meta-analysis showed that, of all the widely used psychological variables (including trust propensity) other than SVO, RWA was the strongest correlate of distrustful behaviour in the trust game (Thielmann et al., 2020; supplemental materials).

Further evidence comes from studies that explore moral values. The mean of the binding moral foundations (in-group loyalty, respect for authority, and purity) that are associated with social conservatism (Nilsson & Erlandsson, 2015; Federico et al., 2013) significantly negatively correlates with behaviour in the trust game (Clark et al., 2017). Furthermore, secular values (non-traditional, non-religious), a proxy of social progressivism, in the World Values Survey are related to trusting (and efficient) behaviour in a property rights game (Kistler et al., 2017). This is in line with work showing that religiosity (an important correlate of social conservatism) seems to be associated with less trust and is not consistently associated with other kinds of pro-sociality (e.g. Jacquet et al., 2021). For example, a recent study found that religiosity is inversely related to trust in the trust game and not related to helping people in third-party games (Galen et al., 2020). This evidence suggests that social conservatives are relatively suspicious of anonymous strangers in economic games, which makes sense because social conservatism is conceptualised as relatively parochial and fearful, reflecting trust only for in-group members and wariness of outsiders (Claessens, Fischer et al., 2020).

3.2.2   Norm Following

Fischer, Chaudhuri, Fišar et al. (2021) use the Rule Following Task, developed by Kimbrough and Vostroknutov (2018), to measure whether social conservatives are willing to forego monetary gains in order to comply with an explicit rule they have been told to follow (see Section 2.2 for details on the task). They find that measures of the social dimension of ideology, such as RWA, support for cultural tightness (Jackson et al., 2019), and security and conformity values (Schwartz et al., 2012), are significantly related to rule-following behaviour (whereas SDO is only weakly negatively related to this).

Based on this result, indirect evidence on the social dimension of ideology can be garnered from how people who tend to follow rules in the Rule Following Task behave in subsequent public goods games. In one study (Gürdal et al., 2020), participants could choose between three groups with different rules (to put all, half, or any amount of their endowment into the common pool). Compared to rule breakers, rule followers tended to prefer groups with the strict rule to contribute the entire endowment and they followed the rules more (i.e. they cooperated more). In Kimbrough and Vostroknutov (2016), participants were either sorted into groups based on their rule-following behaviour or placed into groups at random. Groups of rule followers maintained higher levels of cooperation for longer periods compared to unsorted groups or groups of rule breakers. However, in unsorted groups, individual rule followers did not tend to contribute more than individual rule breakers. Combined, these studies show that rule followers prefer having strict rules in place, and when these rules state that they should cooperate at high levels, they do, and groups of rule followers are particularly good at maintaining high levels of cooperation.

There is also some evidence that, like rule followers, authoritarians contribute more in public goods games with strict, exogenously imposed contribution rules. In a study conducted in China – which is more collectivistic and accepting of authority and inequality compared to Western countries (Vollan et al.,

2017) – 300 people, including workers with a rural background and university students, played public goods games in three conditions: (1) normal, (2) authoritarian (with an exogenously imposed rule to contribute the entire endowment), and (3) democratic (players could vote to implement the rule). In contrast to previous work in the West that finds that democratically chosen rules work best at maintaining cooperation, the main result was that the exogenously imposed rule worked best, and participants higher in RWA cooperated more in this authoritarian condition; meanwhile, participants lower in RWA cooperated more in the democratic condition.

3.2.3   Norm Enforcement

Yamagishi et al. (2012) and a recent meta-analysis (Thielmann et al., 2020) show that RWA and the personality trait openness, which is linked to social progressivism (Duckitt & Sibley, 2017; Hirsh et al., 2010; Osborne et al., 2013), are related to punitive responses in the ultimatum game where participants are willing to forego money to punish another who is considered to be engaging in unfair behaviour. Moreover, Baumert et al. (2014) found that the "authority" moral foundation (linked to social conservatism) was positively associated with punishment in the ultimatum game (but not in a third-party punishment game). Moreover, Chuah et al. (2009) report that valuing individual freedom (corresponding to social progressivism) was associated with less punitiveness in the ultimatum game, while parochial attitudes (corresponding to social conservatism) were associated with more punitiveness.

Finally, threat sensitivity is a well-known correlate of social conservatism, and a recent study found that exposure to threat (violent crime) predicted punitive, not cooperative, behaviour across a battery of economic games (Littman et al., 2020). That is, threat coming from within the community seems to activate a norm-enforcing, punitive phenotype but not a cooperative one. However, Claessens, Sibley et al. (2020) did not find that RWA and conservation/openness values (that correspond to social conservatism/progressivism) generally predict a norm-enforcing, punitive phenotype.

The evidence covered here broadly supports the view that, compared to the economic dimension of ideology, the social dimension is more consistently related to punitiveness, at least in the ultimatum game. The reason that social conservatism and related variables are often associated with punitive behaviour in the ultimatum game may be that punitiveness in this game seems to reflect normative rather than pro-social or anti-social behaviour (Brañas-Garza et al., 2014; Brethel-Haurwitz et al., 2016; Yamagishi et al., 2012).[3]

3.2.4   In-Group Bias

Given that social conservatives are theoretically in-group-focussed and wary of cooperating with anonymous strangers, they should only cooperate with trusted in-group members with whom they feel interdependent, and not with out-group members in intergroup economic games. Those games (mentioned in Section 3.1.3), which ask participants to choose from self-interest, "in-group love", "out-group hate", and universalism, allow us to study the relationship between group mindedness and social conservatism. Recently, Fischer, Claessens, Chaudhuri et al. (2021) found that right-wing authoritarians tended to engage in in-group love (as well as identify with the artificial in-group) and out-group hate; RWA was unrelated to self-interest and universalism. An older study (also mentioned in Section 3.1.3) looked at the behaviour in single-group (measuring self-interest vs. in-group love) and intergroup (measuring self-interest vs. out-group hate) prisoner's dilemmas and found that vertical collectivists, similar to social conservatives (see Claessens, Fischer et al., 2020), were inclined to choose in-group love and disinclined to choose out-group hate (Probst et al., 1999).

4.   Conclusion

Overall, studies on unidimensional political ideology using economic games paint conservatives as less pro-social than liberals. However, many studies also show that there are no large differences between liberals and conservatives in pro-sociality (especially in-group-focussed pro-sociality) as well as norm compliance and punitive behaviour. We argue that the likely explanation for this is that unidimensional measures of ideology are too crude to reveal underlying behavioural differences between people with different ideologies.

Indeed, studies that examine the two primary dimensions of ideology reveal important differences. The evidence on the economic dimension of ideology clearly points to an underlying behavioural phenotype characterised by competition vs. cooperation. That is, economic conservatism seems to be underpinned by a predisposition for within-group competition (self-interest and a behavioural disposition that enhances inequality between individuals) and between-group competition (out-group hate). In contrast, economic progressivism seems to be underpinned by cooperation extending beyond group boundaries (universalism), egalitarianism, compassion for the disadvantaged, and a tendency to punish selfish people who exploit others. Less research has been conducted on the social dimension of ideology, but social conservatism seems to be characterised by a drive to maintain group conformity. In economic games, social conservatives distrust anonymous strangers, follow rules/norms, punish more (at least in some games), and display both in-group love and out-group hate. These results are consistent with the fact that people high in SDO view the world as a competitive jungle or zero-sum game, whereas people high in RWA view the world as dangerous and uncertain and therefore turn inwards to their groups for protection and lash out at threatening out-groups.

Findings based on the dual dimensions of ideology also help to explain results from unidimensional studies. They suggest that the pro-sociality associated with liberalism is driven by economic, rather than social, progressivism. Moreover, when unidimensional measures of ideology are used, the social dimension of ideology may mask the effect of the economic dimension on pro-sociality, which would explain why many studies fail to find greater pro-sociality among those classified as liberal on unidimensional measures. Moreover, experiments on the dual dimensions suggest that the negative relationship between unidimensional conservatism and trust is driven by social conservatism. And the similar levels of in-group-biased, normative, and punitive behaviour on both ends of the unidimensional spectrum may be driven by left- and right-wing authoritarians, but this requires further research.

We hope this chapter has laid the foundation for a fruitful dialogue between political science and behavioural economics. The studies reviewed here and the gaps identified should provide ample opportunities for future cross-disciplinary collaboration. As we have seen, incentivised experiments are a valuable tool for uncovering basic dispositional differences and similarities between people with different ideologies. This can foster more understanding across political divides and help experts and laypeople alike to gain a firmer grasp of what fuels our political behaviour.

Acknowledgments

We thank the Royal Society New Zealand Marsden Fund for research support under Grant UOA-17-074. We are also grateful to Scott Claessens, Guy Lavender Forsyth, Chris Sibley, and Ryan Greenaway-McGrevy for feedback on the ideas contained in this chapter.

Notes

1. We have provided a glossary in the Appendix describing all the games discussed in this chapter. Those not entirely familiar with these games may wish to consult the glossary before reading further.
2. It may be useful to address the semantics involved. We refer to those who view the world as a competitive jungle and are more comfortable with hierarchy and inequality as "economic conservatives", and those who are in favour of greater equality, social justice, and redistributive economic policies as "economic progressives". In the literature, what we call "economic progressivism" is often called "economic liberalism", but we avoid using this terminology because "economic liberalism" can also refer to support for free-market capitalism and opposition to the welfare state and other redistributive economic policies, all of which are actually economically conservative positions. Turning to the social dimension of ideology: "social conservatives" are those who favour adherence to established group norms, whereas "social progressives" (who can also be referred to as "social liberals") are those who are in favour of individual freedom (e.g. they tend to support same-sex marriage and marijuana legalisation).
3. In contrast, the reason that economic conservatism (Claessens, Sibley et al., 2020) and its correlates, like self-reported dominance (Pfattheicher et al., 2014) and disagreeableness (Roberts et al., 2013), are sometimes related to punitiveness in games other than the ultimatum game may be that punitive behaviour in these games is often driven by self-interest, spite, competitiveness, and power (Hilbe & Traulsen, 2012; Houser & Xiao, 2010; Raihani & Bshary, 2019). This is the case for prisoner's dilemma (Falk et al., 2005), third-party (Delton & Krasnow, 2017; Leliveld et al., 2012), and public goods games (Herrmann et al., 2008; Hoeft & Mill, 2017; Krasnow et al., 2012; Pfattheicher et al., 2014), and even for the punishment phenotype found across games (Chierchia et al., 2017).

References

Aaldering, H., & Böhm, R. (2020). Parochial versus universal cooperation: Introducing a novel economic game of within- and between-group interaction. *Social Psychological and Personality Science*, 11(1), 36-45.

Alford, J. R., & Hibbing, J. R. (2007). Personal, interpersonal, and political temperaments. *The Annals of the American Academy of Political and Social Science*, 614(1), 196-212.

Anderson, L. R., Milyo, J., & Mellor, J. M. (2004). Do liberals play nice? The effects of party and political ideology in public goods and trust games. In J. Morgan (Ed.), *Experimental and Behavorial Economics* (*Advances in Applied Microeconomics*, Vol. 13, pp. 97-106). Bingley: Emerald Group Publishing Limited.

Antonioni, A., Pereda, M., Cronin, K. A., Tomassini, M., & Sánchez, A. (2018). Collaborative hierarchy maintains cooperation in asymmetric games. *Scientific Reports*, 8(1), 1-9.

Balliet, D., Tybur, J. M., Wu, J., Antonellis, C., & Van Lange, P. A. (2018). Political ideology, trust, and cooperation: In-group favoritism among Republicans and Democrats during a US national election. *Journal of Conflict Resolution*, 62(4), 797-818.

Barclay, P., & Barker, J. L. (2020). Greener than thou: People who protect the environment are more cooperative, compete to be environmental, and benefit from reputation. *Journal of Environmental Psychology*, 101441.

Baumert, A., Schlösser, T., & Schmitt, M. (2014). Economic games: A performance-based assessment of fairness and altruism. *European Journal of Psychological Assessment*, 30(3), 178-192.

Bergh, R., & Sidanius, J. (2020). Domineering dispositions and hierarchy preferences: differentiating the impact of traits and social values in economic games. *Personality and Social Psychology Bulletin*. doi: 10.1177/0146167220965292

Brañas-Garza, P., Espín, A. M., Exadaktylos, F., & Herrmann, B. (2014). Fair and unfair punishers coexist in the Ultimatum Game. *Scientific Reports*, 4(1), 1-4.

Brethel-Haurwitz, K. M., Stoycos, S. A., Cardinale, E. M., Huebner, B., & Marsh, A. A. (2016). Is costly punishment altruistic? Exploring rejection of unfair offers in the Ultimatum Game in real-world altruists. *Scientific Reports*, 6(1), 1-10.

Cappelen, A. W., Halvorsen, T., Sørensen, E. Ø., & Tungodden, B. (2017). Face-saving or fair-minded: What motivates moral behavior? *Journal of the European Economic Association*, 15(3), 540-557.

Chaudhuri, A. (2009). *Experiments in Economics: Playing Fair with Money*. London and New York: Routledge.

Chiao, J., Mathur, V., Harada, T., & Lipke, T. (2009). Neural basis of preference for human social hierarchy versus egalitarianism. *Annals of the New York Academy of Sciences*, 1167(1), 174-181.

Chierchia, G., Lesemann, F. P., Snower, D., Vogel, M., & Singer, T. (2017). Caring cooperators and powerful punishers: Differential effects of induced care and power motivation on different types of economic decision making. *Scientific Reports*, 7(1), 1-10.

Chirumbolo, A., Leone, L., & Desimoni, M. (2016). The interpersonal roots of politics: social value orientation, socio-political attitudes and prejudice. *Personality and Individual Differences*, 91, 144-153.

Chuah, S. H., Hoffmann, R., Jones, M., & Williams, G. (2009). An economic anatomy of culture: Attitudes and behaviour in inter- and intra-national ultimatum game experiments. *Journal of Economic Psychology*, 30(5), 732-744.

Claessens, S., Fischer, K., Chaudhuri, A., Sibley, C. G., & Atkinson, Q. D. (2020). The dual evolutionary foundations of political ideology. *Nature Human Behaviour*, 4, 336-345.

Claessens, S., Sibley, C., Chaudhuri, A., & Atkinson, Q. D. (2020). Cooperative phenotype predicts economic conservatism, policy views, and political party support [working paper].

Clark, C. B., Swails, J. A., Pontinen, H. M., Bowerman, S. E., Kriz, K. A., & Hendricks, P. S. (2017). A behavioral economic assessment of individualizing versus binding moral foundations. *Personality and Individual Differences*, 112, 49-54.

Costello, T. H., & Lilienfeld, S. O. (2020). Social and economic political ideology consistently operate as mutual suppressors: Implications for personality, social, and political psychology. *Social Psychological and Personality Science*. doi: 10.1177/1948550620964679

Cozzolino, P. J., & Snyder, M. (2008). Good times, bad times: How personal disadvantage moderates the relationship between social dominance and efforts to win. *Personality and Social Psychology Bulletin*, 34(10), 1420-1433.

Cronin, K. A., Acheson, D. J., Hernández, P., & Sánchez, A. (2015). Hierarchy is detrimental for human cooperation. *Scientific Reports*, 5, 18634.

Dawes, C. T., Johannesson, M., Lindqvist, E., Loewen, P. J., Ostling, R., Bonde, M., & Priks, F. (2012). Generosity and political preferences. *SSRN Electronic Journal*, 941.

Dawes, C. T., Loewen, P. J., & Fowler, J. H. (2011). Social preferences and political participation. *Journal of Politics*, 73(3), 845-856.

Delton, A. W., & Krasnow, M. M. (2017). The psychology of deterrence explains why group membership matters for third-party punishment. *Evolution and Human Behavior*, 38(6), 734-743.

Deutsch, M. (1960). Trust, trustworthiness, and the F Scale. *Journal of Abnormal and Social Psychology*, 61(1), 138-140.

Duckitt, J., & Sibley, C. G. (2009). A dual-process motivational model of ideology, politics, and prejudice. *Psychological Inquiry*, 20(2-3), 98-109.

Duckitt, J., & Sibley, C. G. (2017). The dual process motivational model of ideology and prejudice. In C. G. Sibley & F. K. Barlow (Eds.), *The Cambridge Handbook of the Psychology of Prejudice* (pp. 188–221). Cambridge: Cambridge University Press.

Esarey, J., Salmon, T. C., & Barrilleaux, C. (2012). What motivates political preferences? Self-interest, ideology, and fairness in a laboratory democracy. *Economic Inquiry*, 50(3), 604-624.

Falk, A., Fehr, E., & Fischbacher, U. (2005). Driving forces behind informal sanctions. *Econometrica*, 73(6), 2017-2030.

Federico, C. M., & Malka, A. (2018). The contingent, contextual nature of the relationship between needs for security and certainty and political preferences: Evidence and implications. *Political Psychology*, 39, 3-48.

Federico, C. M., Weber, C. R., Ergun, D., & Hunt, C. (2013). Mapping the connections between politics and morality: The multiple sociopolitical orientations involved in moral intuition. *Political Psychology*, 34(4), 589-610.

Fehr, E., Fischbacher, U., Von Rosenbladt, B., Schupp, J., & Wagner, G. G. (2003). A nation-wide laboratory: Examining trust and trustworthiness by integrating behavioral experiments into representative survey. IZA Discussion Paper No. 715, Bonn, Germany.

Fietzer, A. W., Ponterotto, J. G., Jackson, M. A., & Bolgatz, J. (2016). Cultural adjustment and social justice behaviour: The role of individual differences in multicultural personality. *European Journal of Personality*, 30(6), 552-563.

Fischer, K., Chaudhuri, A., & Atkinson, Q. D. (2020). Responses to the COVID-19 pandemic reflect the dual evolutionary foundations of political ideology [working paper].

Fischer, K., Chaudhuri, A., Fišar, M., Sibley, C., Špalek, J., Tremewan, J., & Atkinson, Q. D. (2021). Right- and left-wing authoritarianism predict different measures of conformist, disgust/threat-sensitive phenotype [working paper].

Fischer, K., Claessens, S., Chaudhuri, A., Sibley, C., & Atkinson, Q. D. (2021). The dual dimensions of political ideology differently predict "ingroup love", "outgroup hate", universalism, and self-interest [working paper].

Fosgaard, T. R., Hansen, L. G., & Wengström, E. (2019). Cooperation, framing, and political attitudes. *Journal of Economic Behavior & Organization*, 158, 416-427.

Fowler, J. H., & Kam, C. D. (2007). Beyond the self: Social identity, altruism, and political participation. *Journal of Politics*, 69(3), 813-827.

Galen, L. W., Kurby, C. A., & Fles, E. H. (2020). Religiosity, shared identity, trust, and punishment of norm violations: No evidence of generalized prosociality. *Psychology of Religion and Spirituality*. doi: 10.1037/rel0000320

Gärling, T. (1999). Value priorities, social value orientations and cooperation in social dilemmas. *British Journal of Social Psychology*, 38(4), 397-408.

Grünhage, T., & Reuter, M. (2020). Political orientation is associated with behavior in public-goods- and trust-games. *Political Behavior*. doi: 10.1007/s11109-020-09606-5

Gürdal, M. Y., Torul, O., & Vostroknutov, A. (2020). Norm compliance, enforcement, and the survival of redistributive institutions. *Journal of Economic Behavior & Organization*, 178, 313-326.

Haesevoets, T., Folmer, C. R., & Van Hiel, A. (2015). Cooperation in mixed-motive games: The role of individual differences in selfish and social orientation. *European Journal of Personality*, 29(4), 445-458.

Haesevoets, T., Reinders Folmer, C., Bostyn, D. H., & Van Hiel, A. (2018). Behavioural consistency within the prisoner's dilemma game: The role of personality and situation. *European Journal of Personality*, 32(4), 405-426.

Häkkinen, K., & Akrami, N. (2014). Ideology and climate change denial. *Personality and Individual Differences*, 70, 62-65.

Halali, E., Dorfman, A., Jun, S., & Halevy, N. (2018). More for us or more for me? Social dominance as parochial egoism. *Social Psychological and Personality Science*, 9(2), 254-262.

Halevy, N., Chou, E. Y., Cohen, T. R., & Livingston, R. W. (2012). Status conferral in intergroup social dilemmas: Behavioral antecedents and consequences of prestige and dominance. *Journal of Personality and Social Psychology*, 102(2), 351-366.

Herrmann, B., Thöni, C., & Gächter, S. (2008). Antisocial punishment across societies. *Science*, 319(5868), 1362-1367.

Hilbe, C., & Traulsen, A. (2012). Emergence of responsible sanctions without second order free riders, antisocial punishment or spite. *Scientific Reports*, 2, 458.

Hilbig, B. E., Zettler, I., & Heydasch, T. (2012). Personality, punishment and public goods: Strategic shifts towards cooperation as a matter of dispositional honesty–humility. *European Journal of Personality*, 26(3), 245-254.

Hirsh, J. B., DeYoung, C. G., Xu, X., & Peterson, J. B. (2010). Compassionate liberals and polite conservatives: Associations of agreeableness with political ideology and moral values. *Personality and Social Psychology Bulletin*, 36(5), 655-664.

Hoeft, L., & Mill, W. (2017). Selfish punishers: An experimental investigation of designated punishment behavior in public goods. *Economics Letters*, 157, 41-44.

Houser, D., & Xiao, E. (2010). Inequality-seeking punishment. *Economics Letters*, 109(1), 20-23.

Jackson, J. C., Van Egmond, M., Choi, V. K., Ember, C. R., Halberstadt, J., Balanovic, J., ... & Gelfand, M. J. (2019). Ecological and cultural factors underlying the global distribution of prejudice. *PLoS One*, 14(9), e0221953.

Jacquet, P. O., Pazhoohi, F., Findling, C., Mell, H., Chevallier, C., & Baumard, N. (2021). Predictive modeling of religiosity, prosociality, and moralizing in 295,000 individuals from European and non-European populations. *Humanities and Social Sciences Communications*, 8(1), 1-12.

Jones, D. N., & Figueredo, A. J. (2013). The core of darkness: Uncovering the heart of the Dark Triad. *European Journal of Personality*, 27(6), 521-531.

Jost, J. T. (2017). Ideological asymmetries and the essence of political psychology. *Political Psychology*, 38(2), 167-208.

Jost, J. T., Glaser, J., Kruglanski, A. W., & Sulloway, F. J. (2003). Political conservatism as motivated social cognition. *Psychological Bulletin*, 129(3), 339-375.

Kaiser, F. G., & Byrka, K. (2011). Environmentalism as a trait: Gauging people's prosocial personality in terms of environmental engagement. *International Journal of Psychology*, 46(1), 71-79.

Kerschbamer, R., & Müller, D. (2020). Social preferences and political attitudes: An online experiment on a large heterogeneous sample. *Journal of Public Economics*, 182, 104076.

Kimbrough, E. O., & Vostroknutov, A. (2016). Norms make preferences social. *Journal of the European Economic Association*, 14(3), 608-638.

Kimbrough, E. O., & Vostroknutov, A. (2018). A portable method of eliciting respect for social norms. *Economics Letters*, 168, 147-150.

Kistler, D., Thöni, C., & Welzel, C. (2017). Survey response and observed behavior: Emancipative and secular values predict prosocial behaviors. *Journal of Cross-Cultural Psychology*, 48(4), 461-489.

Krasnow, M. M., Cosmides, L., Pedersen, E. J., & Tooby, J. (2012). What are punishment and reputation for? *PLOS One*, 7(9), e45662.

Leliveld, M. C., van Dijk, E., & van Beest, I. (2012). Punishing and compensating others at your own expense: The role of empathic concern on reactions to distributive injustice. *European Journal of Social Psychology*, 42(2), 135-140.

Littman, R., Estrada, S., Stagnaro, M. N., Dunham, Y., Rand, D., & Baskin-Sommers, A. (2020). Community violence and prosociality: Experiencing and committing violence predicts norm-enforcing punishment but not cooperation. *Social Psychological and Personality Science*, 11(2), 276-283.

Mattan, B. D., Barth, D. M., Thompson, A., Feldman-Hall, O., Cloutier, J., & Kubota, J. T. (2020). Punishing the privileged: Selfish offers from high-status allocators elicit greater punishment from third-party arbitrators. *PLOS One*, 15(5), e0232369.

Milfont, T. L., Bain, P. G., Kashima, Y., Corral-Verdugo, V., Pasquali, C., Johansson, L. O., … Bilewicz, M. (2018). On the relation between social dominance orientation and environmentalism: A 25-nation study. *Social Psychological and Personality Science*, 9(7), 802-814.

Milfont, T. L., Richter, I., Sibley, C. G., Wilson, M. S., & Fischer, R. (2013). Environmental consequences of the desire to dominate and be superior. *Personality and Social Psychology Bulletin*, 39(9), 1127-1138.

Müller, D. (2019). The anatomy of distributional preferences with group identity. *Journal of Economic Behavior & Organization*, 166, 785-807.

Müller, D., & Renes, S. (2020). Fairness views and political preferences: Evidence from a large and heterogeneous sample. *Social Choice and Welfare*. doi: 10.1007/s00355-020-01289-5

Nettle, D., Colléony, A., & Cockerill, M. (2011). Variation in cooperative behaviour within a single city. *PLOS One*, 6(10), e26922.

Nilsson, A., & Erlandsson, A. (2015). The Moral Foundations taxonomy: Structural validity and relation to political ideology in Sweden. *Personality and Individual Differences*, 76, 28-32.

Osborne, D., Wootton, L. W., & Sibley, C. G. (2013). Are liberals agreeable or not? *Social Psychology*, 44, 354-360.

Oxley, D. R., Smith, K. B., Alford, J. R., Hibbing, M. V., Miller, J. L., Scalora, M., … Hibbing, J. R. (2008). Political attitudes vary with physiological traits. *Science*, 321(5896), 1667-1670.

Petersen, M. B., & Laustsen, L. (2019). Upper-body strength and political egalitarianism: Twelve conceptual replications. *Political Psychology*, 40(2), 375-394.

Peysakhovich, A., Nowak, M. A., & Rand, D. G. (2014). Humans display a "cooperative phenotype" that is domain general and temporally stable. *Nature Communications*, 5(1), 1-8.

Pfattheicher, S., Landhäußer, A., & Keller, J. (2014). Individual differences in antisocial punishment in public goods situations: The interplay of cortisol with testosterone and dominance. *Journal of Behavioral Decision Making*, 27(4), 340-348.

Pisor, A. C., Gervais, M. M., Purzycki, B. G., & Ross, C. T. (2020). Preferences and constraints: The value of economic games for studying human behaviour. *Royal Society Open Science*, 7(6), 192090.

Ponsi, G., Panasiti, M. S., Aglioti, S. M., & Liuzza, M. T. (2017). Right-wing authoritarianism and stereotype-driven expectations interact in shaping intergroup trust in one-shot vs multiple-round social interactions. *PLOS One*, 12(12), e0190142.

Pratto, F., Tatar, D. G., & Conway-Lanz, S. (1999). Who gets what and why: Determinants of social allocations. *Political Psychology*, 20(1), 127-150.

Probst, T. M., Carnevale, P. J., & Triandis, H. C. (1999). Cultural values in intergroup and single-group social dilemmas. *Organizational Behavior and Human Decision Processes*, 77(3), 171-191.

Putterman, L., Tyran, J. R., & Kamei, K. (2011). Public goods and voting on formal sanction schemes. *Journal of Public Economics*, 95(9-10), 1213-1222.

Raihani, N. J., & Bshary, R. (2019). Punishment: One tool, many uses. *Evolutionary Human Sciences*, 1. doi: 10.1017/ehs.2019.12.

Reese, G., Proch, J., & Cohrs, J. C. (2014). Individual differences in responses to global inequality. *Analyses of Social Issues and Public Policy*, 14(1), 217-238.

Roberts, S. C., Vakirtzis, A., Kristjánsdóttir, L., & Havlíček, J. (2013). Who punishes? Personality traits predict individual variation in punitive sentiment. *Evolutionary Psychology*, 11(1), 186-200.

Sagiv, L., Sverdlik, N., & Schwarz, N. (2011). To compete or to cooperate? Values' impact on perception and action in social dilemma games. *European Journal of Social Psychology*, 41(1), 64-77.

Schwartz, S. H., Cieciuch, J., Vecchione, M., Davidov, E., Fischer, R., Beierlein, C., ... Dirilen-Gumus, O. (2012). Refining the theory of basic individual values. *Journal of Personality and Social Psychology*, 103(4), 663.

Shaffer, B., & Duckitt, J. (2013). The dimensional structure of people's fears, threats, and concerns and their relationship with right-wing authoritarianism and social dominance orientation. *International Journal of Psychology*, 48(1), 6-17.

Sheldon, K. M., & Nichols, C. P. (2009). Comparing Democrats and Republicans on intrinsic and extrinsic values. *Journal of Applied Social Psychology*, 39(3), 589-623.

Smirnov, O., Dawes, C. T., Fowler, J. H., Johnson, T., & McElreath, R. (2010). The behavioral logic of collective action: Partisans cooperate and punish more than nonpartisans. *Political Psychology*, 31(4), 595-616.

Smith, V. L. (1976). Experimental economics: Induced value theory. *American Economic Review*, 66(2), 274-279.

Smith, V. L. (1982). Microeconomic systems as an experimental science. *American Economic Review*, 72(5), 923-955.

Stanley, S. K., Milfont, T. L., Wilson, M. S., & Sibley, C. G. (2019). The influence of social dominance orientation and right-wing authoritarianism on environmentalism: A five-year cross-lagged analysis. *PLOS One*, 14(7).

Tajfel, H., & Turner, J. C. (1979). An integrative theory of intergroup conflict. In S. Worchel, & W. G. Austin (Eds.), *The Social Psychology of Intergroup Relations* (pp. 33-47). Monterey, CA: Brooks/Cole.

Thielmann, I., Spadaro, G., & Balliet, D. (2020). Personality and prosocial behavior: A theoretical framework and meta-analysis. *Psychological Bulletin*, 146(1), 30-90.

Thomsson, K. M., & Vostroknutov, A. (2017). Small-world conservatives and rigid liberals: Attitudes towards sharing in self-proclaimed left and right. *Journal of Economic Behavior & Organization*, 135, 181-192.

Tomasello, M., Melis, A. P., Tennie, C., Wyman, E., Herrmann, E., Gilby, I. C., ... Melis, A. (2012). Two key steps in the evolution of human cooperation: The interdependence hypothesis. *Current Anthropology*, 53(6), 673-692.

Van Lange, P. A., Bekkers, R., Chirumbolo, A., & Leone, L. (2012). Are conservatives less likely to be prosocial than liberals? From games to ideology, political preferences and voting. *European Journal of Personality*, 26(5), 461-473.

Vollan, B., Landmann, A., Zhou, Y., Hu, B., & Herrmann-Pillath, C. (2017). Cooperation and authoritarian values: an experimental study in China. *European Economic Review*, 93, 90-105.

Weng, H. Y., Fox, A. S., Hessenthaler, H. C., Stodola, D. E., & Davidson, R. J. (2015). The role of compassion in altruistic helping and punishment behavior. *PLOS One*, 10(12), e0143794.

Yamagishi, T., Horita, Y., Mifune, N., Hashimoto, H., Li, Y., Shinada, M., ... Simunovic, D. (2012). Rejection of unfair offers in the ultimatum game is no evidence of strong reciprocity. *Proceedings of the National Academy of Sciences*, 109(50), 20364-20368.

Zhao, K., Ferguson, E., & Smillie, L. D. (2017). Politeness and compassion differentially predict adherence to fairness norms and interventions to norm violations in economic games. *Scientific Reports*, 7(1), 1-11.

Appendix: Glossary of Games

Below, we provide a description of some behavioural economic games commonly deployed to investigate social preferences related to ideology. All dollar amounts are examples to help illustrate the structure of the game and the approximate relative size of incentives.

Dictator Game

This is a sequential two-player game. The first mover has $10; the second mover has no initial endowment. The first mover decides how much of this $10 to send to the second mover. The second mover has no decision to make. The amount sent by the first mover is considered a measure of the first mover's level of generosity/altruism.

Ultimatum Game

This is a sequential two-player game. The first mover has $10; the second mover has no initial endowment. The first mover decides on a split of the initial endowment of $10 (say $7 and $3). This decision is then conveyed to the second mover, who can either accept or reject the offer. If the second mover accepts, then each gets the split offered by the first mover (first mover gets $7, second mover gets $3). But, if the second mover rejects, then both get nothing. This game (and the second mover's decision to reject small offers) is often used to measure preferences regarding fairness.

Trust Game

This is a sequential two-player game. Typically, both players start with an initial endowment of $10. The first mover can choose to send any or all of $10 to the second mover. Any amount ($X) sent is multiplied typically by 3, and this tripled amount ($3X) is given to the second mover. (If the amount is doubled/quadrupled, then the second mover gets 2X, 4X, etc.) The second mover then decides whether to send anything back to the first mover. The latter amount is not multiplied. The amount sent by the first mover is considered a measure of "trust", while the proportion returned by the second mover is considered a measure of trustworthiness/reciprocity. (Since different second movers get different amounts, one cannot look at the absolute amount returned by the second mover, but rather the proportion returned.)

Public Goods Game

This is a group decision-making game, typically with more than two players. Let us say that a group consists of five players. Each player has $5 and can keep this entire amount or contribute any or all to the public (group) account. Decisions are made simultaneously. The amount put in the public account is multiplied by M. This can be any number higher than 1 but less than the number of players such that M/5 is less than 1 (i.e. the multiplied amount divided by the number of players is less than 1). If there are five players, then M could be 2, 3, or 4 (implying that the marginal per capita return = $0.4, $0.6, or $0.8, respectively). This makes it a dominant strategy to free-ride by keeping the entire $5 in one's private account. The social optimum is for every player to contribute everything to the public account, as this generates the highest return for every player.

Prisoner's Dilemma Game

Table 8.1   Prisoner's dilemma game

		Player #2	
		Cooperate	Defect
Player #1	Cooperate	$3, $3	$0, $4
	Defect	$4, $0	$1, $1

This is a paired game with decisions made simultaneously. Each player can choose from one of two strategies, generically referred to as "Cooperate" or "Defect". If both players choose "Cooperate", then they each get $3. If they both choose "Defect", then each gets $1. If one player chooses "Cooperate" while the other chooses "Defect", then the player choosing to cooperate gets $0 while the defecting player gets $4. Defect is the dominant strategy for both players resulting in a unique dominant strategy Nash equilibrium of {Defect, Defect}, where each gets $1, even though {Cooperate, Cooperate} is socially optimal and maximizes payoff for both players with each getting $3. This is because, regardless of what the other player chooses ("Cooperate" or "Defect"), the other player is better off choosing "Defect". For each player "Defect" yields $4 as opposed to $3 (from "Cooperate") if the other player chooses to "Cooperate". Meanwhile, "Defect" yields $1 as opposed to $0 (from "Cooperate") if the other player also chooses "Defect".

Payoff Ranked Coordination (Stag Hunt) Game

Table 8.2   Payoff ranked coordination (stag hunt) game

		Player #2	
		Hunt Stag	Hunt Rabbit
Player #1	Hunt Stag	$8, $8	$0, $5
	Hunt Rabbit	$5, $0	$5, $5

This is a paired game with decisions made simultaneously. Each player can choose from one of two strategies: hunt stag or hunt rabbit. If both players choose "hunt stag", then they both get $8 each. If they both choose "hunt rabbit", then they both get $5 each. If one player chooses "hunt stag" while the other chooses "hunt rabbit" then the player choosing "hunt stag" gets $0, while the player choosing "hunt rabbit" gets $5. This game has two Nash equilibria: one where both players choose to hunt stag and a second where both players choose to hunt rabbit. The former is the payoff-dominant equilibrium in the sense that both players get a higher payoff of $8 each at this equilibrium. The latter is the secure (or risk-dominant) equilibrium. This is because a player can guarantee a payoff of $5 for themselves by choosing "hunt rabbit" (yields $5 regardless of what the other player chooses).

Second-Party Punishment Game

There are two players, each with $10. This game has two stages: the transfer stage, and the penalty stage. In the transfer stage, each player decides whether to transfer $3 to the other player. Any amount transferred is doubled and given to the other player. Decisions are made simultaneously. Players get to see the outcome of the transfer stage. Next, there is a penalty stage with decisions made simultaneously again. Both players can pay up to $1 to reduce the other player's payoff, depending on the decisions made in the transfer stage: $1 given by one player reduces the other player's payoff by $5.

Third-Party Punishment Game

Three players, A, B, and C, all start with $10. First, Player A decides whether to "take" from Player B. If Player A takes, Player B loses $5, and Player A gains $3 (taking is inefficient). If Player A takes, Player C can then pay up to $2 to reduce Player A's payoff. Each \$1 given by Player C reduces \$5 from Player A. Player B is passive in the interaction.

Random Income Game

In the random income game, participants are put into groups of four and given a random endowment that their peers can see. Players can then pay a cost to take money away from or give money to their groupmates. Decisions are made simultaneously.

9 Neuroeconomics

Sarah Cowie, Ian Kirk, and Olav Krigolson

1.   Introduction

Neuroeconomics is the study of how the economic theories of decision-making and learning are implemented by the neural mechanisms identified from neuroscience research. In this chapter, we explore how a combination of neuroscientific, psychological, and economic approaches has shed light on why we behave in particular ways, over and above what any one of these individual approaches can reveal. Rather than providing a broad, scoping review of the different areas of research within neuroeconomics, or trying to describe completely the neural basis of decision-making and learning, we focus here on specific examples of research that has contributed to the broad understanding of neuroeconomics either because the research provides answers to key questions or because it poses novel questions that set the direction for future research.

2.   Decision-Making

2.1   Expected Value and Dual-Process Accounts of Decision-Making

How do we make decisions, especially when the outcomes are probabilistic? From a neuroeconomics perspective, the simplest account of decision-making involves the computation of "expected values" – a multiplicative combination of the value of a choice and the probability of attaining that choice if selected (von Neumann & Morgenstern, 1944). Once an expected value is computed for each possible choice, one simply chooses the highest expected value as their decision. For example, consider the choice of whether or not one should play the lottery. While lottery prizes can soar into the millions of pounds or dollars, the odds of winning the lottery push the expected value of playing below that of not playing, thus, one should never play the lottery. Perhaps it is easier to think of expected values in situations such as choosing what to eat or what career to pursue, where the values and odds of attaining a choice are difficult to ascertain and/or there is a wide range of available choices. In any event, from a theoretical perspective, the computation of expected values is thought to underlie human decision-making.

But is this what actually happens in the brain? Are expected-value calculations the basis of our decisions? Experimental evidence suggests that this is indeed true. For instance, in a seminal work, Platt and Glimcher (1999) trained monkeys to respond to visual cues to earn rewards. In a key manipulation, rewards were framed within the context of expected value – the amount of juice given to the monkey for a given choice was a product of the magnitude of juice and the probability of receiving the juice. Using single unit recordings, where neural activity is directly measured via a wire implanted into the monkey's brain, Platt and Glimcher demonstrated that the firing rate of neurons in the lateral intraparietal area scaled to the expected values of the presented choices. In other words, the results showed that choices with large expected values evoked greater neuronal firing than choices with small expected values. Further, the amount of firing in the lateral intraparietal area did not encode reward value or reward probability, but instead encoded the multiplicative of the two – the expected value of the choice. Subsequent studies in monkeys and in humans demonstrated similar results and highlight that multiple regions within the brain compute expected values to facilitate decision-making (e.g. Rolls et al., 2008).

While there is no doubt that the computation of expected values plays a key role in the neural basis of decision-making, decision-making is, of course, not that simple. While it does appear that decision-making processes rely on the computation of expected values, individual decisions stem from a two-system process (Evans, 2003; Evans & Frankish, 2009; Kahneman, 2011) wherein a given decision reflects either a rapid, unconscious, intuitive response (henceforth called System One; see Kahneman, 2011) or a slower, conscious, deliberative process (henceforth called System Two).

For example, when asked, "What is two plus two?", we instantly know the answer (four), thanks to System One. However, if asked, "What is the square root of 2 119 936?", System Two would engage to help solve the problem (the answer is 1 456, for the curious). Typically referred to as dual-process theory, the hypothesis is that the brain relies on two systems to make decisions (Evans, 2003).[1] When a given context affords a well-learned response, System One quickly provides a well-learned answer – which would be the choice with the highest expected value. However, when there is uncertainty or conflict in a given context, System Two is recruited to arrive at a decision by forcing an effortful computation of expected values. The early basis for dual-process theory stems from a pupillometry study by Kahneman et al. (1968) who had participants listen to a series of numbers presented to the beat of a metronome. In the first experimental condition, participants simply had to remember the numbers that they heard and repeat them back when prompted – a condition that the authors argued was synonymous with a System One decision process. In the second experimental condition, participants had to add one to each digit they heard and then hold these newly computed numbers in memory until instructed to repeat back the numbers, a condition proposed to engage System Two. The key measurement the researchers used was pupil diameter – which was found to be larger in the "Add One" condition (proposed to engage System Two) and smaller in the "Add Zero" condition (proposed to engage System One). As a result of these data, Kahneman et al. proposed that situations that require greater mental effort engage System Two, whereas situations that require little to no mental effort engage System One. It is worth noting that, for some time, pupil diameter was held as the "gold standard" methodology for probing whether or not someone was engaged in System One or System Two thinking.

Advances in the technology used by neuroscientists have provided further means for examining System One and System Two decision processes within the brain. For example, electroencephalography (EEG) reflects the electrical activity of large numbers of cortical neurons and was first recorded in humans in 1924 by Hans Berger (Haas, 2003). Over the past 100 years, researchers have used EEG to probe the full spectrum of cognitive processes, including attention, decision-making, learning, memory, and sensory perception. In recent work, Williams et al. (2019) sought to replicate the 1968 study by Kahneman and colleagues while also measuring neural activity via EEG. The results of this specific study demonstrated a replication of the pupil diameter findings reported by Kahneman et al. – a larger pupil diameter was observed in the Add One experimental condition that engaged System Two than in the Add Zero condition that engaged System One. Moreover, Williams et al. observed that the Add One condition evoked more EEG activity in the theta band (neural oscillations between 4 and 7 Hz) over the prefrontal cortex, and that the Add Zero condition evoked more EEG activity in the alpha band (neural oscillations between 8 and 12 Hz) over posterior regions of the brain. Importantly, frontal theta EEG oscillations have been linked specifically to the engagement of cognitive control (Cavanagh & Frank, 2014), a neural process related to the deployment of mental effort and thought to play a key role in System Two decision-making (Williams et al., 2019). Indeed, the role of cognitive control with regard to dual-process accounts of decision-making is interesting as it has been proposed that cognitive control is the mechanism by which System Two decision-making is engaged (Pennycook, 2018). The increased posterior alpha oscillations Williams and colleagues observed in the Add Zero condition are also of interest. Specifically, a prominent explanative theory of alpha oscillations suggests that increases in alpha power are associated with a reduction in the use of attentional processes (Clayton et al., 2015), which one might expect to see during System One decision-making.

Some might feel that the classic Kahneman "Add One" paradigm is not an ecologically valid task with which to probe dual-process accounts of decision-making. To address this, recent work, again by Williams et al. (in revision), used EEG to explore the neural correlates of System One and System Two decision-making while participants performed a clinical reasoning task. Specifically, Williams and colleagues had participants learn to diagnose a series of virtual patients using a presented medical reading ("AST") while EEG was recorded. In this task, there were two possible diagnoses, each of which was associated with a specific range of AST values. In the key manipulation, case difficulty was manipulated using medical readings that either clearly were indicative of one of the diagnoses (an "easy" case) or were on the borderline between the two diagnoses (a "hard" case).[2] The authors proposed that easy cases would be mediated with a System One decision process whereas hard cases would be mediated with a System Two decision process. In line with their previous work, Williams et al. found that the hard clinical cases evoked more frontal theta EEG oscillations than their easy counterparts. Recall that frontal theta oscillations are thought to reflect the engagement of cognitive control and, thus, by proxy are associated with System Two decision-making. However, counter to their previous work, Williams et al. did not observe an increase in posterior alpha EEG oscillations when easy clinical cases were presented to participants.

In sum, evidence suggests that the brain computes expected values as part of the decision-making process. However, as stated above, human decision-making is complicated, with experimental evidence suggesting that it is a result of two processes, one responsible for fast, intuitive, and reflexive responses and the other engaged when a slow, analytical, and effortful process is required to resolve conflict or uncertainty. While the evidence for a dual-process account of decision-making that is presented here is from studies using pupillometry and electroencephalography, it is important to note that there is a wide body of evidence using functional-magnetic resonance imaging that highlights the role of the prefrontal cortex in decision-making and dual-process theory (e.g. Sul et al., 2010).

2.2   The Ultimatum and Dictator Games: The Role of Emotion in Decision-Making

When faced with a choice to keep resources or share them with others, the rational choice is to be selfish. Yet, we often choose to make sacrifices that benefit others. The Dictator Game, where a proposer must decide whether, and how much, to give to a responder, may be used to explore the decision-making processes underlying altruistic acts. In this game, proposers typically share some of their money with the responder (Andreoni & Miller, 2008; Zaki & Mitchell, 2011; Weiland et al., 2012; Rodrigues et al., 2015). The game is played only once, so there is no opportunity for consequences; this apparent altruism thus occurs in the absence of any direct or potential future benefit to the proposer. In the Ultimatum Game, participants also typically play just one round, but the responder decides whether to accept or reject the proposer's offer and, hence, whether or not the two players get to keep any money – thus, the Ultimatum Game is a model of cooperation rather than pure altruism. Rationally, a proposer in the Ultimatum Game should give the smallest possible proportion to the responder, and the responder should accept that amount. Surprisingly, proposers tend to give more than they have to – on average, about 40% of the total amount on offer – and responders tend to reject offers of 20% or less (Güth et al., 1982; Güth, 1995; Thaler, 1988; Camerer, 2003; Camerer & Thaler, 1995; Hoffman et al., 1996). That is, responders will forgo small amounts of money to punish the proposer when the offer is perceived as unfair. Decisions in the Dictator and Ultimatum Games are sensitive to personality variables, situational variables (Rodrigues et al., 2015), and emotional states (Fiori et al., 2013). Yet, the cause of these seemingly irrational decisions remains a subject of debate; why would a proposer give any more than they absolutely have to, and why would a responder choose no money over a small, albeit unfair, amount?

Dual-process theories predict that intuitive and deliberative decision-making processes compete to determine choices made. If giving is intuitive – perhaps because of an innate bias towards potential reciprocation, or because altruism is, in itself, rewarding – altruistic decisions should be fast, and selfish ones (which require a more deliberative process) slow. This reaction-time-based logic has led to much confusion and debate (see Krajbich et al., 2015, for example), with the ultimate conclusion that reaction times alone are insufficient to infer underlying decision-making processes. Brain activity underlying fair and selfish offers in the Ultimatum and Dictator Games adds an extra dimension to choices made by proposers and responders, and may thus be key to uncovering the processes leading to seemingly irrational choices.

Extensive investigation into the brain's response to fair and unfair offers in economic games, using fMRI, implicates brain areas that deal with fast, intuitive processes like subjective value assessment and emotional responses (see Feng et al., 2015, for a meta-analysis; Weiland et al., 2012). Similar brain areas are also activated during more lifelike decisions about moral dilemmas (Green & Myerson, 2004); thus, economic games appear to be a good model for moral decision-making generally. These findings suggest that human prosocial preferences are driven by intuitive decision-making processes (Haidt, 2001; Roch et al., 2000; Sanfey & Chang, 2008; Scheele et al., 2012; Zaki & Mitchell, 2011). More deliberative processes likely monitor and respond to conflict between intuition and economic self-interest (Feng et al., 2015; Weiland et al., 2012), reaching a resolution either by regulating and suppressing intuitive emotional responses (Civai et al., 2012; Grecucci et al., 2013; Tabibnia et al., 2008), or by using executive control to override self-interest (Baumgartner et al., 2011). Although each method of reaching a resolution involves similar components of the deliberative decision-making system, the resulting actions are different; suppressing emotion may result in a tendency to choose selfishly, whereas suppressing self-interest may result in a tendency to choose pro-socially.[3] The relation between different brain structures, decision mechanisms, and outcomes again underscores the importance of looking beyond behavioural data to understand complex decision-making processes.

Although proposers and responders in economic games both have the same aim – to maximise gain, and conform to social norms – the nature of their decision differs. Responders react to the fairness of a proposal, whereas proposers decide on the fairness of the proposal. A comparison of proposers and responders in the Ultimatum Game reveals systematic differences between the timing and intensity of brain activity locked to a stimulus, derived from EEG signals (event-related potentials, or ERPs). Horat et al. (2017) found that ERPs consistent with conflict resolution occurred earlier in the decision-making process for proposers than responders, and responders showed more pronounced ERP activity relating to fairness judgements. ERPs reflecting higher-order cognitive control were higher in amplitude, and occurred earlier in a decision, for proposers than responders. Clearly, both the task requirements and the way decision-making processes unfold differ between responders and proposers. The greater potential for variation in the proposer's decision, and the fact that proposers are not responding to someone else's actions, may mean that the decision-making processes of the proposer have the greatest potential to shed light on why we behave pro-socially.

Although the Dictator and Ultimatum Games both involve decisions about generosity, the motivation for such decisions differs. Decisions of proposers are likely to be driven by intrinsic rewards in the Dictator Game, and some combination of intrinsic and extrinsic rewards in the Ultimatum Game. Understanding both the differences and the similarities between decisions in both games has the potential to uncover much about how intrinsic and extrinsic rewards weigh on decision-making. In a meta-analysis, Cutler and Campell-Meikeljohn (2019) showed that decisions to give, in both the Dictator and Ultimatum Games, activate brain regions associated with reward processing and value computation, suggesting that the same system deals with both extrinsic and intrinsic rewards. In contrast, much less overlap was found between the structures involved in selfish decisions, perhaps because selfishness in the Dictator Game reflects a personal preference for loss by others rather than the self, while in the Ultimatum Game, selfishness results at least partly from predictions about how others will behave. When combined with neuro-imaging, the Dictator and Ultimatum Games are thus powerful tools for understanding decision-making processes.

Why is it that decisions are sometimes selfish and other times fair or generous? Answering this question requires assessment of how different components of the decision-making process interact. One specific frequency band of brain activity – midfrontal theta – may hold particular promise for revealing the interplay between intuitive and deliberative processes. Midfrontal theta indexes both deliberative and intuitive decision-making processes (Cavanagh & Frank, 2014; Mitchell et al., 2008); it predicts behaviour in strategic games (Cohen & Ranganath, 2007) and responder decisions in the Ultimatum Game (Hewig et al., 2011). Rodrigues et al. (2015) showed that different decisions of proposers playing the Dictator Game are associated with different degrees of theta power. Participants, acting as proposers, could choose to split eight cents various ways across a series of trials – keeping all, giving all, splitting equally, or splitting unequally to favour either the proposer or the responder. Participants were told they would get to keep the total amount they chose to keep for themselves across all trials – thus, in each trial, participants were making a decision between keeping their own money and giving it away. Before the experiment, participants were assessed on the personality dimension of altruism, and split into two groups based on whether they scored low or high on this dimension, allowing the experimenters to understand how personality differences influenced decision-making. In some trials, the proposer was told that their choice would be observed and rated by others; in other trials, proposers were told that their choice would not be observed. In all trials, participants were shown the income level of the responder – low, medium, or high.

Examining brain activity before participants made a choice allowed the researchers to determine whether brain activity predicted fair and unfair offers, and how situational factors – like the income level of the responder and the likelihood of being judged by others – affected the decision. High- and low-altruism proposers both rated choices where more money was allocated to the proposer as unfair, choices where the split was equal as fair, and choices where the split favoured the responder as hyper-fair – thus, any differences in behaviour or brain activity could not be attributed to different perceptions about fairness norms. Overall, proposers made higher offers to receivers with lower income levels. Higher-altruism dictators made fewer unfair offers, and more over-fair offers than did low-altruism dictators. Having the decision observed increased the likelihood that low-altruism dictators would make an offer favouring the responder, and decreased the likelihood that high-altruism dictators would make an offer favouring the receiver. Theta power predicted different choices for high and low altruists; the greater the theta power, the more likely low altruists were to offer nothing, and the more likely the high altruists were to offer an even split.

What decision-making processes are reflected in these different patterns of theta for different personality types? One's degree of altruism will influence the perceived rewards for different choices, and the degree of conflict between selfishness and fairness. For high altruists, generosity (rather than fairness, since participants tended to give fairly when they were being watched, and generously when they were not) may be intrinsically rewarding; hence, conflict between a choice that is intrinsically rewarding and a choice that is socially acceptable would be greatest in the lead-up to a decision to be fair. In contrast, selfishness might be the more rewarding option for low altruists, and conflict between rewards and social norms would be greatest before a selfish decision. Certainly, theta activity is associated with increased conflict in a range of decisions. In a separate study that did not assess personality (Chen et al., 2019), theta activity after an unfair decision was similar to that associated with conflict, deviation from social norms, and sub-optimal choices (Polezzi et al., 2008; Boksem & De Cremer, 2010; Hewig et al., 2011; Wu et al., 2011; Wang et al., 2016). Thus, the theta activity observed in Rodrigues et al.'s (2015) study may suggest that separate decision-making systems compete with one another in terms of the expected utility they predict for different possible choices.

Rodrigues et al.'s (2015) study underscores the depth of complexity of altruistic decisions – one that extends beyond reaction times and brain structures. Because distinct psychological processes should each have their own unique signature, one way that neuroeconomics may contribute to understanding why we sometimes sacrifice our own resources for the good of others is to map out such signatures and look for their occurrence during decisions. The advantage of EEG over other methods like fMRI is its high temporal resolution, as well as its multi-dimensionality; EEG permits measures of frequency and power and changes in these elements across time, as well as source estimation. That is, a multi-dimensional EEG signature would allow assessment of the interplay between psychological processes. Unravelling the decision-making processes that lead us to behave in an apparently irrational manner clearly requires the use of all elements of the EEG signature.

3. Learning

3.1 Reward Prediction Errors and Learning

To survive and thrive in its environment, any animal (including humans) must engage in behaviours that result in obtaining what is necessary for that survival (food or money, for example). Rewards induce these behaviours. Rewards can be considered positive reinforcers that induce learning, or are the attractive or motivational aspect of a stimulus that induces appetitive, approach, and consummatory behaviour (Schultz, 2015). Decades of electrophysiological work in rats, mice, and monkeys has established that neurons in the midbrain dopamine system, striatum, and orbitofrontal cortex process rewards. The amount and value of a reward and the probability of it occurring can be signalled and used in learning and decision-making (Gershman & Uchida, 2019). The most remarkable properties of dopaminergic cells gained widespread attention with the publication of two papers over 20 years ago. These papers (Montague et al., 1996; Schultz et al., 1997) describe recordings from dopaminergic cells in the brain while a variety of behaviours were observed, and tied these together using a reinforcement learning computer model that appears to capture accurately how animals predict and respond to rewards.

For example, electrodes were implanted in areas of monkeys' brains that contain numerous dopaminergic cells. Monkeys were given an unexpected reward (e.g. fruit juice), and these cells briefly (but significantly) increased their discharge rate. When the researchers repeatedly associated the reward with a tone or a light that signals that the reward is imminent, the neuron stops firing on presentation of the reward, but fires instead on presentation of the tone or light (i.e. on the prediction of the reward). Next, the researchers presented the tone or light but not the subsequent juice. There was a spike in neuron firing in anticipation of the juice, followed by a significant reduction of firing (below baseline levels) or a complete cessation in firing when the juice did not arrive. From these data, it appears that dopamine neurons code both the expectation of reward as well as the response to reward.

Thus, dopamine neurons encode what is known as a reward prediction error (RPE). They send a signal that can indicate that the reward was as expected (zero RPE), better than expected (positive RPE), or absent or less than expected (negative RPE). Learning occurs when prediction errors are signalled. A positive or negative error is used to update value estimates that will lead to more accurate prediction of future rewards. The studies mentioned above have been repeatedly replicated and extended in non-human primates so that we now have a clear picture of how RPE is generated in dopaminergic cells in the ventral tegmentum of the midbrain, transmitted to the striatum and neocortex, and used to update stimulus values and goal-directed behaviour (Lak et al., 2016). Employing fMRI in humans, translational descriptions of the RPE have been described in the midbrain, striatum, and prefrontal cortex, and the fMRI-derived activations altered by the same manipulations that affect dopaminergic neuron response in animals (Chase et al., 2015; Garrison et al., 2013).

Again, with respect to human research, the relatively low temporal resolution of fMRI limits the extent to which the dynamics of activity in neural networks can be mapped onto trial-by-trial behaviour. However, in a parallel endeavour to that described for exploration/exploitation above, EEG can be used to finely track these network neural dynamics, albeit only the dynamics of the neocortex. Nevertheless, and in combination with modelling, this mapping can be used to gauge learning in the system, and the extent to which this changes future behaviour. That the cortical end of a reward-processing network can be accessed by EEG in general has had considerable support from work using EEG-derived stimulus-locked ERPs. Here, many stimulus-locked EEG signals from many repeated single trials are averaged to form the ERP. Many researchers have found relative negative or positive deflections in the ERP in response to negative relative to positive prediction error (e.g. Holroyd & Coles, 2002; Holroyd et al., 2008). A useful technique though it is, ERP analysis does not give trial-by-trial resolution. For this we need to analyse the ongoing EEG being tracked simultaneously to behaviour. Studies of this sort have begun to appear over the last decade and, as noted above, the occurrence of frontal midline theta seems indicative of reward processing in these paradigms. As an example, Cavanagh et al. (2012) found that midfrontal theta power correlated with unsigned prediction error, although greater power was found in negative prediction errors relative to positive prediction errors. In general, however, frontal midline theta seemed to correlate more strongly with the unexpectedness of punishment and, thus, may not reflect negative prediction error per se. It is possible that it reflects instead the need for system tuning in response to an unexpected outcome – that is, a need for cognitive control (a process thought to be indexed by theta; Cavanagh & Frank, 2014). In a similar vein, Cavanagh (2015) investigated ongoing EEG during positive reward prediction error and found that parietally distributed delta (oscillations in the 1 to 4 Hz range) were correlated with prediction errors.

There is still some work to do regarding the interpretation of these cortically derived signals. It has been argued, for instance, that different frequencies of slow waves likely involve the recruitment of different cortical-subcortical re-entrant neural loops, thus, different frequencies within the delta-theta range, for example, likely reflect the selection of different neural networks (Kirk & Mackay, 2003). Thus, one of the next challenges is to determine the extent to which slow oscillations (theta and delta, for instance) recorded over different areas of the neocortex represent "windows" through which to infer the networks that are active in any given situation. This is a general challenge but one that has particular relevance in the current context. To what extent are these cortical signals representative of network processing of contextual reward, uncertainty, and prediction errors?

3.2   Temporal Discounting

Many of the decisions we make in life involve outcomes in the future – choices between immediate gratification and longer-term payoffs relating to health (diet, exercise, alcohol consumption), career (writing a neuroeconomics chapter versus watching a rugby game), or the environment (whether or not to recycle, use public transport, buy energy-efficient appliances). The more delayed an outcome, the smaller its subjective value in the present, and the less heavily it weighs in our decision-making process. The process by which an outcome systematically loses value over time is called discounting. Choices between immediate and delayed outcomes – intertemporal choice – pose an interesting challenge to economics because they often violate axioms of normative models of decision-making (see Kalenscher & Pennartz, 2008, for a detailed discussion).

Discounting means we will often choose a more immediately available item of lesser value over a delayed item of greater value. Indeed, we will choose a smaller, more immediate option even when told that the larger, delayed outcome is more likely to occur (Cowie et al., 2020). We will even pay more to have an item sooner, opting for the increased cost of overnight delivery of our online purchases. The effect of delay on subjective value means that, when faced with a choice between the same outcomes or items, we may arrive at different decisions depending on the time at which we make a choice – termed preference reversal (Green et al., 1994). Given the choice between fruit or junk food, you would be more likely to opt for fruit if you were choosing a week in advance than if you were choosing right before eating (VanEpps et al., 2016).

Delay appears to reduce the value of different types of rewards, for different populations, in different settings in the same way (e.g. Odum, 2011), but there is still debate about the exact mathematical form of the reduction in delay. Presently, discounting of subjective value is most commonly described using a hyperbolic function (Green & Myerson, 2004; van den Bos & McClure, 2013), but the reduction in subjective value with delay may also be described by other equations with potentially different theoretical implications (e.g. McClure et al., 2007). Not all outcomes are discounted at the same rate; money holds its subjective value more than other commodities like food, drugs, and cigarettes (Odum, 2011); larger outcomes lose their value less rapidly than smaller outcomes (the magnitude effect; Benzion et al., 1989; Green et al., 1994; Thaler, 1981), and positive outcomes are discounted more steeply than losses (the sign effect; Chapman, 1996; Thaler, 1981). The rate of discounting may also be increased or reduced by the way the question is framed (see Appelt et al., 2011; Loewenstein, 1988), and by the perceived reliability of the environment (Dixon et al., 2006; Kidd et al., 2013). These complexities mean the decision-making processes underlying delay discounting remain something of a mystery.

While the choices we make between different outcomes are observable, the decision-making processes that underlie such choices are less easily examined. Behaviour alone is not enough to determine how we arrive at choosing junk food over fruit in some situations and not others. It is impossible to tell from the choice alone – or the time that choice takes – how subjective value is arrived at in a way that allows preference reversal. In this section, we explore one way that the analysis of brain and behaviour has contributed to decisions between outcomes in the future. One possibility is that two decision-making systems – fast, intuitive System One, and slow, deliberative System Two – are recruited for intertemporal choice; parameters of the choice itself determine how these systems interact and, hence, which option is chosen.

McClure et al. (2004) used fMRI to explore how different structures in the brain responded to different intertemporal choices. In a series of trials, participants chose to receive either a smaller, more immediate amount of money, or a larger, more delayed amount of money. In some trials, the more immediate option was available without a delay; in others, it was delayed. The longest delay was six weeks. Parts of the limbic system, associated with reward processing (Breiter & Rosen, 1999; Knutson et al., 2001), were activated to a greater extent when one of the options was available immediately, relative to when both options were delayed. Areas associated with higher-level cognition and goal-oriented decisions – lateral prefrontal areas – were not preferentially responsive to immediacy; instead, these areas showed greater activation when the dollar amounts were more similar and, hence, decisions more difficult.

McClure et al. (2007) showed an almost identical pattern of differential activation of brain areas when choices were made between amounts of fruit juice and water[4] over much shorter delays of up to 30 minutes. The likelihood of choosing the smaller, sooner option was greater when activity in the limbic system was greater, and when activity in the prefrontal areas was less. These results suggest the involvement of two dissociable decision-making systems: a fast system that tends to prefer more immediate options, and a more deliberative system that (at least under some circumstances) is more willing to delay gratification and wait for larger rewards.

Having established the involvement of two systems in the brain, the next step is to understand how the systems interact to arrive at a choice. Since decisions occur rapidly, a different neuroimaging tool – EEG – is ideally suited to exploring the dynamics between processes because it affords temporal resolution on the scale of milliseconds. Indeed, the amplitude of different components of EEG oscillations, occurring at different times, is differentially affected by different task manipulations (e.g. Gui et al., 2016; Liu et al., 2020). One particular frequency of brain activity – frontal midline theta – shows promise. Theta captures activity relating to reward processing and to cognitive control (e.g. see Mitchell et al., 2008), and correlates with behaviour in intertemporal choice tasks; for example, theta is enhanced when decisions favour the smaller, more immediate option over the larger, more delayed option (Gui et al., 2018). Lin et al. (2018) established that frontal midline theta is also sensitive to the components of inter-temporal decisions.

Lin et al. asked participants to choose between receiving a smaller amount of money today, or a larger amount after a delay. Combinations of delay and amount for the larger–later option were selected for each participant on the basis of how they had chosen in a preliminary delay-discounting task, such that all participants made choices across the same range of differences in subjective value. As the difference in subjective value became smaller, frontal midline theta power increased shortly after the two options were presented, and shortly before a participant chose an option. Surprisingly, theta power in "no-brainer" trials where conflict was low was similar to theta power in trials with the greatest level of subjective conflict, suggesting that theta power reflects general cognitive control and attentional processes, rather than a simple reaction to conflict (see also Gui et al., 2018). Event-related potentials, which show the average amplitude of brain activity as a function of time since an event (stimulus onset, or response), add further insight. Subjective conflict modulated a component associated with stimulus evaluation in other decision-making tasks (a component resembling the early P3 component), but not a component that in other decision-making tasks is usually associated with conflict effects (the N2 component; Yeung et al., 2004). The only signal that tracked subjective conflict but not delay or the no-brainer surprise was a response-locked component that typically follows correct responses in inhibitory-control tasks (Vidal et al., 2000). Taken together, these findings show that EEG has the potential to provide a highly sensitive measure of brain activity underlying intertemporal choices. Hence, EEG is a promising tool for investigating the dynamics of decision-making processes underlying intertemporal choice – particularly if its depth of measurement (in terms of its ability to yield high-temporal-resolution measures of power, frequency, and source and network estimations) can be harnessed to isolate signatures of different decision-making networks.

3.3   Cognitive Load, Perceived Ownership, and Learning

As noted previously, feedback dependent learning appears to rely on the computation of RPEs within the brain to drive behavioural adaptation. As we have noted, as well, the neural signals associated with decision-making and the computation of RPEs are sensitive to temporal discounting, but what else? What other factors influence the neural systems that underlie human learning? While it is impossible for us to cover within this chapter all of the factors that influence learning, we review two here that have a negative and a positive impact on the computation of RPEs – cognitive load and self-relevance.

Cognitive load refers to the demand on a neural system or systems. For instance, cognitive load underpins the real issue with talking on your cellular phone while driving an automobile – both of these tasks place a demand on the neural systems within your brain, and the cognitive load of multitasking results in reduced performance and an increased likelihood of accidents. Krigolson and colleagues (2012) examined the impact of cognitive load on the human learning system within the medial-frontal cortex – the one that is thought to play a key role in generating the aforementioned dopaminergic RPEs that drive subsequent behavioural modification (see Holroyd & Coles, 2002, for more details). In their study, Krigolson et al. had participants perform a simple experimental task in which they had to accurately guess the duration of one second while EEG data were recorded. In the key manipulation, the task was performed in blocks in which cognitive load was either low or high. During low-load experimental trials, the feedback provided to participants informing them of the accuracy of their guess was simple – either a check mark indicating they had accurately guessed one second, or a cross indicating that their guess was inaccurate. During high-load experimental trials, the feedback was more challenging to interpret – two single-digit numbers that had to be added to determine response accuracy. Importantly, Krigolson et al. found that the amplitude of the reward positivity (see Proudfit, 2015), a component of the human ERP associated with the evaluation of RPEs in the medial frontal cortex, was reduced by the increased cognitive load in the complex-feedback condition. In principle, this reduction in the amplitude of the reward positivity suggests that the efficacy of medial-frontal learning is impacted negatively by increased cognitive load, thus, feedback-dependent learning is impaired.

In a follow-up study, Krigolson and colleagues (2015) further investigated the impact of cognitive load but, in this instance, sought to examine the impact of multitasking on neural learning signals. In this experiment, the authors again had two groups of participants perform the same time-estimation task that they used in 2012, but this time they only provided the simple feedback – the check mark and the cross. However, one of the experimental groups also had to perform a second task at the same time as the first – a task that required them to self-monitor their own eye movements while performing the time-estimation task. In line with their previous work, Krigolson and colleagues found that the amplitude of the reward positivity was reduced in the multitasking condition, again suggesting that increased cognitive load reduces the efficacy of neural learning systems.

What drives the negative impact that increased cognitive load has on neural learning systems? Perhaps the most prominent account is resource theory, which posits that neural systems utilise "cognitive resources", and when two tasks compete for the same resources, performance on one or both tasks is reduced (Wickens, 1981). In terms of the results discussed above – whether it was the processing of the mathematics problem while evaluating feedback, or the dual task situation of temporal guessing and eye monitoring – the amount of resources needed to do both tasks simultaneously was insufficient, thus, neural performance (i.e. feedback evaluation) was reduced. Importantly, the results of these two studies suggest real-world applications – increased cognitive load has a negative impact on learning, thus, cognitive load is something that needs to be monitored and assessed to improve learning environments.

Self-relevance (or ownership) is another factor that can have an impact on neural learning systems. For example, early work in this area by Turk et al. (2011) examined the impact of ownership on the neural systems that underlie human attention – a follow-up to earlier work by Cunningham et al. (2008), who demonstrated that perceived ownership biased human memory, but did not ascertain the neural basis for this effect. Typically, ownership is examined in experiments wherein participants see a series of presented objects, including household items, such as utensils, tools, food, and so on. Presented with the item is a cue that indicates that the item either belongs to the participant or to someone else. After the experiment, the impact of the ownership cue is assessed in terms of memory recall. Results like those put forth by Cunningham et al. demonstrate that perceived ownership results in a greater rate of retention in memory for the items that were identified as belonging to the participant. What Turk et al. did was record EEG data during a standard ownership paradigm. The results of their experiment revealed that the onset of the cue indicating that an item belonged to the participant resulted in an increased neural response associated with the focusing of visuospatial attention. In other words, the invocation of perceived ownership resulted in the brain paying more attention to what was on the computer screen, thus enhancing task-relevant memory.

Extending this work to the neural systems involved in learning, Krigolson et al. (2013) recorded EEGs of participants playing a gambling task in which they won prizes for themselves or others. During the task, participants saw a series of common items in line with the aforementioned experiments in this area by Cunningham et al., Turk et al., and others. However, in Krigolson and colleagues' paradigm, participants "gamble" to win or lose the presented items for themselves or for others. The gamble in itself was simple; participants picked a random response button and then found out if they won or lost. Analysis of the EEG data revealed that the amplitude of the aforementioned reward positivity was enhanced when participants were gambling for themselves relative to when they were gambling for someone else. These data are important as they demonstrate that self-relevance enhances the efficacy of neural learning systems and highlight how high-level constructs like ownership have an impact on lower-level systems, such as the one responsible for feedback evaluation. In follow-up work, Hassall et al. (2016) had participants gamble for themselves or for someone else, for varying amounts of money (which they won or lost[5]). In line with their previous work, the researchers found that the reward positivity was greater when participants gambled for themselves, but it was almost entirely absent when the participants gambled for someone else. This result is particularly interesting when one considers the role of an investment banker – does their reward system care about the outcome if they are not "gambling" with their own money? In any event, it is clear that perceived self-ownership enhances the efficacy of neural learning systems.

4.   Where to from Here?

The intersection of neuroscience, psychology, and economics has shed much light on how we make decisions. Extensive work with fMRI has established the underlying neural correlates of decision-making. Investigations of the activity of different populations of neurons, and different areas of the brain, in response to changing task demands provides further insight into the dynamics of learning and decision-making processes. One challenge that builds on this body of work is to understand commonalities across decision-making para-digms, and how subtle variations of the nature of the task affect outcomes – for example, whether the payoffs for choices are awarded to the participant or to another, and whether such payoffs are intrinsically or extrinsically rewarding. A second challenge involves the extent to which different frequencies and sources of brain activity map onto distinct psychological processes, and how these psychological processes interact in economic decisions. Together, these efforts will be fruitful in revealing why the effects of things like ownership and delay to outcome have apparently identical effects on real and hypothetical choices. Further, and perhaps more importantly, understanding the interplay between psychological factors – emotion, cognition, and personality – and decision-making processes will further reveal why we sometimes make appar-ently irrational decisions – choosing to gamble, accepting items of lesser value, sacrificing our own resources, or persisting with an old choice at the expense of investigating new, and potentially better, options.

Acknowledgements

The authors wish to thank Dr Matthew Miller for his feedback on an earlier version of this chapter.

Notes

1. It is worth noting that there are many names for dual-process theory and System One and System Two, however, a full review of this is beyond the scope of this chapter. It is also worth noting that some argue for a continuous single-system account of decision-making within the brain (see Melnikoff and Bargh, 2018), which again is beyond the scope of this chapter.
2. For example, the first diagnosis might have a range of AST values between 100 and 300, and the second diagnosis might have a range of AST values between 300 and 500. An "easy" diagnosis was a presented case where the AST value was close to the mean value for the first diagnosis (200) or the second diagnosis (400). A "hard" diagnosis was a presented case where the AST value was between these two ranges (300).
3. At least for people whose personal preferences favour self-interest (see Rodrigues et al., 2015). Further, suppressing self-interest does not always result in prosocial

choices; rejecting an unfair offer in the Ultimatum Game might well be considered an anti-social choice.

4.   Indeed, at least behaviourally, intertemporal choice tends to be the same regardless of whether choices are made between actual or hypothetical consequences (see, for example, Madden et al., 2003, 2004), perhaps because the choice itself is real regardless.

5.   An interesting thing to note with ownership tasks is that, in most instances, the participants are aware that they do not actually own the items in question. Yet, in spite of this, there is still a very large statistical effect.

References

Andreoni, J., & Miller, J. H. (2008). Analyzing choice with revealed preference: Is altruism rational? In Plott, C., & Smith, V. (Eds.), *Handbook of experimental economics results*, Vol. 1, 481–487. Amsterdam: North-Holland.

Appelt, K. C., Milch, K. F., Handgraaf, M. J., & Weber, E. U. (2011). The decision-making individual differences inventory and guidelines for the study of individual differences in judgment and decision-making research. *Judgment and Decision Making*, 6(3), 252–262.

Baumgartner T., Knoch D., Hotz P., Eisenegger C., & Fehr E. (2011). Dorsolateral and ventromedial prefrontal cortex orchestrate normative choice. *Nature Neuroscience*, 14, 1468–1474.

Benzion, U., Rapoport, A., & Yagil, J. (1989). Discount rates inferred from decisions: An experimental study. *Management Science*, 35(3), 270–284.

Boksem, M. A. S., & De Cremer, D. (2010). Fairness concerns predict medial frontal negativity amplitude in ultimatum bargaining. *Social Neuroscience*, 5(1), 118–128. https://doi.org/10.1080/17470910903202666

Breiter, H. C., & Rosen, B. R. (1999). Functional magnetic resonance imaging of brain reward circuitry in the human. *Annals of the New York Academy of Sciences*, 877(1), 523–547.

Camerer, C. F. (2003). *Behavioral game theory: Experiments in strategic interaction*. Princeton, NJ: Princeton University Press.

Camerer, C. F., & Thaler, R. H. (1995). Anomalies: Ultimatums, dictators and manners. *Journal of Economic Perspectives*, 9(2), 209–219.

Cavanagh, J. F. (2015). Cortical delta activity reflects reward prediction error and related behavioral adjustments, but at different times. *NeuroImage*, 110, 205–216.

Cavanagh, J. F., Figueroa, C. M., Cohen, M. X., & Frank, M. J. (2012). Frontal theta reflects uncertainty and unexpectedness during exploration and exploitation. *Cerebral Cortex*, 22, 2575–2586.

Cavanagh, J. F., & Frank, M. J. (2014). Frontal theta as a mechanism for cognitive control. *Trends in Cognitive Sciences*, 18, 65–75.

Chapman, G. B. (1996). Temporal discounting and utility for health and money. *Journal of Experimental Psychology: Learning, Memory, and Cognition*, 22(3), 771.

Chase, H. W., Kumar, P., Eickhoff, S. B., & Dombrovski, A. Y. (2015). Reinforcement learning models and their neural correlates: An activation likelihood estimation meta-analysis. *Cognitive, Affective Behavioral Neuroscience*, 15, 435–459.

Chen, M., Zhu, X., Zhang, J., Ma, G., & Wu, Y. (2019). Neural correlates of proposers' fairness perception in punishment and non-punishment economic games. *Current Psychology*. https://doi.org/10.1007/s12144-019-0129-3

Civai, C., Crescentini, C., Rustichini, A., & Rumiati, R. I. (2012). Equality versus self-interest in the brain: Differential roles of anterior insula and medial prefrontal cortex. *Neuroimage*, 62, 02–112.

Clayton, M. S., Yeung, N., & Kadosh, R. C. (2015). The roles of cortical oscillations in sustained attention. *Trends in Cognitive Sciences*, 19(4), 188–195.

Cohen, M. X., & Ranganath, C. (2007). Reinforcement learning signals predict future decisions. *Journal of Neuroscience*, 27(2), 371–378.

Cowie, S., Gomes-Ng, S., Hopkinson, B., Bai, J. Y., & Landon, J. (2020). Stimulus control depends on the subjective value of the outcome. *Journal of the Experimental Analysis of Behavior*, 114(2), 216–232.

Cunningham, S. J., Turk, D. J., Macdonald, L. M., & Macrae, C. N. (2008). Yours or mine? Ownership and memory. *Consciousness and Cognition*, 17(1), 312–318.

Cutler, J., & Campbell-Meiklejohn, D. (2019). A comparative fMRI meta-analysis of altruistic and strategic decisions to give. *Neuroimage*, 184, 227–241.

Dixon, M. R., Jacobs, E. A., & Sanders, S. (2006). Contextual control of delay discounting by pathological gamblers. *Journal of Applied Behavior Analysis*, 39(4), 413–422.

Evans, J. S. B. (2003). In two minds: Dual-process accounts of reasoning. *Trends in Cognitive Sciences*, 7(10), 454–459.

Evans, J. S. B., & Frankish, K. (Eds.). (2009). *In two minds: Dual processes and beyond* (Vol. 10). Oxford: Oxford University Press.

Feng, C., Luo, Y. J., & Krueger, F. (2015). Neural signatures of fairness-related normative decision making in the ultimatum game: A coordinate-based meta-analysis. *Human Brain Mapping*, 36(2), 591–602.

Fiori, M., Lintas, A., Mesrobian, S., & Villa, A. E. P. (2013). Effect of emotion and personality on deviation from purely rational decision-making. In Guy, T., Kárný, M., & Wolpert, D. (Eds.), *Decision making and imperfection*, Vol. 474, 129–161. Berlin: Springer.

Garrison, J., Erdeniz B., & Done, J. (2013). Prediction error in reinforcement learning: A meta-analysis of neuroimaging studies. *Neuroscience and Biobehavioral Review*, 37, 1297–1310.

Gershman, S. J., & Uchida, N. (2019) Believing in dopamine. *Nature Reviews Neuroscience*, 20, 703–714.

Grecucci, A., Giorgetta, C., van Wout, M., Bonini, N., & Sanfey, A. G. (2013) Reappraising the ultimatum: An fMRI study of emotion regulation and decision making. *Cerebral Cortex*, 23, 399–410.

Green, L., Fristoe, N., & Myerson, J. (1994). Temporal discounting and preference reversals in choice between delayed outcomes. *Psychonomic Bulletin & Review*, 1(3), 383–389.

Green, L., & Myerson, J. (2004). A discounting framework for choice with delayed and probabilistic rewards. *Psychological Bulletin*, 130(5), 769.

Gui, D. Y., Li, J. Z., Li, X., & Luo, Y. J. (2016). Temporal dynamics of the interaction between reward and time delay during intertemporal choice. *Frontiers in Psychology*, 7, 1526.

Gui, D. Y., Yu, T., Yan, J., & Li, X. (2018). Dissociable functional activities of cortical theta and beta oscillations in the lateral prefrontal cortex during intertemporal choice. *Scientific Reports*, 8(1), 1–8.

Güth, W. (1995). On ultimatum bargaining experiments—A personal review. *Journal of Economic Behavior & Organization*, 27(3), 329–344.

Güth, W., Schmittberger, R., & Schwarze, B. (1982). An experimental analysis of ultimatum bargaining. *Journal of Economic Behavior & Organization*, 3(4), 367–388.

Haas, L. F. (2003). Hans Berger (1873–1941), Richard Caton (1842–1926), and electroencephalography. *Journal of Neurology, Neurosurgery & Psychiatry*, 74(1), 9. https://doi.org/10.1136/jnnp.74.1.9. PMC 1738204. PMID 12486257.

Haidt, J. (2001). The emotional dog and its rational tail: A social intuitionist approach to moral judgment. *Psychological Review*, 108(4), 814–834.

Hassall, C. D., Silver, A., Turk, D. J., & Krigolson, O. E. (2016). We are more selfish than we think: The endowment effect and reward processing within the human medial-frontal cortex. *Quarterly Journal of Experimental Psychology*, 69(9), 1676–1686.

Hewig, J., Kretschmer, N., Trippe, R. H., Hecht, H., Coles, M. G., Holroyd, C. B., & Miltner, W. H. (2011). Why humans deviate from rational choice. *Psychophysiology*, 48(4), 507–514.

Hoffman, E., McCabe, K. A., & Smith, V. L. (1996). On expectations and the monetary stakes in ultimatum games. *International Journal of Game Theory*, 25(3), 289–301.

Holroyd, C. B., & Coles, M. G. (2002). The neural basis of human error processing: Reinforcement learning, dopamine, and the error-related negativity. *Psychological Review*, 109, 679–709.

Holroyd, C. B., Pakzad-Vaezi, K. L., & Krigolson, O. E. (2008). The feedback correct-related positivity: Sensitivity of the event-related brain potential to unexpected positive feedback. *Psychophysiology*, 45, 688–697.

Horat, S. K., Prévot, A., Richiardi, J., Herrmann, F. R., Favre, G., Merlo, M. C., & Missonnier, P. (2017). Differences in social decision-making between proposers and responders during the Ultimatum Game: an EEG study. *Frontiers in Integrative Neuroscience*, 11, 13–25.

Kahneman, D., Peavler, W.S, & Onuska, L. (1968). Effects of verbalization and incentive on the pupil response to mental activity. *Canadian Journal of Psychology/Revue Canadienne de Psychologie*, 22(3), 186–196.

Kahneman, D. (2011). *Thinking, fast and slow*. London: Penguin.

Kalenscher, T., & Pennartz, C. M. A. (2008). Is a bird in the hand worth two in the future? The neuroeconomics of intertemporal decision-making. *Progress in Neurobiology*. doi:10.1016/j.pneurobio.2007.11.004

Kidd, C., Palmeri, H., & Aslin, R. N. (2013). Rational snacking: Young children's decision-making on the marshmallow task is moderated by beliefs about environmental reliability. *Cognition*, 126(1), 109–114.

Kirk, I. J., & Mackay, J. C. (2003). The role of theta-range oscillations in synchronising and integrating activity in distributed mnemonic networks. *Cortex*, 39, 993–1008.

Knutson, B., Fong, G. W., Adams, C. M., Varner, J. L., & Hommer, D. (2001). Dissociation of reward anticipation and outcome with event-related fMRI. *NeuroReport*, 12(17), 3683–3687.

Krajbich, I., Bartling, B., Hare, T., & Fehr, E. (2015). Rethinking fast and slow based on a critique of reaction-time reverse inference. *Nature Communications*, 6(1), 1–9.

Krigolson, O. E., Hassall, C. D., Balcom, L., & Turk, D. (2013). Perceived ownership impacts reward evaluation within medial-frontal cortex. *Cognitive, Affective and Behavioral Neuroscience*, 13(2), 262–269.

Krigolson, O. E., Hassall, C. D., Satel, J., & Klein, R. M. (2015). The impact of cognitive load on reward evaluation. *Brain Research*, 1627, 225–232.

Krigolson, O. E., Heinekey, H., Kent, C. M., & Handy, T. C. (2012). Cognitive load impacts error evaluation within medial-frontal cortex. *Brain Research*, 1430, 62–67.

Lak, A., Stauffer, W. R., & Schultz, W. (2016) Dopamine neurons learn relative chosen value from probabilistic rewards. *Elife*, 5, 1–19.

Lin, H., Saunders, B., Hutcherson, C. A., & Inzlicht, M. (2018). Midfrontal theta and pupil dilation parametrically track subjective conflict (but also surprise) during intertemporal choice. *NeuroImage*, 172, 838–852.

Liu, Q., Yi, W., Rodriguez, C., McClure, S., & Turner, B. (2020). Frontoparietal dynamics and value accumulation in intertemporal choice. BioRxiv.

Loewenstein, G. F. (1988). Frames of mind in intertemporal choice. *Management Science*, 34(2), 200–214.

Madden, G. J., Begotka, A. M., Raiff, B. R., & Kastern, L. L. (2003). Delay discounting of real and hypothetical rewards. *Experimental and Clinical Psychopharmacology*, 11(2), 139.

Madden, G. J., Raiff, B. R., Lagorio, C. H., Begotka, A. M., Mueller, A. M., Hehli, D. J., & Wegener, A. A. (2004). Delay discounting of potentially real and hypothetical rewards: II. Between-and within-subject comparisons. *Experimental and Clinical Psychopharmacology*, 12(4), 251.

McClure, S. M., Ericson, K. M., Laibson, D. I., Loewenstein, G., & Cohen, J. D. (2007). Time discounting for primary rewards. *Journal of Neuroscience*, 27(21), 5796–5804.

McClure, S. M., Laibson, D. I., Loewenstein, G., & Cohen, J. D. (2004). Separate neural systems value immediate and delayed monetary rewards. *Science*, 306(5695), 503–507.

Melnikoff, D. E., & Bargh, J. A. (2018). The mythical number two. *Trends in Cognitive Sciences*, 22(4), 280–293.

Mitchell, D. J., McNaughton, N., Flanagan, D., & Kirk, I. J. (2008). A review of frontal midline theta from the perspective of hippocampal "theta." *Progress in Neurobiology*, 86, 156–185.

Montague, P. R., Dayanm P., & Sejnowski, T. J. (1996). A framework for mesencephalic dopamine systems based on predictive Hebbian learning. *Journal of Neuroscience*, 16, 1936–197.

Odum, A. L. (2011). Delay discounting: Trait variable? *Behavioural Processes*, 87(1), 1–9.

Pennycook, G. (2018). A perspective on the theoretical foundation of dual process models. In De Neys, W. (Ed.), *Current issues in thinking and reasoning. Dual process theory 2.0*, 5–27. New York: Routledge.

Platt, M., & Glimcher, P. (1999). Neural correlates of decision variables in parietal cortex. *Nature* 400(6741), 233–238.

Polezzi, D., Daum, I., Rubaltelli, E., Lotto, L., Civai, C., Sartori, G., & Rumiati, R. (2008). Mentalizing in economic decision-making. *Behavioural Brain Research*, 190(2), 218–223. https://doi.org/10. 1016/j.bbr.2008.03.003

Proudfit, G. H. (2015). The reward positivity: From basic research on reward to a biomarker for depression. *Psychophysiology*, 52(4), 449–459.

Roch, S. G., Lane, J. A., Samuelson, C. D., Allison, S. T., & Dent, J. L. (2000). Cognitive load and the equality heuristic: A two-stage model of resource overconsumption in small groups. *Organizational Behavior and Human Decision Processes*, 83, 185–212.

Rodrigues, J., Ulrich, N., & Hewig, J. (2015). A neural signature of fairness in altruism: A game of theta? *Social Neuroscience*, 10(2), 192–205.

Rolls, E. T., McCabe, C., & Redoute, J. (2008). Expected value, reward outcome, and temporal difference error representations in a probabilistic decision task. *Cerebral Cortex*, 18(3), 652–663.

Sanfey, A. G., & Chang, L. J. (2008). Multiple systems in decision making. *Annals of New York Academy of Sciences*, 1128, 53–62.

Scheele, D., Mihov, Y., Kendrick, K. M., Feinstein, J. S., Reich, H., Maier, W., & Hurlemann, R. (2012). Amygdala lesion profoundly alters altruistic punishment. *Biological Psychiatry*, 72, e5–e7.

Schultz, W. (2015). Neuronal reward and decision signals: From theories to data. *Physiological Reviews*, 95, 853–951.

Schultz, W., Dayan, P., & Montague, P. R. (1997). A neural substrate of prediction and reward. *Science*, 275, 1593–1599.

Sul, J. H., Kim, H., Huh, N., Lee, D., & Jung, M. W. (2010). Distinct roles of rodent orbitofrontal and medial prefrontal cortex in decision making. *Neuron*, 66(3), 449–460.

Tabibnia, G., Satpute, A. B., & Lieberman, M. D. (2008). The sunny side of fairness preference for fairness activates reward circuitry (and disregarding unfairness activates self-control circuitry). *Psychological Science*, 19, 339–347.

Thaler, R. (1981). Some empirical evidence on dynamic inconsistency. *Economics Letters*, 8(3), 201–207.

Thaler, R. (1988). Anomalies: The ultimatum game. *Journal of Economic Perspectives*, 2(4), 195–206.

Turk, D. J., van Bussel, K., Brebner, J. L., Toma, A., Krigolson, O. E., & Handy, T. C. (2011). When "it" becomes "mine": Attentional biases triggered by object ownership. *Journal of Cognitive Neuroscience*, 23(12), 3725–3733.

Van den Bos, W., & McClure, S. M. (2013). Towards a general model of temporal discounting. *Journal of the Experimental Analysis of Behavior*, 99(1), 58–73.

VanEpps, E. M., Downs, J. S., & Loewenstein, G. (2016). Advance ordering for healthier eating? Field experiments on the relationship between the meal order–consumption time delay and meal content. *Journal of Marketing Research*, 53(3), 369–380.

Vidal, F., Hasbroucq, T., Grapperon, J., & Bonnet, M. (2000). Is the "error negativity" specific to errors? *Biological Psychology*, 51(2–3), 109–128.

von Neumann, J., & Morgenstern, O. (1944). *Theory of games and economic behavior*. Princeton, NJ: Princeton University Press.

Wang, G., Li, J., Li, Z., Wei, M., & Li, S. (2016). Medial frontal negativity reflects advantageous inequality aversion of proposers in the ultimatum game: An ERP study. *Brain Research*, 1639, 38–46. https://doi.org/10.1016/j.brainres.2016.02.040

Weiland, S., Hewig, J., Hecht, H., Mussel, P., & Miltner, W. H. (2012). Neural correlates of fair behavior in interpersonal bargaining. *Social Neuroscience*, 7(5), 537–551.

Wickens, C. D. (1981). Processing resources in attention, dual task performance, and workload assessment (no. epl-81-3/onr-81-3). *Illinois University at Urbana Engineering-Psychology Research Lab*.

Williams, C. C., Kappen, M., Hassall, C. D., Wright, B., & Krigolson, O. E. (2019). Thinking theta and alpha: Mechanisms of intuitive and analytical reasoning. *Neuroimage*, 189, 574–580.

Williams, C. C., Ferguson, T. D., Hassall, C. D., Wright, B., & Krigolson, O. E. (in revision). Dissociated neural signals of conflict and surprise in effortful decision making. *Neuropsychologia*.

Wu, Y., Leliveld, M. C., & Zhou, X. (2011). Social distance modulates recipient's fairness consideration in the dictator game: An ERP study. *Biological Psychology*, 88(2), 253–262. https://doi.org/10. 1016/j.biopsycho.2011.08.009

Yeung, N., Botvinick, M. M., & Cohen, J. D. (2004). The neural basis of error detection: Conflict monitoring and the error-related negativity. *Psychological Review*, 111(4), 931.

Zaki, J., & Mitchell, J. P. (2011). Equitable decision making is associated with neural markers of intrinsic value. *Proceedings of the National Academy of Sciences*, 108(49), 19761–19766.

10 Sleep and decision-making

David L. Dickinson

1.   Introduction

This chapter is aimed at introducing the reader to experimental research on sleep and decision-making. While the literature in this area is extensive, the goal here is to highlight the usefulness of studying adverse sleep conditions as a real-world example of cognitive constraints or bounded rationality. In doing so, I will note the benefits of the experimental economics approach, present an organizing framework for examining the effects of sleepiness on decision-making, highlight the various methodologies that have been used to study adverse sleep state effects, and discuss key published research that has used these methodologies to study higher-level decision-making.

This chapter will not discuss literature on economics and sleep that is not directly related to decision-making. The choice of how much one chooses to sleep fits into the classic work on time allocation (Becker, 1965), but we will not cover theoretical work on sleep choice or the sizable economic impacts that insufficient sleep and circadian disruption have on economy-wide losses (e.g., productivity losses, health expenditures related to poor sleep; see Hafner et al., 2017; Giuntela & Mazzonna, 2019). There is also some literature connecting adverse sleep states to final outcome measures, but where identifying the components of decision-making is not a focus. Examples of this type of study include those linking poor sleep and educational attainment (e.g., Baert et al., 2015), automobile accidents (e.g., Varughes & Allen, 2001; Pérez-Chada et al., 2005), or stock returns (e.g., Kamstra et al., 2000).[1] In other words, the focus in this chapter is on how sleep impacts the building blocks of decision-making, so the emphasis is on studies that are more suited to the identification of precise components of choice. Other relevant research that is not the focus of this chapter includes work in the sleep-science and psychology literatures. The interested reader may wish to see useful reviews from the sleep literature for a starting point in this area (e.g., Harrison & Horne, 2000; Lim & Dinges,

2010). These other strands of literature on sleep and decisions or cognition often use different methodologies, focus on real-world scenarios that sacrifice task attribute control, and/or may not focus on tasks that can directly speak to precise decision components of interest to economists. I do my best to include in this chapter those studies that use more traditional economics decision paradigms, but that derive from the sleep and psychology literature. As will be noted later, many of the protocols in the literature have used at-home sleep manipulations such that there is a "field experiment" element to some of the existing sleep studies that assess decisions in the lab (i.e., field-in-the-lab). Some researchers are also actively working on sleep-related field experiments in developing countries (e.g., Bessone et al., 2020), but this is only more recent, and such field experiment research is subject to additional challenges (see note 1).

There has been considerable research in recent years examining how cognitive load may impact decision-making, which is somewhat relevant to our interests in this chapter. Such research is usually done via a couple of standard manipulations: time pressure (e.g., Kocher & Sutter, 2006; Rand et al., 2012) and multi-tasking via digit memorization (see the recent review in Deck & Jahedi, 2015). Another recent study asked participants to perform a difficult version of the Stroop task for several minutes in order to deplete self-control (Kocher et al., 2019). Models of "ego depletion" present self-control as a resource that can be used up and unavailable for other tasks (e.g., Baumeister et al., 1998; Muraven et al., 1999),[2] and this resource may be replenished with sleep. These distinct methodologies can all be seen as alternative approaches aimed at understanding limits to rationality, or decision impairment or deficit, in a general sense.

Herbert Simon (1955) is generally considered to have first proposed the theory of bounded rationality as an alternative to rational-choice decision-making theories. This chapter is not a review of that vast literature, but we mention it to highlight that other researchers have shown interest in developing applied experimental methodologies to study these problems. Cognitive load manipulations are useful in furthering our understanding of decision-making under those specific conditions (e.g., time-pressured decision-making, or choice when our minds are occupied with other items). What this chapter offers is a look at the experimental research and methodologies used to study the influence of another common and highly relevant real-world cognitive state on decision-making: sleepiness. In some sense, it is more challenging to work with sleep restriction or deprivation because these impact one's physical and cognitive states. Regarding decision-making specifically, sleepiness compounds higher-level cognition effects with some lower-level deficits (e.g., slower reaction times, motor skills, inattentiveness) that may play a role in executing one's decision. This may result in challenges to the identification of precise mechanisms, but a carefully chosen task can limit the role that these factors play—the simpler the task the better, in most instances, for just such reasons. The benefits of a systematic study of how sleep impacts decision-making are that it can provide insights into behavior and choice that are more directly applicable to real-world decision-makers given the prevalence of insufficient sleep in modern society.

Evidence suggests that insufficient sleep is a condition that affects large segments of the population across the globe. In the U.S., insufficient sleep has been recently labeled a public health problem by the U.S. Centers for Disease Control and Prevention. This is not surprising given that 30% of adults are considered to be chronically sleep deprived due to habitual sleep levels of 6 hours or less per night (Schoenborn & Adams, 2010). Additionally, more than 20 million adults perform shift work each year, which implies an additional challenge to being well-rested physically (McMenamin, 2007). Note also that such shift work is often concentrated in sectors where public health is at stake, such as emergency service workers, long-haul trucking, and air traffic control, to name a few. This problem of sleepy decision-makers is not reserved for the U.S., however, as similar levels of insufficient sleep have been found in recent survey data from Mexico, Canada, the U.K., Germany, and Japan. At the country-wide level, Figure 1 highlights the variation in average adult sleep levels compiled for this chapter from the recent literature (with publication dates ranging from 2005 to 2018).

The studies represented in Figure 1 used reported survey-based data on average sleep levels, either as a primary outcome variable of interest or as a secondary variable collected as a co-variate for other analysis. In total, the identified studies provided information on recent adult average sleep levels in 33 countries across the globe. When data were available on sleep levels in a particular country from more than one study, only the more recent study or the study with the larger sample size was included. Nevertheless, Figure 1 should be viewed with caution given the different primary research questions across studies that led to these average-sleep-level data (often as a secondary variable of interest). Keep in mind that average sleep combines both above- and below-average-level sleepers; thus, it is clear that the global concern over recommended sleep levels is far from trivial, given that many countries may not even have average sleep at recommended levels. In other words, average sleep of 7.5 hours per night in a country implies a significant proportion of individuals with less than this amount (as well as others with higher sleep levels, to be fair). Regarding the theme of this chapter, if insufficient sleep is

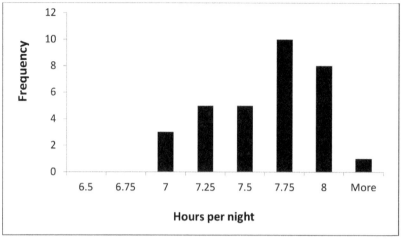

Note: Countries included (with the number of observations on which their data were based in parenthesis) were the following: Australia (1011), Austria (490), Belgium (6832), Brazil (1999), Bulgaria (713), Canada (250), China (12 794), Colombia (703), England (702), France (634), Germany (2646), Ghana (3679), Greece (721), Hungary (539), Iceland (631), India (6526), Iran (3515), Ireland (426), Italy (1733), Japan (10 424), Korea (648), Mexico (2130), Netherlands (679), Poland (702), Portugal (862), Romania (702), Russia (3506), Slovak Republic (1174), South Africa (3507), Spain (1999), Thailand (826), United States (1532), and Venezuela (632). Reference information for the published studies from which these sleep quantities were extracted are available from the author on request.

Figure 10.1   Worldwide average adult sleep levels (n = 33 countries)

somewhat prevalent, then sleepiness is also common. Furthermore, if sleepy decision-making is commonplace, then a systematic study of choice with variation in sleepiness can help further our understanding of the cognitive underpinnings of decision-making in general.

As we shall see, a main theme of the studies identified in this chapter is that adverse sleep states typically promote less deliberative decision-making. While an obvious simplification, the popular dual-systems approach to decision-making (Shiffrin & Schneider, 1977; Stanovich & West, 2000; Camerer et al., 2005) considers that the two major contributing processes to decision-making are the automatic (System 1) or deliberative (System 2) decision processes. Neural networks activated during decisions often involve overlapping regions among those typically implicated in each type of decision-making. For predictive validity, it is enough to consider that the relative impact of one decision-making process (compared to the other) may be influenced by state-level decision-maker changes, such as sleepiness. Carefully selected decision tasks can therefore help illuminate the precise mechanisms involved in choice by systematically examining how adverse sleep states impact key task outcome measures. We review several examples in detail in this chapter.

2. Sleep and Decision-Making

Our understanding of how sleep affects decision-making is greatly aided by exploiting the benefits of experimental methods to randomly assign sleep levels, or randomly manipulate when decision-making occurs during one's circadian rhythm. Sleep scientists have been active in studying decision-making in the context of laboratory-induced sleep deprivation for many years (i.e., how sleep impacts both the behavioral outcomes and neural activation relevant to decision-making). Generally, the sleep literature has concluded that deliberative processing areas of the brain (so-called "executive function" regions) are disproportionately impacted when we are sleep deprived (Chee & Chua, 2008; Drummond et al., 1999, 2013; Horne, 1993; Muzur et al., 2002). Thus, it seems clear that sleep likely changes the relative contribution of Systems 1 and 2 processes on decision-making. One study (Libedinsky et al., 2011), for example, showed that sleep deprivation altered value signals in the ventromedial prefrontal cortex—a deliberative System 2 process area of the brain—in a way that was directly proportionate to observed behavioral outcomes.

In short, sleep scientists have led the charge in early research on sleepy decision-making. Many sleep scientists come from a background in psychology, however, which means that the decision paradigms used may suffer from criticisms raised by experimental economists. For example, a lack of incentives directly tied to decision outcomes implies a lack of outcome saliency, and the attractively packaged paradigm aimed at engaging the decision-maker may suffer from the lack of task precision. In other words, previous studies may limit our ability to make clear conclusions due to the absence of incentives (part of the expected methodology in experimental economics) or a lack of decision tasks free from confounds. This is not universally true of all decision-making studies conducted by sleep scientists, but a useful example on task design can be made by focusing on the widely used Iowa Gambling Task (IGT).

The IGT involves the selection of cards from a series of decks that contain both green and red cards that either monetarily reward or penalize, respectively, the decision-maker. This task is commonly used to make claims regarding risk attitude of a decision-maker, and the task stimuli are engaging. However, a careful examination reveals at least two problems with the IGT (independent of whether or not the task is incentivized with real earnings or potential for losses). First, it is unknown to the decision-maker the proportion of green versus red cards in each deck. Thus, it is a not a pure test of risk preference, but rather ambiguity preference (uncertainty). Secondly, a given choice can produce a loss or a gain, thus crossing an important reference point considered to toggle preferences from risk aversion to risk seeking (as per the prospect theory of Kahneman & Tversky, 2013). While I am not claiming that nothing useful has been learned from research using the IGT, my point is that the task lacks the precision to cleanly identify unique components of decision-making that are affected by an experimental manipulation like sleep restriction. To make a useful comparison, the research limitation would be similar to observing that a sleep-deprived driver crashes in a driving simulation more frequently than a well-rested driver. Such a result has taught us something important about the link between sleep deprivation and the likelihood of an automobile accident. In the end, however, the mechanism(s) producing the outcome (i.e., crash rate) would remain unclear without a more precise task design. Additional basic research would still be needed to identify the impact of sleep deprivation on reaction times (motor skills), risk attitude, information processing, and others, or some combination of many factors that could all play a contributing role in increased accident risk.

To organize our thinking of how the brain makes decisions, consider a dual-systems framework that speaks of an automatic (System 1) as well as a more deliberative (System 2) process at work in decision-making (e.g., Shiffrin & Schneider, 1977; Camerer et al., 2005). Of course, a dual-systems framework is inherently an oversimplification (see also Kahneman, 2011, on this point), but a general idea of how brain inputs or neural circuitry might respond to a cognitive challenge like sleep restriction can be given a bit more formal structure by borrowing from production theory (see Dickinson & McElroy, 2017). Such an approach can also be consistent with more current views of modulatory/reciprocal interactions between decision inputs because one can easily accommodate complementarity between cognitive inputs.

For example, consider that the accuracy of decisions, D, is a function of two cognitive inputs, x_1 and x_2: $D = D(x_1, x_2)$. Within the dual-systems framework, these could be loosely thought of as automatic and deliberative system inputs, but x_1 and x_2 could also represent distinct neural circuits of interest. Let the cognitive costs of using these inputs be w_1 and w_2, respectively. Now consider the constrained maximization problem at hand. For example, if $D(x_1, x_2)$ is assumed to have a common functional form, such as the Cobb–Douglas function $D = x_1^{\alpha} x_2^{1-\alpha}$, then α represents the factor share of the brain's resources that will be devoted to cognitive input 1, and $(1-\alpha)$ is therefore the factor share devoted to cognitive input 2. Such a framework would imply that the brain's optimal usage of prefrontal inputs or resources, x_2^*, would satisfy

$x_2^* = \dfrac{(1-\alpha)}{\alpha} \dfrac{w_1}{w_2} x_1$. The typical result is that the level of deliberation, or neural

circuit activity of the prefrontal region, used at the optimum, x_2^*, would be both decreasing in α (the brain's technological bent toward cognitive input 1) as well as decreasing in w_2 (the costliness of cognitive input 2, x_2). Sleep restriction, for example, can be thought of as increasing the cost of deliberation (or, increasing the cost of a neural pathway activity), w_2, and/or shifting the decision production function toward a relatively higher use of more automatic cognitive input 1, x_1, via an increase in the factor share parameter, α.[3] There may be instances, such as with the fight/flight/freeze response, where System 1 may entirely dictate one's choice, but in most instances a partial substitutability of these two main decision processes is a reasonable assumption.

3.   Methodologies to Study Sleepiness

The body of research where sleep state or sleepiness is manipulated prior to decision-making has used several methodologies. Across the studies surveyed below, we see the following methodologies used to study sleep impacts on decisions: observational, sleep deprivation or restriction in the sleep lab, sleep restriction outside of the lab, circadian manipulations, or other approaches.

An observational study does not involve a manipulation of one's sleep state; rather, these types of studies measure home-grown variation in sleep levels across the study sample. The researcher then examines the relationship between decision-making and the observational sleep variable. While useful, an observational study obviously does not benefit from randomization and experimental manipulation of one's sleep state, thus limiting one's ability to make causal inferences. At a minimum, the most rigorous observational study would include an objective and validated measurement of the key variable, such as sleep levels. For example, wrist-worn sleep trackers (i.e., actigraphy devices) that have been validated against polysomnography, or a diurnal-preference (morningness–eveningness) instrument validated against physiological measures (e.g., saliva-based melatonin levels) are common in these studies. Modern actigraphy devices used by sleep researchers boast impressive battery life (implying the user need not worry about recharging the battery) and can be worn for most daily activities like dish-washing and showering (i.e., they can be worn almost 24/7 and need only be removed for swimming, contact sports, working with chemicals, etc.).

Less common, and potentially less valid, is sleep measurement that uses self-report measures or commercial but non-validated sleep tracking devices— these devices are not as monetarily costly to the researcher to obtain, but may be costly down the road in the form of increased scrutiny over the data valid- ity. Regarding increasingly popular commercial sleep tracking devices, the researcher would be wise to consider whether such a device has been validated in the literature, and whether its features are suitable for the planned design— features like battery life, sleep feedback during the study (which may not be desirable), or varied data output measures should all be carefully considered. While several validation studies exist to compare wrist-worn sleep trackers to polysomnographic measures, a recent study noted some of these trade-offs while also reporting on a direct data comparison of a research-grade actigra- phy device to a common commercial sleep tracker (Dickinson, Cazier, & Cech, 2016). Perhaps the best advice here is to keep in mind that the burden of proof is and should be on the researcher to convince others regarding the validity of the measures used for any study, including observation research. A recent review offers advice regarding the use of lower-cost consumer "wearables" in sleep research (De Zambotti et al., 2019), and the Sleep Research Society recently published a position statement that includes guidelines on the use of more commercial consumer devices in research (Depner et al., 2020).

Studies that manipulate one's sleep level may take place inside or outside of a sleep lab. A sleep lab is typically used for more extreme sleep manipulations that would prove unsafe to administer outside of the protection of a lab environment. The sleep laboratory is also useful when more comprehensive controls are desired, such as control over physical activity, light exposure, food intake, or the exact type of sleep manipulation (e.g., selective deprivation of REM sleep). As for the level of sleep manipulation that researchers administer in a sleep lab, this can vary from a partial sleep restriction to total sleep depri- vation of one (or more) nights. If one is willing to sacrifice some experimental control for the sake of real-world parallelism, an at-home sleep restriction protocol can be used. Here, the participant may be randomly assigned to a prescribed sleep level over one or several nights. The sleep level prescribed may be a restricted sleep level or a more well-rested sleep level. Typically, a passive but objective measurement of sleep level is part of a good at-home sleep protocol (i.e., validated actigraphy device measurements). The passive measurement of sleep levels using actigraphy is typically also completed with simple sleep diaries that can help assess compliance of participants with the prescribed sleep treatment. Finally, the experimenter may require daily texts or emails from each participant to record bed and wake times. The purpose is to provide another piece of complementary data to help the researcher most accurately score the beginning and end-points of the participant's attempted sleep period in the event the sleep diary data are unclear, blank, or the actigraphy data have not been marked on the device at bed/wake times as requested (this happens). While this may sound rather involved, it is relatively simple for the participant. In addition to wearing the sleep-tracking actigraphy device 24/7 (with few exceptions), the participant answers a few simple sleep diary questions at bed/wake time each day, sends a short email to the experimenter, and presses a marker button on the actigraphy device to note bed and wake times. Regarding the decision-making component of the study, the decision tasks can be administered at desired time points with little difficulty in a sleep lab study that involves the participant physically staying in the lab. For an at-home study, the participant may complete online decision tasks during the manipulation (once sufficiently "treated" by the manipulation), but almost certainly would return to the lab for a decision session once having completed the sleep manipulation. It is during this post-manipulation decision session when the participant would likely be asked to return the completed sleep diaries and the actigraphy devices so that sleep data may be downloaded and scored by the experimenter.[4]

Because sleepiness may result from either cumulative wake hours or one's circadian rhythm that dictates a daily cycle to one's sleepiness and alertness, circadian manipulations can also be used to study sleepy decision-making. This may or may not be done in conjunction with information on one's diurnal preference, but including a diurnal preference measure increases the power of the circadian manipulation. For example, if one has a validated measure of morningness–eveningness preferences, then increased power in a circadian design might involve recruitment of only morning- or evening-type participants to participate in experiments at a randomly assigned early morning or late evening time. Figure 2 shows how typical alertness ratings vary by diurnal preference type. Here, it is apparent that decision-making between, say, 4 a.m. and 5 a.m. would be at an unfavorable or at a suboptimal point in time, no matter one's diurnal preference type. On the other hand, at a time such as 1 a.m., an evening-type would be, on average, at a more circadian-preferred (alert) point in time compared to a morning-type individual, which implies heterogeneity in the circadian optimality of the decision time if one recruits participants that differ in diurnal preference. In-lab studies may administer more controlled manipulations of circadian misalignment such that cumulative wake hours or time since last sleep are also kept constant, but most existing research studying economic decision-making using circadian manipulations has used a second-best approach of time-of-day differences in decision-making.

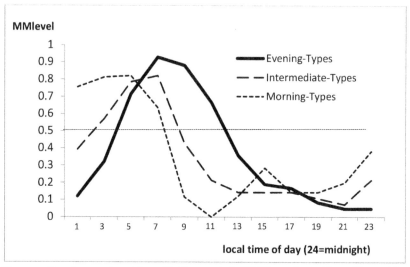

Source: Graph reproduced from Dickinson et al. (2019) as adapted from Figure 1 in Smith et al. (2002).
Note: Diurnal preference patterns were validated against alertness ratings and used to construct a measure of one's mismatch (MM) level $\in [0 , 1]$.

Figure 10.2   Mismatch level, based on self-reported alertness

Finally, other methodologies have been creatively used to examine sleep impacts on decision-making. For example, the daylight saving time clock change represents an exogenous shift in sleep that occurs two nights each year. Decision studies not using laboratory methods or economic decision paradigms have leveraged this annual shift to study topics such as cyberloafing (using Internet access at work for personal use; see Wagner et al., 2012) and severity of punishment in judicial decisions (Cho et al., 2016); this points to an opportunity for future research involving economic decision-making. Another example involves time-zone boundaries, which have been shown to shift the nightly sleep of those living on the immediate eastern side of the time zone by approximately 20 minutes per night (or more for those with early work schedules; see Giuntella & Mazzonna, 2019). This allows for a regression discontinuity design that can be useful if some type of decision-making data exist that can be matched with the geolocation of the individual. Such studies require relatively larger sample sizes (e.g., thousands of observations) that are only available in some survey data sets. In short, while certain methodologies involving sleep restriction or time of day may be the most typical of studies surveyed in this chapter, other creative approaches allow additional possibilities. The next two sections highlight existing sleep and decision-making studies, both individual choice and interactive decisions, that have focused on task paradigms common in experimental economics.

4.   Sleep and Decision-Making: Individual Choice

Risky choice was the focus in McKenna et al. (2007) and Castillo et al. (2017). McKenna et al. (2007) studied both pure risk and ambiguity preferences over gains and losses following total sleep deprivation. The within-subjects design required each participant to complete the task both well-rested and following a full night of total sleep deprivation (TSD). The results showed that the participants, whose well-rested choices were consistent with risk aversion in gambles over gains but risk loving over losses, became less risk averse in the risky gains domain and less risk loving in the losses domain under TSD. These results are consistent with sleep deprivation effectively desensitizing the participants to monetary risk (TSD had few if any impacts on choices over ambiguous gambles). Using a different risky-choice paradigm in conjunction with a circadian match/mismatch protocol, Castillo et al. (2017) also reported that subjects at a circadian off-peak time of day made choices consistent with being desensitized to risk. Specifically, participants chose riskier asset bundles using a novel task developed by Choi et al. (2007). Interestingly, their study also allowed for a test of choice consistency with standard preference axioms. The authors concluded that, though risky choice differed at a circadian off-peak time of day/night, choices were not less consistent with rationality, defined in common ways in economics (i.e., choices did not simply become irrational or random when at a circadian off-peak time).[5] These results contrast with those in Sundelin et al. (2019), who reported no impact of sleep restriction on risky choice, but it is noteworthy that sleep restriction in Sundelin et al. (2019) lasted only two nights and was therefore considerably more mild than that studied in McKenna et al. (2007).[6]

The typical conclusion in the literature has been consistent with the McKenna et al. (2007) study, with generally robust findings that indicate that sleep deprivation/restriction increases preference for risk or desensitizes one to bad risky-choice outcomes.[7] This includes findings across many studies more familiar to the sleep-science literature that have used tasks or methodological approaches not generally considered by experimental economists (see Womack et al., 2013). One mechanism that may be responsible for these sleep deprivation effects on risky choice could be increased impulsivity. The evidence on sleep deprivation and impulsivity has been mixed in the domain of delayed monetary rewards (Libedinsky et al., 2013), but a more recent study found a significant impact of naturalistically measured habitual short sleep and poor sleep quality on increasing impulsivity in choice (Curtis et al., 2018). Other possible mechanisms linking sleep and risky choice are that TSD or sleepiness affect anticipation of rewards (i.e., overconfidence) and/or feedback learning from loss events in ways that make risky choice seem more attractive (see Venkatraman et al., 2007, 2011).

Another individual decision task domain that has been studied in the context of sleep deprivation and sleep restriction is Bayesian choice. Using a Bayesian task that involved integration of new information and base rate probabilities, TSD was found to reduce the decision weight that individuals placed on new information relative to base rate information in making assessments (Dickinson & Drummond, 2008).[8] This result was extended to observational levels of insufficient sleep in a follow-up study that examined two distinct samples of college students (one sample was military cadets; Dickinson, Drummond, & Dyche, 2016). While this result was robust, neither study identified a reduction in the Bayesian accuracy of subject choices, even though the analysis indicated altered decision weights by sleep level. However, a more recent study using a different Bayesian paradigm identified a reduction in the accuracy in more difficult assessment environments (Dickinson & McElroy, 2019), which is consistent with other recent work concluding that sleep restriction or circadian mismatched timing of decision-making harms decision-making quality in complex, but not easy-choice, environments (McElroy & Dickinson, 2019).[9]

Framing effects, whereby the style in which one presents a choice influences decisions made in otherwise identical scenarios (in terms of the relevant final outcome information), are a decision bias that is frequently studied by psychologists. If framing effects are considered the result of reduced attentiveness, then it is natural to hypothesize that sleepy individuals will be more subject to the framing of choice in decision-making. McElroy and Dickinson (2010) examined data from a classic framing task paradigm (the "Asian Disease" problem; see Tversky & Kahneman, 1981) using a circadian timing protocol. While the nature of this task does not make it possible to incentivize the choices, the authors followed more standard experimental economics methodology by offering fixed monetary compensation for participation and by not recruiting solely from the set of psychology research methods students.[10] Over 600 young adults (college students with an average age of 23.3 years) were recruited to complete the short framing task during a randomly assigned one-hour time slot during the day or night. All 24 of the possible 1-hr time slots were assigned. Interestingly, decisions from the circadian off-peak participants were more likely to display a framing effect, as hypothesized. However, the effects were driven by highly significant effects in the loss condition of the task, while no framing effects resulted from circadian timing in the gains-frame condition. The identification of variation in the strength of framing effects across times of day reiterates the potential for using circadian timing (along with validated measures of morningness–eveningness preferences, as was done in McElroy and Dickinson, 2010) to study sleepiness in decision-making. It also highlights the interesting fact that, while sleepiness may lead to increased sensitivity to some seemingly less pertinent contextual details of a decision (such as with enhanced framing effects), it was also found to decrease sensitivity to other key variables, including the potential for monetary loss (Castillo et al., 2017) and demand sensitivity to prices (Dickinson & Whitehead, 2015).

One last domain of individual choice to note in this chapter is the area of ethical or moral choice, and again our focus is on studies involving incentivized tasks of the sort used in experimental economics. Barnes et al. (2011) provided evidence linking lack of sleep to unethical behavior in both lab and field contexts, but their lab study specifically identified a link between lack of sleep and over-reporting results of an incentivized trivia quiz. Kouchaki and Smith (2014) showed that time of day may influence honesty in messages sent or in self-reported outcomes of a cognitive-style task, although there was no explicit consideration of one's diurnal preference. Rather, their focus was on the likely depletion of self-control resources hypothesized to be necessary for one to resist a temptation to be dishonest. Other evidence may not be laboratory based, but it has examined how exogenous shocks, like daylight saving time changes, affect field-relevant outcomes, such as cyberloafing (see Wagner et al., 2012) or decreased search activity related to moral topics (Barnes et al., 2015). As a whole, there is relatively little in the area of incentivized ethical choice in conjunction with explicit manipulation of sleep levels or sleepiness.

5. Sleep and Decision-Making: Interactive Decisions (Social/Group/Market Outcomes)

Interactive decision-making, as examined here, implies decisions that may affect others or are made in conjunction with others. A most basic version of interactive decision-making would involve simple two-person social interactions. The first study to examine how sleep impacts social decision-making, to our knowledge, is the study by Anderson and Dickinson (2010), which examined outcomes in classic ultimatum, dictator, and trust games of individuals in both well-rested and TSD states (sleep laboratory controlled). The authors reported that TSD reduced trust and increased minimum acceptable offers in ultimatum games, although the ultimatum game is notoriously messy to analyze given that offers may be due to kindness or the simple aversion to having one's offer rejected. A more recent study examined this same suite of tasks using the at-home partial sleep restriction and circadian match/mismatch paradigm reported in Dickinson et al. (2017). This study found that mild but chronic (within-subjects manipulated) sleep restriction decreased prosocial behaviors in the form of reduced dictator offers, lower trust, and lowered trustworthiness (Dickinson & McElroy, 2019). Yet another study (Holbein et al., 2019) extended those results to include the practically relevant domain of civic engagement behaviors (e.g., likelihood of voting, signing a petition, donating to the Red Cross). Results here were congruent among survey-based, regression discontinuity design (using time-zone boundary impacts), and an online time-of-day manipulation (nighttime assignment required response in the middle of the night) combined with a civic engagement survey. Across all methodologies (not just the randomized experiment study), the results from Holbein et al. (2019) showed that reduced sleep decreased prosocial behaviors of the sort that are important in democratic societies.

The existing research examining how sleep impacts small-group decision-making is even more limited. Clark and Dickinson (2017) examined how a full week of at-home sleep restriction affected contribution and punishment decisions in a classic voluntary contribution mechanism (VCM) public-good-provision environment. Their key finding was that the availability of norm enforcement through punishment led to higher contribution levels among sleep-restricted group members, as if sleep restriction leads one to contribute more to avoid punishment. Though not robust across different measures of sleep restriction, they also reported some suggestive evidence that even though sleep-restricted individuals punish less overall, they may be more inclined to punish antisocially (i.e., to punish those who contributed more than they did). Another recent working paper utilized the same set of participants as Clark and Dickinson (2017). This paper (Castillo & Dickinson, 2020) explored choices in classic minimum-effort coordination games using three-person groups. Their evidence showed that groups containing sleep-restricted members suffered higher levels of costly miscoordination. Furthermore, the miscoordination resulting from sleep-restricted group members was enough to negate the beneficial impacts of repeated interactions with the same group members.

A different type of interactive decision potentially affected by adverse sleep states is the domain of anticipation or "theory of mind"-type tasks. One such task involves the "guessing game" first introduced by Nagel (1995). Successfully anticipating others' decisions involves a type of mentalizing that requires medial prefrontal cortex activation (Coricelli & Nagel, 2009), which is harmed by sleep deprivation. Dickinson and McElroy (2010) administered the Guessing Game in an online survey that was sent to 684 participants who completed the task at a randomly assigned 1-hr time slot. All hours of the day and night were assigned, survey time stamps were used to validate response times, and the authors organized results by scoring 1:00 a.m.–5:00 a.m. as Bad Time = 1, and noon–7:00 p.m. as Bad Time = 0 (using information in Figure 2 as a guide, they discarded some of the time slots for their analysis). While main time-of-day effects were not found, they reported that combining Bad Time with additional adverse sleep states of high daytime sleepiness (from a validated metric) and not having slept much the prior night produced significant differences. Specifically, guesses from those in an "adverse sleep state" combination, compared to a "favorable sleep state" combination, were further from equilibrium.

In a follow-up study, Dickinson and McElroy (2012) examined a multi-period version of the same game, with feedback after each period administered to validated morning types or evening types at either 8:00 a.m. or 8:00 p.m., respectively, to create a randomly assigned set of circadian-matched and mismatched participants. Objective actigraphy sleep measures were also obtained for the week prior to the decision experiment, though sleep was not manipulated. Their study reported that circadian mismatch led to decisions further from the rational equilibrium prediction only in the first period of play, when the game was novel and participants had yet to receive feedback. The feedback made mimicry an easy strategy to employ for circadian mismatched participants, but their results highlighted the importance of circadian state in this anticipation task, at least when the task is novel to the participants.[11] One drawback of Dickinson and McElroy (2012) is that the 8:00 p.m. evening time chosen in their design likely did not pose as serious of a circadian mismatch for morning-type participants as intended (see Figure 2 above, for example). Later circadian mismatch protocols of Dickinson and co-authors utilized a 10:00 p.m. evening time for in-lab evening sessions (see, for example, the protocols in Castillo et al., 2017, and Dickinson et al., 2017).

While distinct, a recent study with some relation to the decision area of "anticipation" involved a time-of-day manipulation across subjects in a market-based asset trading experiment (Dickinson, Chaudhuri, & Greenaway-McGrevy, 2020). This study was designed to examine how globally dispersed market

participants behave in a classic asset trading market experiment that produces price bubbles (see Bostian & Holt, 2009). The premise in Dickinson,
Chaudhuri, and Greenaway-McGrevy (2020) was that successful trading
strategies require successful anticipation of others' behavior, as is the case in
the Guessing Game. Here, the authors designed asset market experiments that
were administered online at different times of the day in two local markets,
East Coast U.S. and New Zealand. Experiments were administered at local
times of noon, 8:00 p.m., and 4:00 a.m. in each location. Additionally, several
"global" markets sessions were designed to put traders at the two locations
together in real time. For the global market sessions, participants in the two
locations were 16 time zones apart, so these sessions introduced heterogeneity
of circadian timing into each asset market. These global markets involved
local-time trading at each location at noon, 4:00 p.m., 8:00 p.m., midnight, 4:00
a.m., and 8:00 a.m.. This logistically complex experiment showed that markets
having more circadian mismatch heterogeneity across traders exhibited longer
lasting price bubbles, and individual traders at more suboptimal times of day
engaged in riskier trading strategies.[12]

6.   Concluding Remarks

The available research on sleep and decision-making reveals this as a fruitful
area for research that is open to multiple methodologies and decision domains.
The interest in how adverse sleep states impact decision-making stems from
research interest in bounded rationality or limits to cognition and how those
impact decisions. These are standard building blocks in behavioral economics,
so this research area has an audience well-versed in the general question of
how less-than-perfectly rational agents make decisions. While many clever
techniques have been developed to induce bounds to rationality in the lab
(or to limit or deplete available cognitive resources), the interest in inducing
adverse sleep or circadian states lies in how commonplace such conditions are
in the real world. The traditional concerns over external validity in experimental methodology are therefore not only decision task concerns, but also concerns that extend to the methods by which we induce the cognitive condition
of interest.

Here, we find that manipulations of time of day or sleep levels often score high
marks in our ability to transfer these conditions to real-world decision-makers
outside the lab. We have seen that both sleep-restriction and circadian-timing
protocols exist that can reasonably recreate the commonplace conditions
experienced by many. While such protocols sacrifice some internal controls

enjoyed in the hyper-controlled sleep laboratory environment, it is easier to make a real-world connection with findings from more ecologically valid protocols that allow the participant to remain in a naturalistic setting. That being said, the existing research that has induced more commonly experienced states of insufficient sleep or suboptimal circadian timing has generally found that inducing sleep restriction over multiple days has been a more effective and powerful experimental manipulation than circadian timing manipulation. This is not only evident in the less significant circadian timing effects found in some studies, but also in the few studies that included both types of "sleepiness" manipulations in a mixed design. Such studies (e.g., Dickinson & McElroy 2017, 2019) generally reported stronger findings and more precise estimates of the sleep restriction effects, compared to circadian mismatch effects, on decision-making.

As we have seen in this chapter, the decision tasks studied within the various sleep protocols are varied. Because this line of research was largely initiated by sleep scientists trained as psychologists, perhaps a disproportionate amount of their early interests are in the domain of individual choice. That being said, the more recent use of task methodologies familiar to experimental economists (e.g., simple tasks, often void of context, no deception, incentivized decision paradigms, etc.) have surely improved the state of the science in this area. It is this author's view that the disciplines of behavioral sleep science and experimental/behavioral economics have benefited from the recent interdisciplinary work highlighted in this chapter. Sleep science has benefitted from a new set of decision paradigms, rigorous decision experiment methodologies, and more varied choice domains. Experimental and behavioral economics has progressed through the use of common physiological states, such as restricted sleep and suboptimal time of day as a means of examining how constraints on decision-making capacity and cognition impact choice in simple building-block decision environments.

As with all science, the robustness of the results that have emerged from this literature depend on an overall body of research that engages the same question from different angles as a type of sensitivity analysis. Future meta-analyses may be useful here, but certain results seem to be consistent across the sleep and decision studies that have used different sleep methodologies or decision paradigms. Specifically, there seems to be some consistency across multiple studies showing that insufficient sleep harms prosociality in some ways, reduces one's use of new information in updating beliefs, increases preference for or tolerance to monetary risk, and reduces the ability to deliberate in ways that may increase the reliance on heuristics.

There may also be more general and yet underappreciated ways in which this emerging area of interdisciplinary research can further knowledge among economists. For example, health economics is not typically concerned with "behavioral health," but it should be considered an important part of understanding the full impact of sleep concerns (e.g., insufficient sleep) that clearly go beyond physical health. Additionally, some of the identified behavioral effects here may also reveal potentially important, yet underappreciated, impacts of modern sleep habits on societies, more generally. For example, social capital has been shown to relate to important macroeconomic outcomes, such as GDP growth (Knack & Keefer, 1997) and corruption (La Porta et al., 1997). In other words, while a clear identification of causation between social capital and macroeconomic outcomes is lacking, the negative impact of insufficient sleep on trust, prosociality, civic engagement, and others likely has a multiplier effect throughout society that is difficult to measure but not necessarily trivial. It is the job of each researcher to help highlight the implications of their findings to the most general audience possible, but hopefully this chapter helps position the existing body of research on this topic area in a broader context. The goal of this chapter has been to stimulate interest and offer a useful nudge toward the unique and rewarding area of research in sleep and economic decision-making.

Acknowledgements

I want to thank Sean Drummond, Martin Kocher, and Marco Castillo for helpful comments on an earlier draft of this chapter.

Notes

1. As another example, a recent working paper in Bessone et al. (2020) reports results from a field experiment that administered a sleep-improvement manipulation. Here, the impact of sleep improvements on labor productivity, savings, and health outcomes were of particular interest. Some classic incentivized economic decision tasks (risk-preference lotteries, dictator, ultimatum, trust, discounting) were also administered, though findings were mostly null results. The lack of robust effects in their study may be due to the severe levels of insufficient sleep identified in their sample of interest (5–6 hr/night, on average, as measured by actigraphy). As such, even their treatment improvements of approximately 30–50 min/night still left the treated individuals below recommended sleep levels. Sleep fragmentation was

also a noted concern in their study, so their population more likely approximated a clinical population rather than a "normal sleepers" population.

2. This line of research on ego-depletion has been met with some criticism over its replicability or validity (e.g., Job et al., 2010). However, the idea that cognitive resources can be used or replenished does allow an alternative, and yet still simple, narrative for how sleepiness may differentially impact decisions requiring top-down executive control from pre-frontal brain regions.

3. If decision output, D, is defined as "accuracy" or quality of decisions, then an increase in the cost of cognitive input 2 with no corresponding increase in overall cognitive "brain budget" will produce a constrained optimal choice at a lower level of D (i.e., optima on lower isoquants would imply lower levels of choice accuracy or quality). In the case of simple decisions, the optimal choice might be to only use cognitive input 1, assuming it is less costly ($w_1 < w_2$)—in such a case, use of cognitive input 2 could be loosely thought of as "overthinking," which moves one's outcome to lower decision output levels (isoquants). It may be that costs, w, and technology, α, are context specific (as suggested in Phelps et al., 2014). Of course, in some contexts, there is no objectively accurate decision or quality is hard to measure, in which case D may be more generally defined as "decisions made." Here, it would make sense that only the cognitively less costly neural inputs be used for decision-making if simply making a decision is the only outcome that matters.

4. Because the experimenter has an interest in the return of the valuable actigraphy devices, a recommended compensation approach is to have a fixed compensation amount (separate from the variable compensation that derives from decisions in the decision tasks administered) promised to the participants that is only issued after the data have been downloaded and scored to at least verify good-faith efforts toward compliance. As a relevant side note, this author did have difficulty once in retrieving an actigraphy device from a participant who had withdrawn from a study in the middle of the sleep protocol. In such instances, I usually grant partial fixed compensation to the participant for simply returning the device, and this is successful in almost every instance. In this one instance, however, it became clear that the participant's incentives to return the device were not aligned with mine. I felt my only remaining option was to inform the participant that if the device was not returned, because it was research property of the university I would have to report it as stolen. Furthermore, as a matter of fact, I also indicated that the retail value of the device, which was over $1 000, would classify it as a felony theft. After many days of unsuccessful attempts to get the device returned, within hours of sending out that particular email the device was finally returned!

5. The results in Castillo et al. (2017) were not intended to imply that choices may never become irrational if circadian mismatch becomes more extreme. In their study, validated morning and evening type participants were randomly assigned to a lab decision session at either 7:30 a.m. or 10:00 p.m. Thus, the circadian mismatch studied (e.g., a morning-type decision-maker at 10 p.m.) was significant but not extreme (e.g., 4 a.m. decision-making).

6. There is a longer stream of research in sleep examining risky choice, but where gains and losses are possible within the same stimulus (e.g., Killgore et al., 2006; Venkatraman et al., 2007, 2011), which McKenna et al. (2007) noted as a confound within the choice task if one believes differences may exist across the gain/loss domain divide. Nevertheless, the general view from such studies is that sleep deprivation increases one's propensity to take monetary risk (Womack et al.,

2013). For this reason, the nuanced difference presented in McKenna et al. (2007) is important (namely, that TSD desensitizes one to monetary risk because it reconciles the difference in findings when they cleanly separate gains versus losses trials).

7.   One recent study found that sleep deprivation effects on risky choice were gender specific, with only males making riskier choices following TSD (females did the opposite; see Ferrara et al., 2015). These authors also reported that only females became more selfish dictators following TSD, so their work has some connection to the other cited research on sleep and social decision-making. The possibility of systematic gender differences in how individuals are impacted by sleep deprivation merits further investigation in the behavioral literature.

8.   Outcomes in the exact same Bayesian decision paradigm were analyzed using well-rested participants to identify that overlapping as well as distinct frontoparietal brain regions were involved in decision-making by those who integrated both sources of information into their choice (Poudel et al., 2017).

9.   One other recent study used a vignette approach to examine circadian timing and Bayesian-type decision-making in the legal context of guilt assessment (Dickinson, Smith, & McClelland, 2020). Though clearly related to the Bayesian choice studied in other sleep research, and though the randomly assigned Night condition was extreme (response time required between 3 a.m. and 5 a.m.), their task did not involve an objectively "correct" answer that could be incentivized using typical experimental economics methods, thus, it is of less interest here. It is noteworthy, however, that their general result found that compounded adverse sleep states may produce differences in guilt assessments.

10.   Psychology departments typically establish databases of students in their lower-level research methods course, and recruitment through these databases is common. Psychology majors are then required to serve as participants in psychology experiments for course credit. This provides many faculty with a zero-monetary cost-ready set of participants for their research studies, which is not the approach used in experimental economics.

11.   Dickinson and McElroy (2012) noted the significance of the observational sleep levels measured in their participants as well as in footnote 6 of their paper. In fact, they found that observational low-sleep levels had a more robust estimated negative effect on anticipation decisions than did the circadian mismatch. This was not reported in their main text due to the fact that they could not rule out the possibility that other omitted variables may be responsible for the observed sleep level effect (e.g., stress during the week).

12.   Another recent asset market study found that a manipulation to reduce self-control similarly resulted in increased levels of asset mispricing (Kocher et al., 2019). As with other studies, this suggests there may be a relationship between sleepiness and the lack of self-control.

References

Anderson, C., & Dickinson, D. L. (2010). Bargaining and trust: The effects of 36-h total sleep deprivation on socially interactive decisions. *Journal of Sleep Research*, *19*(1-Part-I), 54–63.

Baert, S., Omey, E., Verhaest, D., & Vermeir, A. (2015). Mister Sandman, bring me good marks! On the relationship between sleep quality and academic achievement. *Social Science & Medicine, 130*, 91–98.

Barnes, C. M., Gunia, B. C., & Wagner, D. T. (2015). Sleep and moral awareness. *Journal of Sleep Research, 24*(2), 181–188.

Barnes, C. M., Schaubroeck, J., Huth, M., & Ghumman, S. (2011). Lack of sleep and unethical conduct. *Organizational Behavior and Human Decision Processes, 115*(2), 169–180.

Baumeister, R. F., Bratslavsky, E., Muraven, M., & Tice, D. M. (1998). Ego depletion: Is the active self a limited resource? *Journal of Personality and Social Psychology, 74*(5), 1252.

Becker, G. S. (1965). A theory of the allocation of time. *The Economic Journal, 75*(299), 493–517.

Bessone, P., Rao, G., Schilbach, F., Schofield, H., & Toma, M. (2020). *The economic consequences of increasing sleep among the urban poor.* NBER working paper #26747.

Bostian, A. J., & Holt, C. A. (2009). Price bubbles with discounting: A web-based classroom experiment. *Journal of Economic Education, 40*(1), 27–37.

Camerer, C., Loewenstein, G., & Prelec, D. (2005). Neuroeconomics: How neuroscience can inform economics. *Journal of Economic Literature, 43*(1), 9–64.

Castillo, M., & Dickinson, D. L. (2020). *Sleep restriction increases coordination failure.* IZA Discussion Paper No. 13242.

Castillo, M., Dickinson, D. L., & Petrie, R. (2017). Sleepiness, choice consistency, and risk preferences. *Theory and Decision, 82*(1), 41–73.

Chee, M. W., & Chuah, L. Y. (2008). Functional neuroimaging insights into how sleep and sleep deprivation affect memory and cognition. *Current Opinion in Neurology, 21*(4), 417–423.

Cho, K., Barnes, C. M., & Guanara, C. L. (2016). Sleepy punishers are harsh punishers: Daylight saving time and legal sentences. *Psychological Science, 29*(2), 242–247.

Choi, S., Fisman, R., Gale, D., & Kariv, S. (2007). Consistency and heterogeneity of individual behavior under uncertainty. *American Economic Review, 97*(5), 1921–1938.

Clark, J., & Dickinson, D. L. (2017). *The impact of sleep restriction on contributions and punishment: First evidence.* IZA Discussion Paper No. 1240.

Coricelli, G., & Nagel, R. (2009). Neural correlates of depth of strategic reasoning in medial prefrontal cortex. *Proceedings of the National Academy of Sciences, 106*(23), 9163–9168.

Curtis, B. J., Williams, P. G., & Anderson, J. S. (2018). Objective cognitive functioning in self-reported habitual short sleepers not reporting daytime dysfunction: Examination of impulsivity via delay discounting. *Sleep, 41*(9), zsy115.

De Zambotti, M., Cellini, N., Goldstone, A., Colrain, I. M., & Baker, F. C. (2019). Wearable sleep technology in clinical and research settings. *Medicine and Science in Sports and Exercise, 51*(7), 1538–1557.

Deck, C., & Jahedi, S. (2015). The effect of cognitive load on economic decision making: A survey and new experiments. *European Economic Review, 78*, 97–119.

Depner, C. M., Cheng, P. C., Devine, J. K., Khosla, S., de Zambotti, M., Robillard, R., ... Drummond, S. P. (2020). Wearable technologies for developing sleep and circadian biomarkers: a summary of workshop discussions. *Sleep, 43*(2), zsz254.

Dickinson, D. L., Cazier, J., & Cech, T. (2016). A practical validation study of a commercial accelerometer using good and poor sleepers. *Health Psychology Open, 3*(2). doi: 10.1177/2055102916679012

Dickinson, D. L., Chaudhuri, A., & Greenaway-McGrevy, R. (2020). Trading while sleepy? Circadian mismatch and mispricing in a global experimental asset market. *Experimental Economics*, *23*(2), 526–553.

Dickinson, D. L., & Drummond, S. P. (2008). The effects of total sleep deprivation on Bayesian updating. *Judgment and Decision Making*, *3*(2), 181.

Dickinson, D. L., Drummond, S. P., & Dyche, J. (2016). Voluntary sleep choice and its effects on Bayesian decisions. *Behavioral Sleep Medicine*, *14*(5), 501–513.

Dickinson, D. L., Drummond, S. P., & McElroy, T. (2017). The viability of an ecologically valid chronic sleep restriction and circadian timing protocol: An examination of sample attrition, compliance, and effectiveness at impacting sleepiness and mood. *PLOS One*, *12*(3). doi: 10.1371/journal.pone.0174367

Dickinson, D. L., & McElroy, T. (2010). Rationality around the clock: Sleep and time-of-day effects on guessing game responses. *Economics Letters*, *108*(2), 245–248.

Dickinson, D. L., & McElroy, T. (2012). Circadian effects on strategic reasoning. *Experimental Economics*, *15*(3), 444–459.

Dickinson, D. L., & McElroy, T. (2017). Sleep restriction and circadian effects on social decisions. *European Economic Review*, *97*, 57–71.

Dickinson, D. L., & McElroy, T. (2019). Bayesian versus heuristic-based choice under sleep restriction and suboptimal times of day. *Games and Economic Behavior*, *115*, 48–59.

Dickinson D. L., Smith, A. R., & McClelland, R. (2020). An examination of circadian impact on judgments. *Social Psychology*, *51*(5), 341–353.

Dickinson, D. L., & Whitehead, J. C. (2015). Dubious and dubiouser: Contingent valuation and the time of day. *Economic Inquiry*, *53*(2), 1396–1400.

Drummond, S. P., Brown, G. G., Stricker, J. L., Buxton, R. B., Wong, E. C., & Gillin, J. C. (1999). Sleep deprivation-induced reduction in cortical functional response to serial subtraction. *Neuroreport*, *10*(18), 3745–3748.

Drummond, S. P., Walker, M., Almklov, E., Campos, M., Anderson, D. E., & Straus, L. D. (2013). Neural correlates of working memory performance in primary insomnia. *Sleep*, *36*(9), 1307–1316.

Ferrara, M., Bottasso, A., Tempesta, D., Carrieri, M., De Gennaro, L., & Ponti, G. (2015). Gender differences in sleep deprivation effects on risk and inequality aversion: Evidence from an economic experiment. *PLOS One*, *10*(3). doi: 10.1371/journal.pone.0120029

Giuntella, O., & Mazzonna, F. (2019). Sunset time and the economic effects of social jetlag: evidence from US time zone borders. *Journal of Health Economics*, *65*, 210–226.

Hafner, M., Stepanek, M., Taylor, J., Troxel, W. M., & Van Stolk, C. (2017). Why sleep matters—The economic costs of insufficient sleep: A cross-country comparative analysis. *Rand Health Quarterly*, *6*(4), 11.

Harrison, Y., & Horne, J. A. (2000). The impact of sleep deprivation on decision making: a review. *Journal of Experimental Psychology: Applied*, *6*(3), 236–249.

Holbein, J. B., Schafer, J. P., & Dickinson, D. L. (2019). Insufficient sleep reduces voting and other prosocial behaviours. *Nature Human Behaviour*, *3*(5), 492–500.

Horne, J. A. (1993). Human sleep, sleep loss and behaviour: Implications for the prefrontal cortex and psychiatric disorder. *British Journal of Psychiatry*, *162*(3), 413–419.

Job, V., Dweck, C. S., & Walton, G. M. (2010). Ego depletion—Is it all in your head? Implicit theories about willpower affect self-regulation. *Psychological Science*, *21*(11), 1686–1693.

Kahneman, D. (2011). *Thinking, fast and slow*. London: Penguin.

Kahneman, D., & Tversky, A. (2013). Prospect theory: An analysis of decision under risk. In L. C. MacLean & W. T. Ziemba (Eds.), *Handbook of the fundamentals of financial decision making: Part I* (pp. 99–127). Singapore: World Scientific.

Kamstra, M. J., Kramer, L. A., & Levi, M. D. (2000). Losing sleep at the market: The daylight saving anomaly. *American Economic Review, 90*(4), 1005–1011.

Killgore, W. D., Balkin, T. J., & Wesensten, N. J. (2006). Impaired decision making following 49 h of sleep deprivation. *Journal of Sleep Research, 15*(1), 7–13.

Knack, S., & Keefer, P. (1997). Does social capital have an economic payoff? A cross-country investigation. *Quarterly Journal of Economics, 112*(4), 1251–1288.

Kocher, M. G., Lucks, K. E., & Schindler, D. (2019). Unleashing animal spirits: Self-control and overpricing in experimental asset markets. *Review of Financial Studies, 32*(6), 2149–2178.

Kocher, M. G., & Sutter, M. (2006). Time is money—Time pressure, incentives, and the quality of decision-making. *Journal of Economic Behavior & Organization, 61*(3), 375–392.

Kouchaki, M., & Smith, I. H. (2014). The morning morality effect: The influence of time of day on unethical behavior. *Psychological Science, 25*(1), 95–102.

La Porta, R., Lopez-de-Silanes, F., Shleifer, A., & Vishny, R. W. (1997). Trust in large organizations. *American Economic Review, 87*(2), 333–338.

Libedinsky, C., Massar, S. A., Ling, A., Chee, W., Huettel, S. A., & Chee, M. W. (2013). Sleep deprivation alters effort discounting but not delay discounting of monetary rewards. *Sleep, 36*(6), 899–904.

Libedinsky, C., Smith, D. V., Teng, C. S., Namburi, P., Chen, V. W., Huettel, S. A., & Chee, M. W. (2011). Sleep deprivation alters valuation signals in the ventromedial prefrontal cortex. *Frontiers in Behavioral Neuroscience, 5*, 70.

Lim, J., & Dinges, D. F. (2010). A meta-analysis of the impact of short-term sleep deprivation on cognitive variables. *Psychological Bulletin, 136*(3), 375.

Muraven, M., Baumeister, R. F., & Tice, D. M. (1999). Longitudinal improvement of self-regulation through practice: Building self-control strength through repeated exercise. *Journal of Social Psychology, 139*(4), 446–457.

McElroy, T., & Dickinson, D. L. (2010). Thoughtful days and valenced nights: How much will you think about the problem? *Judgment and Decision Making, 5*(7), 516.

McElroy, T., & Dickinson, D. L. (2019). Thinking about complex decisions: How sleep and time-of-day influence complex choices. *Consciousness and Cognition, 76*, 102824.

McKenna, B. S., Dickinson, D. L., Orff, H. J., & Drummond, S. P. (2007). The effects of one night of sleep deprivation on known-risk and ambiguous-risk decisions. *Journal of Sleep Research, 16*(3), 245–252.

McMenamin, T. M. (2007). A time to work: Recent trends in shift work and flexible schedules. *Monthly Labor Review, 130*(12), 3–15.

Muzur, A., Pace-Schott, E. F., & Hobson, J. A. (2002). The prefrontal cortex in sleep. *Trends in Cognitive Sciences, 6*(11), 475–481.

Nagel, R. (1995). Unraveling in guessing games: An experimental study. *American Economic Review, 85*(5), 1313–1326.

Pérez-Chada, D., Videla, A. J., O'Flaherty, M. E., Palermo, P., Meoni, J., Sarchi, M. I., ... Durán-Cantolla, J. (2005). Sleep habits and accident risk among truck drivers: A cross-sectional study in Argentina. *Sleep, 28*(9), 1103–1108.

Phelps, E. A., Lempert, K. M., & Sokol-Hessner, P. (2014). Emotion and decision making: multiple modulatory neural circuits. *Annual Review of Neuroscience*, *37*, 263–287.

Poudel, G. R., Bhattarai, A., Dickinson, D. L., & Drummond, S. (2017). Neural correlates of decision-making during a Bayesian choice task. *NeuroReport*, *28*(4), 193–199.

Rand, D. G., Greene, J. D., & Nowak, M. A. (2012). Spontaneous giving and calculated greed. *Nature*, *489*(7416), 427.

Schoenborn, C. A., & Adams, P. E. (2010). Health behaviors of adults: United States, 2005–2007. *Vital Health Stat 10*, *245*(1), 132.

Shiffrin, R. M., & Schneider, W. (1977). Controlled and automatic human information processing: II. Perceptual learning, automatic attending and a general theory. *Psychological Review*, *84*(2), 127.

Simon, H. (1955). A behavioral model of rational choice. *Quarterly Journal of Economics*, *69*(1), 99–118.

Smith, C. S., Folkard, S., Schmnieder, R. A., Parra, L. F., Spelten, E., Almiral, H., … Tisak, J. (2002). Investigation of morning-evening orientation in six countries using the preferences scale. *Personality and Individual Differences*, *32*(6), 949–968.

Stanovich, K. E., & West, R. F. (2000). Individual differences in reasoning: Implications for the rationality debate? *The Behavioral and Brain Sciences*, *23*, 645–726.

Sundelin, T., Bayard, F., Schwarz, J., Cybulski, L., Petrovic, P., & Axelsson, J. (2019). Framing effect, probability distortion, and gambling tendency without feedback are resistant to two nights of experimental sleep restriction. *Scientific Reports*, *9*(1), 8554.

Tversky, A., & Kahneman, D. (1981). The framing of decisions and the rationality of choice. *Science*, *221*, 453–458.

Varughese, J., & Allen, R. P. (2001). Fatal accidents following changes in daylight saving time: The American experience. *Sleep Medicine*, *2*(1), 31–36.

Venkatraman, V., Chuah, Y. L., Huettel, S. A., & Chee, M. W. (2007). Sleep deprivation elevates expectation of gains and attenuates response to losses following risky decisions. *Sleep*, *30*(5), 603–609.

Venkatraman, V., Huettel, S. A., Chuah, L. Y., Payne, J. W., & Chee, M. W. (2011). Sleep deprivation biases the neural mechanisms underlying economic preferences. *Journal of Neuroscience*, *31*(10), 3712–3718.

Wagner, D. T., Barnes, C. M., Lim, V. K., & Ferris, D. L. (2012). Lost sleep and cyberloafing: Evidence from the laboratory and a daylight saving time quasi-experiment. *Journal of Applied Psychology*, *97*(5), 1068.

Womack, S. D., Hook, J. N., Reyna, S. H., & Ramos, M. (2013). Sleep loss and risk-taking behavior: A review of the literature. *Behavioral Sleep Medicine*, *11*(5), 343–359.

Index

against women 145–6
diurnal preference 221, 223
dominance value orientation 173
dopaminergic cells 199
Dual-Process Model of political ideology 168
dual-process theories 192–5
dynamic enforcement 73–4
dynamic standards mechanism 76
dynamic tournament mechanism 75

economic conservatism/progressivism 164, 170–71
    inequality 172–3
    pro-sociality 169–72
    within- and between-group competition 173–4
economic/economy
    behaviour, social norms in 19
    incentives, importance of 70
    inequality 168
    progressivism 170–73
educational attainment 215
EEG 198–9, 203
effective enforcement 79
egalitarian behaviour 164, 173
ego depletion 216
electroencephalography (EEG) 193
emissions
    credible estimate of 78
    markets, enforcement in 81
    permit markets 78
    trading markets 78–9
    trading programs 81
emotion/emotional 207
    in decision-making 195–9
    responses 196
empirical expectations 23, 26–7
empirical information 34
endowment effect 48
enforcement 80–81
    cost effectiveness of 79
    in emissions permit markets 77–8
    expenditures 69
    intertemporal complications 80–81
        measurement and penalties 78–9
    underexplored topics 81–2

unique aspects of permit market compliance 79–80
    resources 69–70
    uncertainty 77
enterprise development 100
entrepreneurial choice 101
    alternative explanation for 96
    risk on 95–6
entrepreneurs/entrepreneurship 110–11, 140
    behavioural differences between 95
    choice of 98
    choosing to become 95–8
    constraints on 99
        access to capital 99–100
        access to skills-based business training 100
    external finance for 99
    growth and success 98
    inherent risks associated with 95
    literature 96
environmental compliance 73, 77, 84
environmental enforcement 69
environmental programs 84–5
environmental regulations 69–71
    behavioural levers 82
        encouraging honesty 84–5
        social observability 82–4
        underexplored topics 85–6
    enforcement in emissions permit markets 77–8
        intertemporal complications 80–81
        measurement and penalties 78–9
        underexplored topics 81–2
        unique aspects of permit market compliance 79–80
    standard economic incentives 71–2
        dynamic enforcement 73–4
        general deterrence 72–3
        relative conditional audit mechanisms 74–6
        underexplored topics 76–7
ERP *see* event-related potentials (ERP)
EU ETS *see* European Union Emissions Trading Scheme (EU ETS)